ACPL ITEM
DISCARDED

D0151494

3 1833 01535 5115

Owen, Diana Marie.
Media messages in American
presidential elections

DO NOT REMOVE
CARDS FROM POCKET

ALLEN COUNTY PUBLIC LIBRARY

FORT WAYNE, INDIANA 46802

You may return this book to any agency, branch,
or bookmobile of the Allen County Public Library.

DEMCO

Media Messages in American Presidential Elections

Media Messages in American Presidential Elections

DIANA OWEN

Contributions to the Study of Mass Media
and Communications, Number 25

Bernard K. Johnpoll, Series Editor

Greenwood Press
NEW YORK • WESTPORT, CONNECTICUT • LONDON

Allen County Public Library
Ft. Wayne, Indiana

Library of Congress Cataloging-in-Publication Data

Owen, Diana Marie.
  Media messages in American presidential elections / Diana Owen.
    p.   cm. — (Contributions to the study of mass media and
  communications, ISSN 0732–4456 : no. 25)
    Includes bibliographical references and index.
    ISBN 0–313–26362–0
    1. Presidents—United States—Election.   2. Mass media—Political
  aspects—United States.   3. Electioneering—United States.
  I. Title.   II. Series.
  JK524.094   1991
  324.7′3′0973—dc20   90–43384

British Library Cataloguing in Publication Data is available.

Copyright © 1991 by Diana Owen

All rights reserved. No portion of this book may be
reproduced, by any process or technique, without the
express written consent of the publisher.

Library of Congress Catalog Card Number: 90–43384
ISBN: 0–313–26362–0
ISSN: 0732–4456

First published in 1991

Greenwood Press, 88 Post Road West, Westport, CT 06881
An imprint of Greenwood Publishing Group, Inc.

Printed in the United States of America

∞

The paper used in this book complies with the
Permanent Paper Standard issued by the National
Information Standards Organization (Z39.48–1984).

10 9 8 7 6 5 4 3 2 1

In Memory of Christine von Gruchalla

Contents

Figures

Tables

Acknowledgments

I would like to take this opportunity to thank several people who have been important to me during the writing of this manuscript, an activity that took place in two stages over the course of the 1984 and 1988 election cycles. During the 1984 election, Jack McLeod dedicated a substantial portion of the annual survey conducted by the University of Wisconsin–Madison's Mass Communication Research Center to this project. I am indebted to him for the Dane County data set, as well as for the insights from his own research that provided a foundation for this work. Lauren Burnbauer earns special mention for her invaluable assistance with coding and inputting the 1988 data base. I am also grateful to the numerous Rutgers University graduate students who helped get the surveys in the mail. Murray Edelman, Leon Epstein, and Gina Sapiro have all been sources of great intellectual stimulation, and I appreciate their comments on the original manuscript. I would like to acknowledge the extremely useful comments of anonymous reviewers. I would also like to thank Todd Adkins and the Greenwood Press staff for their valuable assistance with the production of the manuscript.

Sustaining interest in a project that must be put on hold for several years until an election occurs is often difficult. I value the thoughtfulness and support of the friends and colleagues who kept me going throughout the process— Steve Bronner, Sue Carroll, Tom Flanegin, Rene Gibson, Gerry Pomper, and Linda Zerilli. Jack Dennis, who has seen me through the entire process of writing, updating, and rewriting, deserves my sincerest thanks. Most of all, I would like to recognize my husband, Jeffrey, for his support, caring, and love.

Introduction

The mass media are playing an increasingly pervasive and visible role in the American presidential election process. During campaigns, countless media messages are disseminated on television and radio and in newspapers and magazines. Campaign communications differ in content and purpose. Each specific type of election media message, however, structures the strategies used by candidates for office and influences how the public perceives political actors, issues, and processes.

Voters use different types of media messages in formulating their opinions about candidates and issues, as well as their orientations toward the campaign. These types include candidate advertisements, news stories about the election, poll results released through the mass media, and televised debates. While there is much speculation and some evidence that each of these message types plays a role in voter education and opinion formation, their relative importance warrants systematic and thorough exploration.

Since campaigns generate different types of media messages, we cannot assume that all messages will have the same effect on voters or that voters will use them all in the same way when developing their campaign attitudes and opinions. The channel through which specific message types are disseminated should also be considered when examining communication effects. With notable exceptions, scholars have tended to consider the influence of specific forms of campaign communication separately or not to differentiate among types of media messages in campaigns at all.[1] Further, voters as consumers of mass-mediated campaign messages are not an undifferentiated mass; they instead represent a diverse audience whose information needs and tastes in political communication vary.

The purpose of this study is twofold. First, we examine the relative importance of specific types of media messages to voters in the 1984 and 1988
presidential elections. Second, we investigate how individuals make use of
messages in establishing their perceptions of candidates and issues during
election campaigns. The message categories studied here include candidate
advertisements, news stories, poll results, and debates. Messages disseminated through both print and electronic media are included in the analysis.

The first portion of the study addresses these basic research questions:
How do media messages transmitted during presidential elections shape voter
attitudes toward and perceptions of candidates and campaign issues? Do different types of media messages influence voters' feelings about candidates and
elections in different ways? Related to these are more specific questions: Do
voters pay more attention to some types of messages than to others? Do
voters gain different kinds of information from different types of messages?
Are specific types of media messages more salient to some types of voters
than to others?

Another facet of this research ties individuals' general media use habits to
the ways in which they receive and process media messages. The following
questions are addressed in this regard: In what ways do voters make use of
media messages in formulating their orientations toward candidates, issues,
and the electoral process? How do voters' general media use habits relate to
their reception and processing of presidential election campaign messages?

THE MASS MEDIA IN PRESIDENTIAL ELECTION
CAMPAIGNS

The study of the effects of mass communication on elections and voting
behavior dates to the beginning of this century. Early work in this area was
influenced by the propaganda campaigns of World Wars I and II, which were
based on the assumption that media messages have an immediate and direct
effect upon the recipient (Lasswell, 1948). When voting research of the 1940s
and 1950s found little evidence to support this perspective, the "limited effects"
tradition emerged (Lazarsfeld, Berelson, and Gaudet, 1944; Berelson, Lazarsfeld, and McPhee, 1954; Klapper, 1960). From the latter viewpoint, the
media in elections act merely to reinforce rather than to persuade.

Since the era of the early voting studies, changes have occurred in the nature
of the mass media, their role in elections, and in the political context within
which campaigns take place. Most important is the advent of television, which
has the ability to bring the live aspect of campaigns into the homes of voters.
Coinciding with the appearance of technological advances in the mass media is
the decline in the role of political parties in elections. These developments
have influenced how elections are reported, transformed candidates' electoral
strategies, and brought new actors to prominence in the campaign arena.

The striking centrality of television's role in elections, coupled with the growing technological sophistication of reporting techniques and the rise of the role of campaign consultants, have fostered the development of a new type of politics in the mass media age. Today, a salient criterion for the recruitment of presidential candidates is the ability to project a positive media image. Campaign strategies must now combine both political and media components (Arterton, 1978).

This requirement has resulted in campaign consultants and media strategists assuming a central role in elections. Since the 1970s, consultants armed with new-style campaign technologies, such as polling, demographic precinct targeting, and direct mail, have transformed the standards for achieving success in elections. Consultants and campaign organizations work to shape the campaign/mass media environment. In running campaigns, consultants strive for precision and control in publicizing candidates through advertising and news reports. As Sabato (1981:111) states, "Mixing style with substance and imagery with reality, media consultants have developed a wide range of formats, strategies, techniques, and gimmicks both to inform and deceive a television-addicted electorate." In so doing, they attempt to mold the ways in which campaigns are covered by journalists. As demonstrated in congressional elections, the ability of candidates to communicate with the electorate not only affects the outcome of the election, but also determines the amount of information that voters will have when making their decisions. The choice of techniques for disseminating information largely determines the scope and appeal of candidates' messages (Goldenberg and Traugott, 1984).

These factors complicate the job of communications organizations, since they can no longer satisfactorily report elections by merely stating the actions and views of candidates. The press now has to present campaigns in a manner that not only satisfies individuals' expectations in terms of entertainment and information, but also fulfills candidates' needs for communicating to voters. One outgrowth of these media and candidate requirements is the spotlighting of campaign events, such as debates, which then rise to special prominence in elections.

To accommodate their increased role in the electoral process, journalists have incorporated social science techniques into their coverage of campaigns. One result of this phenomenon is the almost continual broadcasting of opinion poll results during presidential races. In addition, reporters delve into the candidates' personal lives and supplement news reports with constant commentary about the political situation that surrounds the election (Leubsdorf, 1976).

Political factors have also contributed to changes in the electoral context, which in turn has influenced the role of mass communications. In particular, scholars have charted the decline of political parties since the 1950s, in terms of both their importance to voters and their organizational vitality.

In earlier times, individuals demonstrated strong attachments to political parties that were organizationally capable of providing voting cues and mobilizing the electorate (Campbell, Converse, Miller, and Stokes, 1960). A great many voters made up their minds early in campaigns and maintained their candidate preference until election day. In recent years, individuals' attachment to political parties has declined, coinciding with an increase in the number of people who call themselves independents, a rise in split-ticket voting, and a greater tendency among voters to switch parties in consecutive elections (Pomper, 1975; Nie, Verba, and Petrocik, 1976; Ladd and Hadley, 1975). In addition, many more people remain undecided until the election campaign is well under way. All of these factors indicate that the party label, as a device for simplifying and organizing voting decisions, is far less salient than it had been in the past.

By most indications, parties have become weaker organizationally, although evidence on this point is mixed. This trend has been exacerbated by attempts to reform the presidential nominating and election processes and the methods of financing campaigns. Generally, the goals of party reform, particularly among Democrats, have been to broaden the political process by encouraging more open participation and to minimize the influence of special interest groups. The reforms of the presidential nominating process, with their emphasis on primaries rather than caucuses for selecting candidates, shift power from the party leaders to the mass public. Campaign finance reforms provide for public funding of major presidential candidates. They have fostered the growth of political action committees that are a fertile source of electoral revenue. Particularly in congressional elections, candidates can raise more money from PACs than from political parties. These developments give rise to more candidate-centered, as opposed to partisan, appeals in both primaries and general elections (Ceasar, 1979; Burnham, 1982). In this era of reform, candidates rely heavily on their own organizations to formulate campaign strategies, raise funds, and organize volunteers, largely to the exclusion of the parties.

The decline in partisan affection and party organization produces an electoral climate in which the mass media's role is likely to be enhanced. The public tends to rely more heavily on the media to provide campaign information and voting cues than it did when parties were predominant. Polsby (1983) suggests that party elites are losing influence in the political system to media elites. Other scholars have asserted that the press has taken on the responsibilities, once assumed by political parties, of recruiting candidates, organizing the issue agenda, and informing and mobilizing voters (Patterson, 1980; Rubin, 1981; Ranney, 1983).

These changes in the electoral context have created new challenges for the mass media, candidates, and voters. Today, voters are bombarded by a constant flow of media messages. In an age of diminished reliance on partisan cues, they are confronted with the challenge of sorting through these messages in order to isolate information relevant to their voting decisions. Voters' perceptions and interpretations of campaign messages are determined largely by their personal attitudes, orientations, and preconceptions. While candidates, campaign organizations, and the mass media are involved in the marketing of electoral communications, the electorate ultimately determines the meaning and relevance of the message.

In keeping with these changes in electoral reality, researchers have adopted new tactics for examining media effects in campaigns. Instead of focusing on the direct persuasive influence of the media, scholars have begun to concentrate on examining the media's role in developing individuals' cognitive and affective evaluations of candidates and issues. Studies have demonstrated that the media have significant direct effects on political learning (Becker, McCombs, and McLeod, 1975). Voters, for example, rely on media messages as significant sources of information about candidates and issues. Thus, more recent trends in political communication research have moved away from the "limited effects" perspective.

THE PRESENT STUDY

Because the mass media have taken on more complex and integral functions in presidential elections, it is important to investigate fully the meaning and implications of their role. The campaign/media environment involves the intricate interaction of the creation, transmission, reception, and processing of messages by three distinct sets of actors with different, although sometimes overlapping, goals. Candidates and their campaign organizations desire to convert undecided voters and to reinforce their bases of existing support. Mass media institutions strive to capture voters' attention by entertaining and informing. Voters use media-based information for making decisions, for fulfilling social expectations (such as participating in conversations about politics), and as a means of taking part in the political process.

Here we will investigate the nature of four specific types of mass media messages and the ways in which they are perceived and utilized by voters in presidential election campaigns. We seek to understand what aspects of campaign communication are most important to citizens for political learning, attitude formation, and decision-making. We also explore why voters relate differentially to various forms of election media.

Researchers concerned with examining the effects of the mass media during elections are confronted with a difficult and often frustrating task. Strong media effects are not easily identified because media signals are frequently entangled with other stimuli in society. Isolating the effects of the mass media in electoral campaigns may be complicated even further by the fact that this type of communication is complex and highly integrated.

One strategy for uncovering mass media effects in a saturated communications environment is to identify specific types of messages. In this research, we employ such a tactic by considering ads, news, poll results, and debates as four distinct message categories. While similar information about campaigns is conveyed in a wide array of formats, it is possible to identify substantive differences in the form and content of mass media messages. By first explicating the unique characteristics of each form, we can then move to assess whether voters make distinctions among types of mass media messages, as well as whether they are more or less receptive to messages disseminated in specific channels. In addition, we can explore whether voters find certain message types more salient than others and if they use messages in different ways and for varying purposes.

The four types of messages selected for study in this research do not comprise an exhaustive list of all the message varieties in campaigns. These four were selected because they represent the most widely disseminated forms of communication and because each has some special identifying characteristics. At an extremely basic level, they all differ in terms of their expressed purposes. Advertisements are designed by candidates expressly to persuade voters. News reports of elections have the explicit, although not exclusive, objectives of informing and engaging the interest of the mass public. Public opinion polls, as reported within the context of news stories and even ads, can be singled out as a unique message form that simplifies reality by reducing the entire campaign to simple percentages. Finally, debates represent special campaign events that are staged through the combined efforts of candidate and mass media organizations. The significance of debates extends beyond their actual occurrence to the media's interpretations of the events both before and after they take place.

Other methods of differentiating campaign media messages have been suggested in past research. One approach divides media messages into two broad categories, consisting of those controlled by the candidates and their campaign committees and those that are not. A distinction is sometimes made between "paid media," which are essentially analogous to controlled media, and "free media." Generally, controlled media include commercial advertisements endorsing candidates and paid for by their committees. Uncontrolled media, for the most part, are news items about candidates reported in print or via the electronic media. While candidates organize their efforts in bids to receive favorable press coverage, they have no direct influence over the news that is reported.

These categories for distinguishing campaign media messages can be misleading. For example, organizations not directly affiliated with a particular campaign have launched political advertising efforts. This type of advertising, by political action committees among others, has historically been negative and is essentially paid media that is uncontrolled by the candidate. In addition, certain types of messages do not fall neatly into one category or another. The content of debates, for instance, is controlled by both the reporters asking the questions and the participants. It is difficult to develop categories of election messages that are mutually exclusive. By focusing on more specific and clearly identifiable message types, we hope to mitigate some of the difficulties associated with broader classification schemes.

OVERVIEW OF THE STUDY

This research focuses on the audience and how it relates to mass-mediated communication during presidential elections. One way of examining individuals' orientations toward the mass media is to investigate the active processes that underlie their decisions to make use of campaign media messages. This study adapts the uses and gratifications approach developed in mass communication research to explore these processes. People's motivations for using the mass media and the gratifications that they receive from specific campaign messages will be determined and related to patterns of media use during the 1984 and 1988 presidential campaigns.

The theoretical framework used to guide this research is outlined in the first chapter. We develop an audience-centered model of communication processes that we use to guide the empirical analysis elaborated in the chapters that follow. We then describe the data base employed in the study.

Chapters 2, 3, 4, and 5 consist of discussions of the unique characteristics of ads, news stories, poll results, and debates respectively, both in general and with regard to the 1984 and 1988 presidential contests. Each chapter begins by discussing the identifying characteristics of the particular message type. The discussion addresses the ways in which the content of the message variety has been shaped through the interplay of candidate and mass media organizations. The implications of these factors for the political process is then explored. A summary of the specific ways in which candidates and the media used each message type during the two elections under study is presented, and voters' use and perceptions of these messages are analyzed. Chapter 6 examines more directly the model of audience mass media use and outcomes presented in Chapter 1. This model serves as a framework for considering voters' motivations for media use in the 1984 and 1988 presidential elections, and it allows us to assess how these motives were satisfied by the four message types under study. The final chapter consists of a summary of the major findings and concluding observations.

NOTE

1. One exception is Patterson and McClure's (1976) study, which examined the effects of television news reports and advertisements. Their work dealt exclusively with televised messages, however, and did not consider radio or print media.

Media Messages in American Presidential Elections

A Model of Audience Mass Media Use and Outcomes

REDEVELOPING MASS COMMUNICATIONS THEORY

The study of the effects of mass communication on elections and voting behavior has passed through distinct phases, each characterized by different theoretical perspectives and research agendas. Early "hypodermic effects" or "bullet theories" gave way to the "limited effects" tradition that emerged from the voting studies of the 1940s. More recently, scholars have reevaluated the role of the mass media in elections. While not returning directly to a full effects perspective, they assert that the media can produce important consequences in the realm of electoral politics. The emergent analytic frameworks demonstrate a greater understanding of the often subtle nature of communication effects and the need to focus on the processes underlying them (see Schramm, 1974; DeFleur and Ball-Rokeach, 1982; McQuail and Windahl, 1981; Lowery and DeFleur, 1988).

The most recent period in political communication research is notable for its attempts to revive the field, which had come to a standstill as a result of the often rigid research perspectives adopted in earlier eras. Yet the challenge of devising adequate theoretical frameworks for studying media effects in elections persists. As early researchers discovered, mass media effects are difficult to isolate. Scholars must take into account a vast array of factors in order to untangle the nature of mass communication and its influence. They must also consider certain contingent conditions under which media effects are likely to occur, including situational, cultural, and historical elements that are frequently difficult to define (O'Keefe and Atwood, 1981; Blumler and Gurevitch, 1980; Hochheimer, 1984).

The problem of developing a coherent body of theory has been compounded by the fact that political communication researchers are spread across a variety of disciplines that frequently follow divergent paths. Work on the mass media's role in elections has been conducted primarily by political scientists and mass communications scholars. For many years, political scientists were greatly influenced by the general premises underlying the full effects theories. Political science research focused more on overt behavioral than on cognitive effects. Mass communications scholars were among the first to move away from searching for behavioral change to examining shifts in attitudes and orientations. This perspective offers greater potential for contributing to our understanding of media influence in elections, and has increasingly been adopted by researchers across disciplines (McLeod and Blumler, 1987). Recent work on agenda-setting, for example, and the present study illustrate this point (Iyengar and Kinder, 1987).

THE MASS MEDIA AND ELECTIONS: A FOCUS ON THE AUDIENCE

While limited effects models generally hindered the development of communication theory, they should not be dismissed out of hand. Important theoretical lessons from the early models of mass communications provide a point of departure for this study. Lasswell's (1948) simple yet elegant formulation of the communications process is shown in the following diagram:

Who → Says What → In Which Channel → To Whom → With What Effect

This model hypothesizes a series of relationships, which extend from the communicator sending a message through a specific medium. The message is received by an audience that experiences specific effects.

Although he did not follow his own advice when applying the model to research, Lasswell stressed that the study of mass communications should be process-oriented, rather than focused on discrete events. He noted that the strength of messages and the consistency of the path along which they are transmitted affect the dissemination of information. These factors lead to differences in the nature and degree of audience effects. Some individuals will receive a particular message and interpret it; others will not. Not all audience members will interpret the message in the same way.

Lasswell also emphasized the role of social context in communicating media messages. The ideological predispositions of certain social groups may run counter to the message content being received, thus producing communication effects unlike those intended by the source or no effects at all. In addition, Lasswell foreshadowed the uses and gratifications theoretical perspective employed in this research. He theorized that communication is used by individuals to meet particular needs. Among these are a desire to reinforce beliefs in societal values and a need to acquire information. These components, together with the accompanying explanation of the model, demonstrate an integration of the full effects perspective with a more realistic view of the audience's power to determine message meaning.

A complete model of the communications process at work in elections should contain the basic components of communicator, medium, content, audience, and effects outlined by Lasswell. It should take into account the roles, motivations, and perceptions of actors at both the disseminating and receiving ends of media messages. The content of communication and the significance of the channel through which it is transmitted should be investigated. Finally, the existing societal conditions that establish the cultural and historical context within which the communication processes are operating should be explored.

THE PRESENT APPROACH

This study incorporates aspects of all the components of Lasswell's model. The dominant focus, however, is on the audience and how it perceives, utilizes, and processes campaign messages. A number of audience-centered models are available in the mass communications field, including those that deal with the internal structure of audience composition, the social interaction among audience members, and the relationship between the audience and the sender of a message. One tradition of research focuses on examining the motivations behind an individual's use of the mass media under different conditions. An adaptation of this perspective, falling into the broadly defined category of the uses and gratifications approach, guides the present investigation. (For an interesting, concise overview of the uses and gratifications field, see Palmgreen, Wenner, and Rosengren, 1985.)

The uses and gratifications framework originally emerged around the time of the early voting studies. It grew out of analyses of readership and viewership conducted during the 1930s, 1940s, and 1950s. Researchers were interested in the functions served by communication forms, such as comic strips and soap operas, as well as by media, especially newspapers and radio (Lazarsfeld, 1940). Attempts were made to ascertain what specific needs were satisfied by audience attention to mediated communications. The basic assumptions of uses and gratifications models ran counter to those of the full effects theoretical frameworks. Thus, during the period when the full effects perspective dominated, little research was conducted employing uses and gratifications approaches. A renewed interest in understanding audience motivations for media use has been developing in recent years.

The uses and gratifications perspective actually encompasses a variety of theoretical orientations. At a basic level, uses and gratifications approaches share several premises. They are all concerned with the "social and psychological origins of needs, which generate expectations of the mass media or other sources which lead to differential patterns of media exposure (or engagement in other activities), resulting in need gratification and other consequences, perhaps mostly unintended ones" (Katz, Blumler, and Gurevitch, 1974:20). In contrast to "hypodermic effects" models, which focus on the influence of communicators on a predominantly passive audience, uses and gratifications perspectives treat the audience as active. The audience member controls the process through which media messages are linked to specific needs. The approach assumes that people can articulate the reasons why they attend to mass communication. Uses and gratifications models can also take into account the fact that other factors satisfy needs that are not media-related. A major goal of this type of research is to examine when and under what circumstances the media play a role in need fulfillment.

Research based on the assumptions underlying the uses and gratifications perspective should not proceed without an awareness of its limitations. First, the approach is not guided by a specific theory of psychological needs, such as those put forth by Freud, Maslow, or Lasswell. Categorization schemes designed by researchers are often too broad to be entirely satisfactory (Katz, Blumler, and Gurevitch, 1974). Uses and gratification research rests on the assumption that motives are determined by basic needs. Not all aspects of media use are need-based, however. Another criticism is leveled at the notion of an active audience, a concept that is central to the framework. Some scholars claim that media use is often passive in nature, based more on factors such as availability than on audience selectivity (Levy, 1983; Levy and Windahl, 1984). Finally, given the functionalist nature of the approach, there is its underlying tendency to support the status quo, and these models sometimes fail to deal adequately with historical change (Rubin, 1986).

Election studies employing the uses and gratifications framework suffer from some specific problems. Research has concentrated predominantly on the channel through which the message is disseminated, rather than on the content or type of message. When taking this approach, the researcher runs the risk that the audience member may be confounding gratifications associated solely with a particular channel, such as television, with those of the content usually disseminated through that channel (Lometti, Reeves, and Bybee, 1977). In addition, most studies to date have treated gratifications as independent variables in research that attempts to explain effects, such as level of political knowledge or attention to specific events portrayed through the media. Analysis has proceeded without establishing a thorough understanding of the nature of motivation measures. Research is particularly unclear about how motivation measures are related directly to other media and political variables. Finally, there has been a failure to consider uses and gratifications in terms of the *processes* by which motives influence mass media effects (Garramone, 1985a).

These difficulties are not entirely insurmountable, as we will demonstrate in the current research. The uses and gratifications approach has the potential to offer useful insights into the ways in which voters attend to campaign communication. It allows researchers to investigate systematically what early

Figure 1.1
Model of Audience Mass Media Use and Outcomes

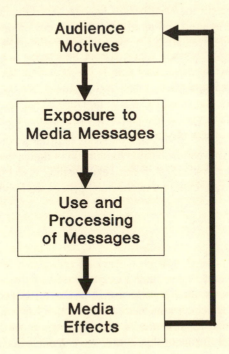

political communications scholars could only speculate about, in terms of the ability of mass media messages to structure, reinforce, and crystallize voter decisions.

A MODEL OF AUDIENCE MASS MEDIA USE AND OUTCOMES

A model that incorporates the uses and gratifications perspective can explain patterns of audience orientations toward the mass media, exposure and attention to communication, processing of messages, and ultimately media effects. Such a model is depicted in Figure 1.1. It will be used to guide the present research as we explore the ways in which voters relate to and use campaign media messages.

The model begins by specifying the factors that are preconditions to conscious, active mass media consumption. From a uses and gratifications perspective, audience motivations form the basic premise upon which media use is based. Audience motivations are shaped by personal traits, predispositions toward particular communication sources, and the needs that individuals feel they can satisfy through the mass media. Media exposure is influenced by individuals' orientations toward specific channels of communication and is an essential component of the process. The form and content of the communication are important to specific media effects. These factors influence which messages will be accepted, rejected, or ignored. The effects of mass communication ultimately have cognitive, affective, and behavioral components. All of these elements of the model will be explained in more detail in the discussion that follows.

The model of audience mass media use and outcomes delineated here focuses on the *conscious* processes that underlie individuals' orientations toward mass communications. While we acknowledge that the processing of media messages can occur at the unconscious level, this study and the guiding model take into account only the active and conscious dimension of media use. While ultimately important to our understanding of the relationship between the audience and the mass media, investigating nonconscious processes is beyond the scope of this research.

Audience Motives

The first component of the model is comprised of the audience's motives for using the mass media. Discovering how the mass audience is oriented toward forms of political communication holds important implications for democratic theory, especially in terms of how such communications affect an informed electorate. In terms of this study, we can explore: (1) who, within the electorate, is motivated to use campaign messages to satisfy particular needs; (2) how voters use campaign media to gratify these needs; and (3) how widespread the active processing of media messages is during presidential elections.

Three basic sets of factors relate to people's conscious motivations for using the mass media. First, specific, characteristic traits of audience members shape their orientations toward the media. Second, individuals' preconceptions about the subject of the communicated messages and the channel through which information is disseminated also inspire media-related motivations. Finally, certain fundamental needs structure individuals' motives for using the mass media.

The Diverse Audience for Political Communication

Defining exactly what the term "audience" comprises with regard to mass communications can be difficult. One common technique is to characterize the mass audience as a single entity that is identified by membership in a society. The audience for mass communication thus represents the total number of persons who have the potential to be reached by a given type of media content. This notion of the audience can be broken down into the categories of those to whom the communication is available, those who receive the messages, and those who process and interpret the content. This view of the audience as basically anonymous, heterogeneous, and disorganized has been challenged for its oversimplification (McQuail, 1981; Escarpit, 1977).

Scholars have assumed widely differing views on the nature of the mass audience and the level of activity that it can exhibit in relation to the communications media. These perspectives run the gamut, from the concept of a highly passive audience that falls prey to the manipulative ideological messages transmitted by ideologues (advocated by mass society and critical theorists), to that of the detached audience (the "limited effects" tradition), and ultimately to a vision of an audience that actively processes, interprets, and creates meaning from mass media messages. In reality, aspects of all of these perspectives are at work. Therefore, it is essential to take into account the diversity of the mass audience in studies of communication effects (Levy and Windahl, 1985).

The relationship between the audience and mass media content is highly complex and should not be treated as constant or universal (McQuail, Blumler, and Brown, 1972). To begin to explore the complexities of the mass media audience, we can differentiate at a rudimentary level on the basis of background characteristics, such as age and education (Blumler, 1985). Yet these distinctions are not rich enough to capture the aspects of individuals' lives that can structure their mass media use (Rosengren and Windahl, 1972). Segments of the mass audience can be identified by their common orientations to political and social life, which in turn influence their motives for using campaign communication (Merrill and Lowenstein, 1971; Friedson, 1974; McCombs and Becker, 1979; Blumler, 1985), as well as their corresponding behavioral patterns (Escarpit, 1977). Audience segments share knowledge, interconnected beliefs, and values. These shared traits and commonalities of interest become relevant when triggered within a particular communication context, such as a presidential election (Hewes and Planalp, 1987).

In terms of voting behavior, certain audiences may be distinguished by their partisan or ideological orientations, their level of interest in the election, and their degree of certainty about their candidate choice. Thus, diverse subgroups may seek different things from communications, which will be reflected in their patterns of media use and ultimately in the ways that they are influenced by mediated messages.

It is important to emphasize that the audience does not behave independently of the content of the communication, the context within which it is disseminated, or the values and intentions of the communicator. The audience can be viewed as a system of "response potentials" with which a communicator must contend under given conditions (Bauer, 1964). Therefore, the communicator will often design messages to appeal to the expectations of diverse audience subgroups (Bauer, 1964; Bauer, 1973; Dervin, 1981).

One could argue that the overt structuring of communicated messages to conform to the perceived desires of specific audience segments is nowhere more obviously pronounced than in American election campaigns. It has become a thriving industry in which political operatives and media wizards seek continually to expose hidden distinctions within the mass audience. In a sense, an underlying goal of this project is to gauge the success and failure of these operatives to meet audience demands and to satisfy their campaign-related media goals.

Audience Predispositions toward Mass Media Elections

Another set of factors that molds audience motives for using the media are preconceived attitudes about the subject of the communication. These predispositions can influence whether an individual will be inclined to seek out media messages or not. Further, they may affect the kinds of needs or desires that individuals seek from the media. An additional consequence is that predispositions may guide the level of attention and exposure to messages that individuals exhibit.

For the current study, individuals' preconceived attitudes about today's mass-mediated presidential contests are important for determining their motivations for media use during a campaign. People approach political campaigns from a variety of perspectives. For some, campaigns represent a time to revitalize passions after a period of political quiescence. Other individuals manage to maintain an awareness of campaigns and exhibit a degree of interest without becoming fully engaged. Still others avoid having any level of involvement in campaigns at all. Related to these characteristics is that individuals may come to political campaigns with different preconceptions based on the degree of prior knowledge that they have about candidates and issues. In addition, campaign orientations can be shaped by voters' levels of certainty about their candidate preferences.

This diversity of attitudes toward election campaigns relates to differential motivations for media use and ties in to the self-selection and selective perception of media content (Lang and Lang, 1959; Sears and Freedman, 1974; McCombs and Becker, 1979). For example, voters who are interested in and attentive to elections and have already decided on a candidate may use the media to reaffirm their attitudes. They may also use the mass media to fulfill a need for social interaction in their lives. These motives may differ from those of voters who need to make up their minds. Undecided voters may rely more heavily on the media to provide them with information that will facilitate their vote choice.

Audience Needs and Motivations

Fundamental to a model based on uses and gratifications are the needs and motivations that influence people's orientations toward mass media. Needs are distinct from motives; they are, in fact, major antecedents of motives. Needs are basic human desires and requirements that stimulate and structure specific motivations. These motivations can then be satisfied, at least in part, through mass media outlets (McLeod and Becker, 1981). Needs encompass both ra-

Figure 1.2
Audience Needs and Motivations

tional and irrational, conscious and unconscious processes. Motivations are more specifically goal-directed (Ball-Rokeach, Rokeach, and Grube, 1984).

Needs stem from social, psychological, and societal factors. Individuals experience needs associated with their personal sense of self, their social interactions, and their connections to the political world (Rosengren and Windahl, 1972). Under some circumstances, political needs are related to personal needs (Katz, Gurevitch, and Haas, 1973; Kippax and Murray, 1980). The event of an election campaign may, in fact, stimulate this connection of personal and political needs.

Motives represent the link between the internal psychological processes associated with needs and the actions taken to satisfy them. Motives for mass media use may be described operationally as the "gratifications sought" (McLeod and Becker, 1981). Motives direct the individual to pursue certain strategies of mass media use. Thus, they relate to behavioral outcomes, which in this model are expressed in terms of individuals seeking exposure to mass communication.

The relationship between needs and motivations is depicted in Figure 1.2. At root are the basic social and psychological sources of needs. These include factors such as self-esteem, self-interest, and the need to understand one's role in a complex and ever-changing society. These basic personal orientations are translated into specific needs that are associated with mass media use.

Researchers have identified a variety of media-related needs that have been organized into a basic typology by McQuail (1981). These include needs for information, for reinforcement of personal values, for social interaction and integration, for entertainment and enjoyment, and for escapism. The motivational manifestations of these needs lead to mass media use. For example, the need for information can reveal itself in individuals continually monitoring the news in order to keep aware of events and to reduce uncertainty about situations that may affect or threaten their lives. They also need information to guide decision-making, form attitudes, and reinforce and crystallize opinions. Informational needs can be linked to needs for social interaction, such as anticipating conversations about a particular topic. We turn now to explore the relevance of these relationships within the context of presidential elections.

Self-esteem forms the basis of one set of needs. People strive to increase their sense of personal satisfaction by appearing competent and moral to themselves and by meeting what they perceive as the expectations of others. During an election campaign, these needs may be grounded in the sense of civic duty that is instilled in Americans from childhood. People may, for example, seek information about an election because they feel it is expected of them in their role as good citizens. In the process, they may look for information that creates a highly positive self-conception and ignore that which fosters feelings of personal disillusionment (Ball-Rokeach, Rokeach, and Grube, 1984).

Needs can also be self-interested, as people act to preserve their personal well-being. One way in which self-interested needs manifest themselves during elections is in the way that individuals selectively attend to issues. Evidence suggests that people seek information predominantly about issues that they perceive will influence their lives directly to the exclusion of those issues that have more far-reaching, societal implications. Voters also tend to look for short-term rewards, as opposed to exploring the long-range consequences of policy issues (Perloff, 1985).

The media can meet the needs of individuals to understand themselves and their society. People act in a wide variety of roles whose definitions and patterns change frequently (Schramm, 1973). These social roles constrain audience needs, opportunities, and choices (Blumler, 1985; Blumler, Gurevitch, and Katz, 1985). The mass media have the potential to assist individuals greatly in their roles as voters. During elections, the media can fulfill voters' informational needs, their need for social interaction, and their need to reinforce personal beliefs, values, and goals.

Exposure to Mass Media Messages

The model of audience mass media use and outcomes that we employ assumes that motivational factors are an essential contingent condition that explains individuals' intentional exposure to mass media messages. When exposure to mass communication is motivationally stimulated, the possibility for media effects is enhanced. Information that does not satisfy a need or stimulate interest is often rejected by the recipient. As Graber (1984) states, "The first step in acquiring information for processing and formulating opinions is attention arousal. Much of the information available in the average home is unused because it has not aroused attention."

Some evidence suggests that exposure and attention to mediated communication are linked to a variety of effects, such as information gain and opinion reinforcement. To some extent, repeated exposure to a message or stimulus serves to enhance an individual's acceptance of the ideas that are communicated. Examples from the political communication field provide illustrations of this point. Studies of political advertising indicate that people who are exposed and pay attention to advertising on behalf of candidates obtain issue and candidate quality information, particularly from shorter ads (Atkin and Heald, 1976; Garramone, 1984; Patterson and McClure, 1976). In addition, individuals who are exposed to television and newspaper news are able to express opinions about political issues and to structure their attitudes toward them in a more meaningful way than those who have not been exposed (Reese and Miller, 1981).

Exposure is linked directly to media reliance, that is, the channel upon which an individual depends most for political information. Studies indicate that there are differences between those who rely on newspapers as their main source of political information and those who depend on television (McLeod, Bybee, and Durall, 1979; Becker and Whitney, 1980; Robinson, 1976). Two basic perspectives guide research incorporating the concept of media reliance. The first treats reliance as the causal component in a relationship linking media use to political knowledge gain and to changes in affective evaluations. These formulations categorize individuals based upon their media use habits and upon which medium they turn to most often. The second perspective, which is gaining in acceptance, treats the individual's tendency to rely on a particular medium to receive messages as suggesting a pattern of orientations toward media use. This conceptualization is well-suited for incorporation into uses and gratifications models, including the perspective adopted here. The underlying assumption is that individuals who view, hear, or read a message in their reliant medium are more likely to be receptive to the message than if they are exposed to the same information through another channel.

Research findings about media reliance and its relationship to politics and elections are confusing and contradictory. Researchers generally consider newspapers to be more effective than television in conveying political information. Newspaper-reliant people have been shown to gain in knowledge and level of political activity during campaigns, while the television-reliant do not (McLeod, Bybee, and Durall, 1979). In addition, studies have demonstrated that individuals who depend on television for election information are lower in levels of political knowledge, efficacy, and trust (Robinson, 1976), as well as more negative in their attitudes toward government than those who rely on print media (Becker and Whitney, 1980). There is also some evidence that the television-dependent are less well-educated and less politically interested (Kessel, 1984). Television, however, has been found to have an integrative effect in connecting political campaigns to individual orientations. More specifically, television-reliant voters make use of the image characteristics that are filtered through the media in making up their minds about candidates. Although newspaper-reliant voters might be expected to make greater use of issue information than image information, they actually do not (McLeod, Glynn, and McDonald, 1983). Still, the media play an integrative role in fostering positive orientations toward the political system for newspaper readers as well (O'Keefe, 1980).

Research findings based upon the assumed connection between reliance and media effects differ. Scholars who subscribe to the view that media reliance causes certain effects have tended to find that television-reliant voters are less politically knowledgeable and active than are the newspaper-dependent (Robinson, 1976). When these findings are taken in conjunction with other research, which indicates that television messages are less informative and more superficial than those appearing in newspapers, the implicit value judgment promotes the superiority of print-reliant individuals. Contradictory evidence has been presented by those who ascribe to the contingent condition perspective. These researchers stress the importance of the integrative role of television in elections, and they have tended to play down the assumption that the newspaper-reliant necessarily have more and better political information (McLeod, Glynn, and McDonald, 1983).

While problems of measurement and conceptualization plague both perspectives (McDonald, 1983), the contingent condition perspective adds a theoretically meaningful component to the model employed in this research. The model assumes that the channel through which communication is disseminated affects the way that voters are oriented toward the media. In addition, the channels through which campaign messages are disseminated influences a person's willingness to accept or reject them. Reliance is central to determining which messages voters will receive. Thus, mass media reliance is a contingent condition for the use and processing of campaign messages.

Use and Processing of Media Messages

According to our model of audience media use and outcomes, the manner in which individuals use and process media information flows from their motives for use and the patterns of exposure to mass communication they exhibit. Audience members possess diffuse orientations toward the social and political environment, as well as toward message content. These orientations structure the ways in which they process communications. First, people approach mediated communications with a backlog of prior information that they have acquired through past experience. During elections, this includes knowledge about the campaign process, types of messages disseminated, issues, and political parties (Graber, 1984). This storehouse of information is a long-term component of information processing, which conditions what voters expect from the media. In addition, individuals bring short-term preconceptions to bear on the situation. In campaigns, these predispositions are usually manifested in their attitudes toward and knowledge about candidates. Often, these preconceptions translate into images. Images can affect the ways in which media messages are perceived and processed.

Images may be defined as "mental images" (Pomper, 1975) or as subjective representations of political objects that act as filtering devices in affecting perceptions about politics (Nimmo and Savage, 1976; Hofstetter, Zukin, and Buss, 1978). A candidate's image is composed of the qualities, traits, attributes, and viewpoints that are conveyed to the public. Two basic and generally opposing theories attempt to explain how candidate images are devised. The first, referred to as the "candidate projection thesis," asserts that voters accept the images of candidates that are presented to them. Candidates thus become what their marketing agents create. This view assumes that people receiving campaign messages are entirely passive and easily manipulated. The "voter projection thesis," by contrast, holds that images are shaped by voters' predispositions about candidates. Image merchants have the option of presenting a candidate who appears neutral and nonthreatening and who keeps a low profile or of tailoring their clients to fit voters' preconceptions about what makes a viable candidate (Nimmo, 1970). In actuality, both of these perspectives offer insights into a suitable explanation of image-making.

We present an alternative conceptualization of image-making in keeping with our beliefs about audience roles in the campaign communication process. Both campaigners and voters contribute to the process via a mutual exchange of perceptions. Candidates attempt to portray themselves and their positions on issues in a particular way to voters, who in turn convey what they expect and desire to see in those seeking office. Voters generally express these expectations in terms of the experience, personal characteristics, and political style of the candidates.

Individuals' prior knowledge about the subject of communication and shorter-term image factors serve as perceptual filters through which messages are interpreted. Thus, the form and the content of communication significantly influence the use and processing of information and the formation of images. At a fundamental level, the technical differences between print and broadcast media are reflected in the way that messages are presented, as well as the content that is offered. Williams (1972) points out that the differences can be traced back to the development of these two basic forms of communication. The purpose of print media, which have predominantly taken the form of newspapers, was to disseminate information. A concern with content preceded consideration of the actual form that the communication took. When radio and television were developed and made available to mass audiences, however, the focus was on the technological aspects of transmission and reception. Content was of only secondary interest and was initially supplied by coverage of public, theatrical, and sporting events.

Print and broadcast communications have a number of distinctive characteristics that are grounded in their form. First, the print media present simultaneously multiple items that may or may not be selected for consumption by the reader. While stylistic techniques give priority to certain articles, consumers may read them in whatever order they determine and in as great or as little detail as they wish. Broadcast media do not allow people this amount of selectivity. They present information in a basically linear fashion, which lends itself to give priority to items that occur early in the broadcast. Beyond the decision to be exposed to a broadcast or not, selectivity is limited to the amount of attention paid by the individual.

Perhaps the biggest distinction between the two forms of communication is that broadcast media introduce outside personalities as a salient factor in the presentation of messages. Television adds a visual dimension to this process. A person's identification with the presenter of a message becomes important to the message's reception, credibility, and processing. In addition, broadcast media bring political forms and debate to life in a manner that cannot be duplicated by print communication.

There is evidence that the form of communication influences its content and ultimately its effect. The type of information presented on television differs from what newspapers and news magazines emphasize. Scholars have noted the existence of "structural bias" in television news stories, which tend to concentrate on action and image rather than on explanation and substance. Television coverage of elections has often been saturated with dramatizations of campaign events and has emphasized the battle between the candidates (Hofstetter, Zukin, and Buss, 1978; Patterson, 1980). While television provides vivid pictures of the election, the print media allow for the discussion of events, issues, and candidates in greater detail (Robinson and Sheehan, 1983).

The format of the presentation of messages affects how they are processed as well. Political learning from televised presidential debates is limited because segments of the audience find the format of the debates unattractive (Graber, 1984). We elaborate upon this point here by assuming that campaign message types have unique characteristics. Voters' perceptions of and experience with message forms shape their expectations in terms of the substance, reliability, and salience of what is communicated. These factors in turn mitigate the effects of campaign communication.

Media Effects

The effects that result from mass-mediated communication are determined in large part by the salience of a particular topic and by individuals' motivations for attending to messages. In elections, these motives will influence the degree to which people are exposed and pay attention to the mass media and to which they use the media for decision-making, information-processing, and campaign involvement (O'Keefe, 1975). Effects can be of two types—subjective and objective. Subjective effects reflect the individuals' feelings about how well particular needs are gratified by mass communications. Objective effects include both cognitive outcomes and behavioral consequences. During campaigns, objective effects can thus take the form of information gain about candidates and issues, as well as active political participation (McLeod and Becker, 1981). Objective effects can be examined on three basic levels: they can be observed through increments in learning; they can confirm or modify attitudes; and they can stimulate overt political behavior (Seymour-Ure, 1974).

The recent trend in mass communication research has been toward examining attitudinal or learning effects rather than the pure behavioral changes that characterized early research (Roberts and Bachen, 1981). During political campaigns, information gain is far easier to discern than are changes in voter preferences linked directly to media messages. Researchers must also be aware of a certain degree of ambiguity about the nature of media effects. For example, are media messages actually providing audiences with new information or simply reminding them of things that they have already processed and stored? Are the media supplying information to individuals or encouraging them to seek more knowledge from other sources? As media effects are extremely complicated phenomena, a "complexity of evidence" is required to make inferences about them (O'Keefe and Atwood, 1981; McLeod and Reeves, 1980). Thus, we need to explore the cognitive, affective, and behavioral dimensions of media effects.

Feedback

One additional outcome of the process is the potential for feedback. The gratifications received from media use can lead to a reinforcement or reevaluation of the needs and motivations for seeking out communicated messages. Gratifications received can also alter the types of predispositions that individuals display when they approach the mass media for need gratification at a later time. These factors would lead once again to exposure to particular forms of mass-mediated communication.

APPLICATION TO THE PRESENT RESEARCH

In this study, the audience-centered model of mass media use and outcomes, which incorporates the general premises set forth in the uses and gratification approach, will guide an examination of the 1984 and 1988 presidential elections. The study will emphasize the implications that the four types of campaign messages presented through different communication channels have for the audience's relationship to the mass media. We assume that individuals bring to these two presidential election contests orientations toward specific message types that they have acquired through past experience. In conjunction with the presentation of messages in 1984 and 1988, these factors will shape the ways in which voters use and process ads, news stories, poll results, and debates to achieve a variety of need-related goals.

RESEARCH DESIGN AND DATA COLLECTION

Survey research was employed as the technique for gathering data for this project during both the 1984 and 1988 presidential elections. Following in the tradition of early studies that sought to explore communication effects in presidential elections (Lazarsfeld, Berelson, and Gaudet, 1944; Berelson, Lazarsfeld, and McPhee, 1954), we conducted surveys on the county level. By administering the questionnaires to voters in limited geographical locations, it is possible to take into account some of the important variations in the political communication environment that exists between samples. Factors such as differences in the type of newspaper and television news coverage available in each county can be assessed.

The 1984 data are from two sources. One is a mail questionnaire sent to residents of Fairfax County, Virginia, a suburb of Washington, D.C. The other consists of a telephone interview survey conducted in Dane County, Wisconsin, which includes the city of Madison, the state capital.[1] Both cities contain a high proportion of well-educated, middle-class voters. The Fairfax and Dane County samples, while perhaps not typical of the American electorate in general, provide two interesting cases for examination in this study. The two counties differ sharply on several important political dimensions, thus providing the opportunity to compare the influence of the media on diverse groups within the electorate.

The analysis of the 1984 presidential contest produced some interesting findings that we hoped to replicate in 1988. Given the limited resources for fielding another another study, a decision was made to broaden the diversity of the data base by including two new counties in the survey and dropping Dane County. A mail questionnaire essentially identical to the one administered in Fairfax County in 1984 (with the exception of specific references to the candidates) was administered to voters in Carroll County, Iowa, and Middlesex County, New Jersey, in addition to Fairfax County. Carroll County was included because it is in the heart of the agricultural region of the United States. In contrast, Middlesex County is highly industrialized and contains a substantial proportion of blue-collar workers. These groups were not represented well in the 1984 study. Fairfax County was included in an effort to gauge the consistency of the initial findings over the course of two election cycles.

The 1984 Dane County data were collected by the Mass Communication Research Center at the University of Wisconsin-Madison. A pre/post-election telephone survey of Dane County residents was conducted using random digit dialing techniques by trained interviewers.[2] Data collection for the first wave of the panel spanned approximately the same time period as the Fairfax County survey. By using the telephone interview technique, response rate problems were minimized. (An exact accounting of the response rate in Dane County is not available, however.) A total of 737 interviews were completed and included in the data set.

The 1984 Fairfax County data set was collected by mailing the questionnaire to a random sample of 1,000 voting-age residents.[3] The first mailing of the questionnaire was scheduled to be received by the intended respondents on the Monday following the second presidential debate, which took place on a Sunday eleven days prior to the election. Thus, the respondents had had the opportunity for exposure to two presidential debates and the vice-presidential debate held in the 1984 election prior to receiving the survey. A single follow-up was sent on the day before the election. Surveys were accepted for two weeks following election day.

The exact same procedure was followed for the 1988 study. Two samples of 750 voting-age residents each were sent surveys in Iowa and New Jersey. A smaller sample of 450 people received surveys in Fairfax County.[4]

While mail surveys often suffer from problems of low response rate, the use of this technique was selected for this sample in 1984 and for the entire 1988 study for a number of reasons. First, many of the questions included in the survey involved complex issues concerning media use habits and perceptions of campaign media messages. A relatively large number of open-ended questions were asked. By answering the questionnaire by mail, respondents were able to give more thought to these questions than they might have if the survey had been conducted over the telephone. The responses provided useful explanatory insights to accompany the close-ended segments of the questionnaire. In addition, the mail questionnaire method was the most cost-effective means of carrying out the research and of gathering the desired information.

In 1984, a total of 478 people (48.7%) returned completed questionnaires that were included in the Fairfax County data set. Given the time constraints involved in fielding this survey, the response rate was quite respectable. The response rates achieved in the three 1988 surveys were more typical of mail questionnaires and thus were somewhat disappointing. A total of 236 individuals (32%) responded to the Carroll County survey, 215 (29%) completed the Middlesex County survey, and 118 (30%) filled out the Fairfax County questionnaire. In short, 569 individuals participated in the 1988 campaign study.

The survey questions were designed to investigate the respondents' knowledge and perceptions of the mass media. More specific questions addressed the role of the mass media in the 1984 and 1988 presidential contests and focused on how individuals perceived and processed specific types of campaign messages. General information about the respondents' media use habits and political orientations was also acquired.

A COMPARISON OF SAMPLE CHARACTERISTICS

Using data from the widely diverse counties that we surveyed over the course of the 1984 and 1988 elections has the benefit of allowing comparisons across samples and therefore strengthens the ability to generalize when consistent findings are uncovered. The counties selected differed on a number of important dimensions, including the nature of the mass media environment, the general political orientations of the respondents, and the participants' attitudes about the elections and candidates. Such structural variations allow interesting contrasts to be made. We move now to compare our samples on a variety of basic demographic, media-related, and political factors.

Several demographic differences appear between the samples. Although attempts were made to include an equal number of men and women in the samples, the 1984 Fairfax County sample contained slightly more male respondents (53%) than females. The opposite was true for Dane County, where 56 percent of those responding were women. In 1988, males answered the questionnaire more often than females in all three counties—56 percent in Carroll County, 60 percent in Middlesex County, and 71 percent in Fairfax County.

The 1984 respondents to the Fairfax County questionnaire averaged more years of formal education than those participating in the Dane County survey. In 1988, the Fairfax County survey participants were very similar in their overall educational profile to the 1984 sample. The average educational levels for participants in the 1988 Carroll and Middlesex County surveys were strikingly similar. They were substantially lower than for both counties in 1984 and for Fairfax County in 1988.

The 1984 Fairfax County respondents had far higher incomes than those in Dane County, even when the cost of living in each county was factored in. Once again, the 1988 Fairfax County participants strongly resembled the 1984 sample in terms of income. The 1988 Iowa, New Jersey, and Virginia samples differed with regard to income. The majority of the Carroll County respondents (59%) had incomes of less than $30,000 per year, compared with 29 percent of the Middlesex County sample and 6 percent of those in Fairfax County. In contrast, 48 percent of the Fairfax County sample had a family income of $70,000 a year, while only 18 percent of those in Middlesex County and 6 percent of those in Carroll County matched that amount. This differential in real dollars still appeared when cost of living was considered.

The 1984 Dane County respondents tended to be somewhat younger than those in Fairfax County. In 1988, the Iowa and New Jersey survey participants were very similar in their age distribution, which was relatively even across age categories. The Virginia sample had a higher concentration of people in the 41–50 age range.

Conducting the study at the county level has a major advantage for this type of research. The respondents in each county sample had access to the same channels of communication and had the potential for exposure to the same media messages. This ability to control for the media environment is crucial. The importance can be illustrated by examining the differences in the newspapers read in each county.

In the 1984 Fairfax County sample, 78 percent of the respondents reported that they read *The Washington Post*, a newspaper with a strong focus on national news events. A far smaller number of people reported reading the local paper, *The Fairfax Journal*, at least once a week. By contrast, most of the Dane County survey participants read the *Wisconsin State Journal* (67%) and *The Capital Times* (18%). Both of these newspapers concentrate heavily on state and local news.

The 1988 Fairfax County sample displayed similar patterns of newspaper choice to that of the 1984 sample, although readership of *The Washington Post* had risen to almost 90 percent. The 1988 respondents reported a tendency to supplement their newspaper reading with *USA Today*, further emphasizing this group's orientation toward national news. The Iowa sample reported a preference for the *Des Moines Register* (59%) and the *Carroll Daily Times* (17%)—newspapers with strong state and local emphasis respectively. New Jersey presented an interesting case, in that the state must struggle continually to maintain its own media identity, particularly in the area of television. The northern New Jersey media market is eclipsed by that of New York City, while south Jersey must contend with the strong influence of Philadelphia. The difficulty in identifying a specific state newspaper, as we found in Wisconsin or Iowa, was evident in the diversity of newspaper preferences indicated by the New Jersey respondents. The largest number of respondents read the *Newark Star Ledger* (36%), followed by the *News Tribune* (21%), the *New York Times* (14%), and the *Home News* (10%), a local paper. A wide variety of other papers, from both in and out of state, were also listed by the respondents.

Respondents to the two 1984 samples differed somewhat on the source of communication on which they relied most for information about the election and politics. Approximately 45 percent of respondents in both Dane and Fairfax Counties reported relying on newspapers for political information. A significantly greater proportion in the Fairfax County sample claimed to depend on television (44%) than in the Dane County sample (35%). Some of the respondents in Fairfax County noted on their questionnaires that while they would have liked to pay more attention to newspapers and the print media in general, the long commute into Washington, D.C., combined with a heavy work schedule, caused them to become reliant on televised information. People in Dane County relied on news magazines and interpersonal communication more than did those in Fairfax County.

The 1988 respondents in all counties relied most heavily on television for their campaign information. The highest proportion of television-reliant respondents came from Carroll County (60%). The Middlesex and Fairfax County samples each reported approximately 45 percent who relied most often on television. Correspondingly, the Iowa respondents were the least reliant on newspapers (27%), as compared to New Jersey (39%) and Virginia (36%).

The media messages received across counties thus differed somewhat in both study years. The counties received differently oriented newspaper accounts of the election and political news depending upon the nature of the community environment. They also varied somewhat in their orientation toward specific mass media channels.

We also found differences between counties along political dimensions. The 1984 Fairfax and Dane County samples were dissimilar in their partisan alignments. There were more Republican identifiers (38%) among Fairfax County respondents than Independents (34%) or Democrats (28%). The majority of participants in the Dane County study were Independents (61%), with the smallest percentage identifying with the Republican Party (14%).

In the 1988 study, there generally appeared to be a more even distribution of partisanship than in 1984. In Iowa, there were slightly more Independents (37%) than Republicans (32%) or Democrats (31%). In New Jersey, there was an equal number of Democrats and Independents—38 percent in each category, while only 22 percent were Republicans. The Republicans in the Fairfax County sample (45%) far outnumbered the Democrats (28%) and Independents (27%).

Most of the respondents in both 1984 samples considered themselves to be ideologically moderate—approximately 60 percent in each sample. The Fairfax County sample, however, contained a greater percentage of conservatives (30%) than did the Dane County sample, which had proportionately more liberals (26%).

In 1988, the majority of respondents again considered themselves to be moderates. All three counties were represented by more self-identified conservatives than liberals. The Fairfax County sample consisted of 32 percent conservatives, followed by Iowa with 27 percent, and New Jersey with 21 percent. Interestingly, Fairfax County also contained the highest proportion of liberals of the three samples (16%), followed by New Jersey (15%), and Iowa (7%).

Attitudes about the specific presidential contests also differed across counties. At the time of the 1984 survey, 14 percent of the Fairfax County and 19 percent of the Dane County residents questioned were undecided about their vote choice. Of those who had made up their minds, a majority of the Fairfax County respondents supported Ronald Reagan for president (55%), while an equal percentage of Dane County participants were committed to Walter Mondale.

In 1988, 14 percent of both the Iowa and New Jersey samples were undecided, while only 6 percent of the Virginia respondents had not yet made up their minds. Candidate preference differed across samples. Michael Dukakis was favored over George Bush by 53 percent of the Iowa respondents who had already decided in the election. The New Jersey and Virginia survey participants supported Bush by proportions of 53 percent and 70 percent respectively.

It is clear that there was an element of self-selection by the respondents to the survey, based on the level of interest that they had in the presidential contests under study. For both years, a substantial proportion of each sample reported a high level of interest in the presidential election. Those surveyed in Fairfax County expressed a far higher level of interest in and attention to the campaign than did those in other counties. Approximately 70 percent of the Fairfax County respondents reported that they were interested in the elections "a lot," as compared to around 50 percent or slightly less for all other counties. This may be explained by the fact that living in the Washington, D.C., area fosters a heightened sense of awareness about politics, particularly at the presidential level. Also, approximately 20 percent of the respondents in the Fairfax County surveys were employed by the government.

Since the goal of this research was to compare the influence of different forms of campaign communication during presidential elections, exposure to the different types of messages was essential. Individuals who were highly interested in and attentive to the election campaigns were also exposed to a wide variety of media messages. This abundance of exposure facilitated our goal of exploring mass media influence by comparing the audience's use of specific message types.

AUDIENCE ORIENTATIONS TOWARD MEDIA MESSAGES IN THE 1984 AND 1988 PRESIDENTIAL ELECTIONS

We have established a theoretical framework that focuses on the audience's use and processing of mass media messages, and we have discussed the data to be employed in our empirical investigation. We now turn to our examination of the 1984 and 1988 presidential elections.

Each of these elections followed general trends that have come to characterize presidential contests in the age of the mass media election. Media messages were abundant during the 1984 and 1988 presidential contests, as they have been in all present-day elections. The candidates pursued vigorous advertising strategies. Both print and television coverage of the campaigns was extensive and included the continual release of poll results predicting the eventual winner. Three sets of candidate debates were held, accompanied by a barrage of media commentary.

Still, the 1984 and 1988 presidential elections were unique political events in many respects. The media environment in a particular election is shaped by a complex interaction of a multitude of factors. These include the technological aspects of campaign communication and coverage; the goals and strategies of the candidate and mass media organizations; and the personal characteristics and appeal of the candidates themselves.

A major assumption underlying this research is that as media messages vary in terms of their form and, to some extent, of their content, they will be treated differently by the electorate. Voters' processing of campaign communications is influenced by their perceptions about specific message types. Individuals' preconceptions about ads, news stories, poll results, and debates can bias their feelings about the information that specific messages contain and can contribute to their displaying different patterns of media use based on their desire to gratify particular election-oriented needs.

Media effects in presidential elections are shaped by a variety of factors. These include voters' level of involvement in the campaign, the degree of certainty that they have reached in their voting decisions, and their familiarity with and feelings about candidates (Atkin, 1980). Generally, those individuals who are highly interested and involved in the presidential campaign will be more likely to be exposed and attentive to campaign communication. Highly involved and interested members of the electorate are also more likely to have made up their minds early in the election. They therefore tend to use the media for political learning, reinforcement, and entertainment. Alternatively, undecided voters need to use media to aid them in decision-making.

Individuals often perceive messages in light of their past experiences with and present evaluations of the source of the message and the channel through which it is disseminated. Some communicated messages may be accorded greater credibility by voters than other message types. The confidence that voters place in the source of a message may affect their willingness to believe it as well. For example, voters may be more willing to believe information presented by news broadcasters than that disseminated by candidates. Finally, media content that is in agreement with voters' preconceptions about candidates and issues may be more readily accepted than dissonant information.

In the chapters that follow, we will explore in detail the defining traits of ads, news stories, poll results, and debates. We will examine the nature of the audience's relationship to each of these message types in general. Finally, we will investigate the specifics of audience orientations toward mass media messages during the 1984 and 1988 presidential elections.

NOTES

1. It was difficult to make the two surveys directly parallel. Certain questions were worded or scaled differently across surveys. Some measures were excluded from one or the other questionnaire entirely because different people were in charge of designing the two instruments. In addition, comparing data that are collected using two different techniques—mail questionnaires and telephone interviews—has the potential to introduce problems into the analysis. Individuals may respond differently depending on the form of the survey. People replying to mail surveys may be more likely to give extreme responses to questions because they are not reporting directly to an interviewer; the feeling of confidentiality is enhanced. One difficulty with the mail questionnaire is the possibility that self-selection bias may enter into the process. Individuals with a higher level of interest in the election are more likely to return questionnaires than those who are less interested. This tendency would inflate the percentage of extreme responses to certain questions, particularly those pertaining to interest in and attention to the campaign.

2. The sample was drawn from the population of private telephone lines in Dane County. Interviewers were given a list of exchanges for Dane County and a list of four digit numbers randomly drawn to complete the phone numbers. Each interviewer was given a quota of surveys to complete. They were instructed to try a telephone number a total of four times before eliminating it from the sample and moving on to another selected at random within the same exchange. Some attention was paid to achieving a balance in terms of gender representation in the sample.

3. The sample was drawn from the population of private home telephone lines in

Fairfax County. In drawing the sample, six communities in Fairfax County were selected at random for inclusion in the study. The use of randomly selected communities simplified the logistics of conducting the survey. The sample was stratified by sex, as an equal number of women and men were sent the questionnaires. Sampling was done with replacement. Cases in which addresses were discovered to be incorrect or individuals returned the survey noting their refusal were replaced by others drawn at random. A total of thirty-six surveys were replaced in this manner.

4. The Carroll County, Middlesex County, and Fairfax County samples were drawn from the population of private home telephone lines in each county. Unfortunately, many questionnaires were returned in 1988 because of incorrect addresses. While we again sampled with replacement, it was virtually impossible to deal with every returned survey. We attribute much of the lowered response rate to this problem.

2

Voter Orientations toward Televised Candidate Advertisements

TELEVISED CANDIDATE ADVERTISING

Televised political advertising forms an integral part of today's presidential campaigns, but there is little agreement about its propriety or influence. Advertising is criticized for manipulating the electorate and trivializing campaigns by promoting image-based politics. At the same time, political commercials are often credited with providing useful information to voters about candidates and issues. Some people blame advertising for driving up the cost of elections, while others praise it as the most inexpensive way of reaching the greatest number of voters. Finally, the fact that political spots are not regulated as product commercials are troubles some observers of the electoral process who feel that this situation facilitates the candidates' ability to mislead the public. Others believe that formal regulation of content is unnecessary because voters are not fools. As Kaid (1981: 249) states, "It is undoubtably true that political advertising is the most controversial, and perhaps, most feared form of political communication."

One indisputable fact remains. Since its advent in the 1952 Eisenhower presidential campaign, the use of advertising has dramatically changed the way elections are run. In that year, Rosser Reeves, a Madison Avenue adman who worked with Eisenhower, pictured candidate spots as emulating product commercials. The advertising approach thus initiated stressed brief, direct, and persuasive messages. The history of advertising in elections demonstrates that ads take on a dynamic quality in campaigns.[1] With each passing contest, changes in the nature and content of spots, as well as the strategies used in advertising, become apparent.

As political advertising evolves in terms of technological innovation and style, and as each election brings into play new challenges and uncertainties, candidates take greater risks with their advertising appeals. The 1984 and 1988 presidential elections illustrate this point well. These two electoral contests provide excellent opportunities to examine whether variations in the style and content of ads are perceived by voters. The "feel good about America" ads produced by the Reagan campaign in 1984 differed sharply from Mondale's ads, which were generally somber in tone and more issue-laden. Bush's hard-hitting attack strategy, coupled with a reprise of the upbeat Reagan-style spots, provided a clear contrast to the more cerebral, often confusing advertising messages of the Dukakis campaign in 1988. Negative advertising was a staple of both elections, allowing us the opportunity to explore voters' reactions to attack strategies.

ADVERTISING AS A CAMPAIGN COMMUNICATION FORM

Advertising in elections has unique characteristics that set it apart from other forms of political communication. For the most part, advertising content is controlled by the candidate's organization[2] and it is not regulated by the Federal Communication Commission (Spero, 1980). Ads are designed to entertain, to persuade, and to create images of candidates that will be perceived favorably by voters. The most prevalent type of campaign ad, the 30- or 60-second spot, emphasizes brevity and repetition. Messages must therefore be simple, concise, and clearly illustrated to be successful. The fact that candidate ads are interspersed throughout regular programming makes them difficult to avoid for many television viewers.

These factors combine to give advertising a potential edge over other campaign media messages. Ads can circumvent viewer selectivity and can reach even the most uninterested and uninformed members of the electorate. Spot ads, in particular, represent only a minor intrusion in a familiar format, which television viewers have come to anticipate through the proliferation of product commercials (Michelson, 1972). For these reasons, ads tend to be recalled by voters.

Candidates attempt to achieve a variety of goals through advertising. Ads are designed to foster recognition of candidates among voters. Strategists strive to convey images of candidates to which voters will respond positively. In some cases, this may constitute the creation of a "secondhand reality," designed to maximize the candidate's position in the race (Buss and Hofstetter, 1976). Political commercials are also used to provide cues to voters and to establish associations between candidates and political objects, goals, and ideals. They can help to set the candidates' issue agendas in an election (Bowers, 1977). In sum, candidates hope that ads will convert the uncommitted, reinforce the convictions of their loyalists, and provide the stimulation necessary to get their supporters to the polls.

In addition to achieving these direct goals, ads can enhance campaign efforts in other ways. They can facilitate candidates' ability to raise funds and to enlist volunteers by providing concrete evidence of campaign activity. Ads are thus a central component of the "meta-campaign" waged for candidate supporters (Diamond and Bates, 1985). Aside from their own media value, ads can generate stories that provide candidates with greater exposure.

Choosing an appropriate and effective advertising strategy is an essential part of a presidential campaign. This situation has greatly enhanced the role played by professional media consultants in the political process. Advertising helps to establish campaign themes designed to inspire positive candidate images; increasingly, it is used to create serious doubts about the opponent. The specific content of ads should support the themes that the candidates and their organizations desire to project in their overall mass media strategy.

THE EFFECTS OF ADVERTISING IN ELECTIONS

Evidence suggests that the potential for political advertising in presidential elections to influence voters' candidate choice directly is perhaps minimal. During presidential campaigns, the media generate a large volume of intensely political information quite apart from that provided in candidate spots. Voters are highly aware of candidates, and they often form concrete attitudes about them fairly early in the campaign. In addition, individuals' defenses are mobilized against candidates' obvious attempts to win their votes (Patterson and McClure, 1974). Under these conditions, advertising appeals are not highly persuasive during general elections for the presidency. Advertising may, however, be more effective in other types of campaigns. Studies have shown that in low-information, low-involvement campaigns, such as congressional, gubernatorial, and primary elections, ads can influence voting intentions (Rothschild and Ray, 1974; Wanat, 1974; Gronbeck, 1989; Payne, Marlier, and Baukus, 1989).

As Patterson and McClure (1973: 60) state, "political commercials are a unique channel of communication. Commercials can deliver a message to the uninterested voter. No other channel of political communication has the power to reach as many of these voters as the televised ad." This observation is supported by the fact that daily television viewing time, not political factors, has been shown to be the primary determinant of individuals noticing political ads (Atkin, Bowen, Nayman, and Sheinkopf, 1973). Evidence suggests that political commercials are an important source of information for voters who have only moderate or very low interest in an election. These voters have lower levels of knowledge about candidates and issues, and they tend to take fewer cues from political parties than those who are highly interested and involved in the campaign. Highly interested voters tend to seek out campaign information from multiple media sources, which is not the case for the uninterested. Advertising effects are greatest where political spots represent a source of new information to the individual. Thus, the potential for ads to influence the politically uninvolved and uninterested is enhanced (Atkin, Bowen,

Nayman, and Sheinkopf, 1973; Atkin and Heald, 1976, Hofstetter, Zukin, and Buss, 1978; McClure and Patterson, 1974; Patterson and McClure, 1974; Joslyn, 1981).

While political ads may reach the uninterested and uninvolved, there is no guarantee that they or other voters will be receptive to spots. In fact, there is some evidence that the continual barrage of ads during presidential elections serves to alienate voters. Atkin, Bowen, Nayman, and Sheinkopf (1973) discovered that people avoid candidate ads because they interfere with prime-time programming. Moderate exposure to ads about candidates seems to produce more favorable ratings than high exposure (Becker and Doolittle, 1975), although there is some evidence to the contrary (Meadow and Sigelman, 1982). In the current study, a number of respondents expressed annoyance at the frequency at which ads were run during the 1984 and 1988 election campaigns. Most of these respondents reported ignoring ads when they appeared on television. Today, more and more people have the capacity to "graze" past political ads by using remote control channel selectors as they do when product commercials are shown.

Attention to political advertising is not necessarily related to exposure to spots. In fact, attention is determined mostly by the entertainment value of the spot, the partisan and candidate predispositions of the viewers, and the level of interest that individuals have in the election. Structural factors in the production value of ads can determine their effectiveness and their ability to hold the audience's attention (Garramone, 1986; Kaid and Davidson, 1986; Shyles, 1986). People who feel that a candidate's ads are entertaining pay more attention, especially uncommitted voters. Partisans tend to pay more attention to ads for their candidate than to spots for the opposition. Finally, individuals who are highly interested in the election are more likely to pay attention to political spots (Atkin, Bowen, Nayman, and Sheinkopf, 1973; Atkin, 1980).

While candidate spots rarely cause people to vote for a candidate, ads do provide individuals with issue information and help them to form effective evaluations of the candidates. Candidates use advertising to establish their issue agendas in elections. Voters often respond to these agendas (Atkin and Heald, 1976; Kaid, 1976). Exposure to advertising is related to learning about issues and formulating images about candidates (Garramone, 1983, 1984; Kaid and Sanders, 1978; Patterson and McClure, 1974, 1976; Hofstetter, Zukin, and Buss, 1978). Spot ads do not contribute any more to issue or image perceptions than other forms of communication (O'Keefe and Sheinkopf, 1974).

Advertising effects vary in relation to different types of voters. The decline in partisan affiliation coincides with the introduction of television ads into the presidential election process (Joslyn, 1981). Individuals who have weak or nonexistent attachments to parties may be more strongly influenced by candidate ads than others are. A number of studies have demonstrated that partisan defectors use televised political spots in making their decisions, particularly those ads that are issue-oriented (DeVries and Tarrance, 1972). Ticket-splitters are more likely to be exposed to the advertising of both parties' candidates (Cohen, 1975; Joslyn, 1981) and to use the information thus obtained to reinforce their decisions than are straight-ticket voters (Patterson and McClure, 1974).

Time of voting decision appears to be relevant to voters' orientations toward political ads. Voters who have made up their minds in an election are less likely to look to ads for information than those who are undecided. Ads are most useful for late campaign deciders and for voters who switch their candidate preference during the election (Patterson and McClure, 1974).

ADVERTISING IN THE 1984 AND 1988 PRESIDENTIAL ELECTIONS

Diamond and Bates (1988) have identified four phases that correspond to candidate advertising strategies in presidential elections. Early in the campaign, candidates are concerned with developing recognition and creating a positive image, so they run "identification" spots. These ads are followed by "argument" spots, in which the candidates attempt to convey what they stand for to the public. Candidates can use these commercials for developing emotional appeals or for conveying their policy positions. Next, "attack" spots highlight the opponent's weak points. In the fourth and final phase, candidates conclude their campaign advertising appeals by presenting their visions of the fate of the nation. In the 1984 and 1988 contests, the candidates' advertising strategies, while employing different tactics, essentially conformed to these temporal patterns (Diamond and Bates, 1985; Diamond and Marin, 1989).

In 1984, Mondale's advertising strategy focused on disseminating issue-oriented themes throughout the campaign. Early in the campaign, the Mondale organization chose to examine economic issues and the need for tax reform in its ads. By early October, a decision was made to use advertising to solidify the Democratic vote by concentrating on matters of interest to Democratic partisans. These included appeals that exposed the plight of the poor and elderly and ads that condemned Reagan's association with right-wing evangelical leaders and their role in policy-making (Schram, 1984). As the campaign drew to a close, the Mondale organization repeatedly aired a five-minute spot that foreshadowed the potential for nuclear war.

Popular accounts suggest that Mondale's advertising effort fell short of achieving its goals for a variety of reasons. First, voters were not receptive to the campaign themes chosen by Mondale's organization. The issues were often presented in a manner that was more complex than most audience members desired. In addition, the Mondale advertising campaign had a highly negative component, stressing the past failures and future dangers associated with the Reagan presidency. The attack strategy was pursued throughout the campaign, but voters did not relate to the themes of Reagan's unfairness and incompetence. Mondale's efforts were launched against a candidate who had a highly appealing television persona, while Mondale himself did not come across well in this medium. In fact, few of the Mondale campaign advertisements featured the candidate, with most employing professionals for voiceovers (Germond and Witcover, 1985).

The Reagan campaign ads provided a marked contrast to the Mondale spots. Reagan's organization collected talent from several top-rated ad agencies, generally specialists in product commercials, to form the "Tuesday Team," which spearheaded its advertising campaign. In May, before the general election, the Tuesday Team began to associate optimism and patriotism with the Reagan administration through a series of televised spots. A controversial 18-minute film aired during prime-time at the Republican National Convention and marked the beginning of the general election advertising effort. The majority of Reagan's spots were upbeat and portrayed American lifestyles, values, and symbols positively. Other spots dealt with specific issues, such as taxes. His most memorable issue spot, the "Bear" ad, focused on the Soviet threat.

As predicted by the Diamond and Bates advertising scenario, the Reagan campaign ran attack spots later in the election. Called "Man-on-the-Street" ads by the Tuesday Team, the Reagan attack spots featured hard-hats and housewives, who expressed their fears at the prospect of a Mondale presidency. These ads were launched primarily in response to Mondale's strong showing in the first televised debate. The tone of the final Reagan ads was once again upbeat, focusing on the country's youth and its potential for a bright future (Bumiller, 1984; Bumiller and Headley, 1984).

While criticized for being too slick, the Reagan ads were consciously designed to fit into the context of an entertainment medium. Their message was simple, generally positive, emotional, and low-key. Extensive market research prior to airing the ads indicated that the audience would be more likely to be receptive and attentive to ads of this sort than to those that were somber and presented complicated messages. The Reagan advertising strategy appeared to conform to the expectations of viewers more than did the techniques employed by the Mondale campaign.

A total of 70 different political ads were aired during the 1984 presidential election, 50 by Reagan and 20 by Mondale. The candidates each spent approximately $25 million to produce and play these ads. In general, the Mondale campaign was slightly more successful in scheduling ads at times when they would be seen by the largest number of people, although both campaigns made good time buys (Diamond and Bates, 1985).

The 1988 presidential contest could well be dubbed "The Year of the Handler" (Goldman and Mathews, 1989; Germond and Witcover, 1989; Runkel, 1989). In this election, image-makers, media consultants, and campaign specialists tested the boundaries of their capacity to manipulate the campaign process. The lessons from this campaign will serve political professionals well. Bush, who willingly turned himself over to a well-organized group of advisors, overcame his early status as the trailing candidate to emerge strongly victorious. Dukakis, by all reports, was a highly contentious candidate toward his advisors and maintained the aura of a hands-on policy while his organization was in a continual state of disarray.

The distinction between Bush's "well-handled" candidacy and Dukakis' "strategic disarray" emerges clearly when we compare their advertising efforts. In many ways, advertising eclipsed news coverage of the campaign. More often than in previous elections, news organizations assigned reporters to do nothing but cover the development and production of campaign spots. The publicity surrounding the candidates' advertising efforts surely enhanced the impact of the spots (Runkel, 1989).

From the outset, the Bush advertising team sought to employ a proactive strategy. The Bush Team was headed by Roger Ailes, a highly experienced media expert who brought with him the knowledge of the successful Reagan effort. Ailes rejected the temptation to accumulate proven talent from past Republican campaigns, however. Instead, he put together a team from small agencies around the country. His goals were to create an environment where fresh ideas could be generated, to take advantage of regional knowledge about advertising appeals, and to make sure that he was completely in charge. From most indications, this gamble paid off.

Bush's advertising strategy had three major objectives. First, the Bush Team wanted to solidify the blurry image that voters had of the candidate and to replace it with a positive one. Bush was portrayed as a warm, personable man. He displayed his skills as a communicator and stressed his leadership ability (Devlin, 1989). The strategy also called for the establishment of clear and coherent campaign themes. These themes emphasized that George Bush represented "mainstream America." Finally, Bush's handlers felt that it was necessary to draw as large a distinction as possible between the two candidates by accentuating the negative aspects of Dukakis and his candidacy while developing the positive side of Bush. In carrying forth this effort, negative campaign spots reached a level never before seen in presidential politics (Runkel, 1989; Devlin, 1989).

The Diamond and Bates scenario continues to provide a useful organizing framework for our discussion of candidate spots in 1988. Bush's identification spots were highly personalized. The candidate was depicted with children and his family against backdrops that reinforced the campaign theme of Bush as the representative of America's heartland (Diamond and Marin, 1989). Other biospots were designed to establish Bush as a communicator and leader. These ads employed footage from Bush's successful Republican National Convention speech, as well as pictures of him in presidential settings, such as in meetings with foreign leaders. They stressed his many years of government service in different capacities.

Bush's advertising strategy was unique in the degree to which it combined the argument and attack phases into one: "1988 marked the first time that attacks on an opponent, rather than the promotion of one's own agenda, became the primary thrust of a presidential campaign" (Morrison, 1988: 260). Bush framed his own campaign agenda in terms of issues that could be cast to reflect negatively on Dukakis, not in terms of issues on which he himself had a positive, programmatic stand. Many of the issues that the Bush Team chose to promote had very little to do with presidential politics (Goldman and Mathews, 1989). The negative ads were designed initially as interim measures while media strategists tried to pinpoint a positive line for Bush to take. Bush's handlers found the attack spots so successful in increasing Bush's standing in the race that these ads aired long after they were scheduled to be pulled off the air.

The four issues that Bush highlighted in his attack strategy were crime, the environment, defense, and taxes. These ads had a dual purpose—to bring these issues to the forefront of the campaign agenda with Dukakis on the defensive and to create an image of Dukakis as a small, rigid, evil technocrat. The two most recognized ads produced by the campaign were the "Boston Harbor" and "Revolving Door" spots. The "Boston Harbor" spot assailed Dukakis' claim to be an environmentalist. The ad took a dramatic and damaging look at the condition of Boston Harbor while chastising Dukakis for missing his chance to clean it up. The "Revolving Door" ad attacked Dukakis for three prison policies—the Massachusetts furlough program, his opposition to the death penalty, and his veto of mandatory sentences for drug offenders. The net result of these policies, the ad proclaimed, was like putting a revolving door on a prison. The point of this ad was driven home further by the now infamous spot made by Americans for Bush, a political action committee using independent expenditures. The ad told the story of Willie Horton, a prisoner who had raped a woman and stabbed her boyfriend while out of jail on a Massachusetts furlough.

From late September into October, Bush experienced a downturn in popularity, as he seemed unable to offer himself as a positive alternative to Dukakis. Additionally, his camp was held responsible for setting the low level of campaign standards that plagued the election. Still, the Bush Team did not have a positive advertising strategy waiting in the wings, so the attack spots continued. For example, six days after the last debate, Bush aired the first "Tank" ads. News footage of a photo opportunity of Dukakis riding in a tank became a backdrop for the message that Dukakis has opposed "virtually every defense system we developed." The goal of discrediting Dukakis' defense policies was compounded here by the unflattering image of Dukakis in a tank looking, as some of our survey respondents reported, "like Snoopy wearing a helmet." When Dukakis protested the inaccuracies of the ads, Ailes retaliated with "Tank II," using the same tank footage. The final attack spot, run just eight days before the end of the campaign, featured a caricature of Mount Rushmore with the faces of George McGovern, Jimmy Carter, Walter Mondale, and Michael Dukakis superimposed (Goldman and Mathews, 1989). The final days of the Bush advertising strategy witnessed the continuation of the attack spots, buffered by warm images of family and country. His plans for the future were for a "kinder, gentler America."

The effectiveness of Bush's attack strategy was facilitated by Dukakis' failure to counter the ads seriously. The strategy's success is difficult to dispute when counting votes. Bush continued to climb in the polls, while his negative ratings decreased and Dukakis' moved upward. At the same time, Bush's negative ads have come under attack for their racist and ethnic prejudices, as well as for their inaccuracies. The content of the spots was compromised by the selective reporting of fragmented "facts," by the misleading visual imagery that was used to manufacture meaning, and by the use of editing techniques designed to make reality appear even grimmer than it is naturally (Goldman and Mathews, 1989; Devlin, 1989; Jamieson, 1989). All of these factors are not new to political advertising, but the extent to which they were used in 1988 has raised serious questions about the propriety of such advertising appeals in American politics.

The inability of the Dukakis advertising effort to put forth a unifying, coherent theme was mirrored by the instability of its media personnel. The original plan was to combine a group of Madison Avenue and political advertising talent much in the style used by past Republican campaigns. Unlike Ailes' role in the Bush campaign, all of the Dukakis advertising personnel were subordinate to the campaign organization. The "Future Group," as it was known, could plan and coordinate ads, but the final approval rested with Dukakis and his campaign managers. As Dukakis nixed script after script and tens of produced commercials failed to make it to the air, members of the "Future Group" quit one after another, to be replaced by others whose tenure with the campaign was equally short-lived. The bureaucracy at Dukakis campaign headquarters made it difficult to deal quickly and effectively with Bush's attack spots. Often, the logistics of getting the finished product to Dukakis before it could be aired resulted in a loss of valuable time (Germond and Witcover, 1989).

Neither the Dukakis campaign nor its advertising component seemed to have a strategy. There was little coordination of what the candidate was saying in his ads with what he was trying to get across in the news. As the campaign failed to provide leadership to the media specialists, ads were created reactively and on a piecemeal basis. Some of the most successful advertising on behalf of Dukakis was produced independently of the campaign at the state level. These independent ads further indicated the lack of cohesion that characterized the Dukakis campaign effort (Devlin, 1989).

During the identification phase, Dukakis failed to provide the voters with a chance to get to know him. He did little to establish either a personal or a political history to which voters could relate (Devlin, 1989). His spots were highly depersonalized and businesslike (Diamond and Marin, 1989). Most ads focused on Dukakis' accomplishments as governor of Massachusetts. Four spots on "Leadership" were aired, which reported Dukakis' record on reducing crime, cutting taxes, and increasing quality health care. The one glimpse of his personal side to which the voters became privy came at the Democratic National Convention in a film narrated by his cousin, Olympia; it featured his vintage snowblower. Plans to use this film as a basis for biospots during the election were scrapped, even though the piece had gone over well with the public (Devlin, 1989).

Dukakis' advertising seemed to become even less effective during the argument and attack phases that were so tightly fused in the Bush strategy. The Dukakis campaign failed to define Bush as an opponent, while the Bush Team did an effective job of defining Dukakis. When Bush began his harsh negative strategy, Dukakis was reluctant to counter-attack directly. This reluctance led to the production and airing of a series of five ads designed to depict Bush as a candidate controlled by handlers. These ads have been widely criticized for being complex, confusing, and even harmful to the Dukakis cause. Some voters even felt that the spots had been run against Dukakis by the Republicans (Devlin, 1989). Other attack spots produced by the campaign were less than memorable.

Instead of fighting back, Dukakis felt that he could explain his position to voters and thereby counter the charges of the Bush campaign. Later in the campaign, after a leadership change in his organization, Dukakis made a series of "face-the-camera" ads in which he revealed his positions. He also made an ad that disparaged Bush for the low road he was taking in the election campaign. The ad depicts Dukakis switching off a television playing the "Tank" ad and stating that he had never seen anything like it in 25 years of public life. This ad was considered to be one of the best Dukakis spots of the campaign, but it did not run soon enough to provide much in the way of damage control.

Dukakis' final spots seemed to be what the campaign had needed all along. They fell into the classic "fate-of-the-nation" category, and they contained a balance of positive and negative content befitting a candidate of the nonincumbent party. The five ads of the "Imagine" series found a campaign theme—the problems squeezing the middle and working classes. The style of these ads brought to mind the successful Reagan pitches and featured touching scenes of children, workers, and middle Americans. These ads were also the only ones to feature candidates Dukakis and Bentsen with their families. While a strong finish, it was too little, too late (Germond and Witcover, 1989).

The two campaigns differed substantially in the amount of money spent on advertising and in how it was used during the 1988 election. The Bush campaign spent approximately $35 million on television advertising, with $31.5 million going to purchase air time. The campaign ran 37 spots, of which 14 were negative. Over 40 percent of the advertising budget went to air negative ads. The Dukakis camp used approximately $30 million of its budget on campaign spots, but only $23.5 million of this was spent on air time. Dukakis expended far more on production costs than did Bush. The campaign produced over 1,000 scripts and 100 ads. Only 47 of these were run, 23 of which were negative (Devlin, 1989). Thus, Bush appeared to better Dukakis in terms of both production value and air time purchases.

Having explored the strategy and content of the candidates' advertising efforts, we turn now to examine the effects of advertising in the two elections under study. We will first examine the degree to which voters were aware of candidate spots. We will then examine their perceptions of advertising content and their reactions to it.

ADVERTISING EFFECTS IN THE 1984 AND 1988 PRESIDENTIAL ELECTIONS

Since the surveys were conducted late in the 1984 and 1988 campaigns, we anticipated that most voters would have come into contact with the candidates' televised advertisements. This was, in fact, the case. The vast majority of respondents—80 percent or more in each county—reported viewing at least one campaign spot.

In 1984, respondents in both samples reported viewing Reagan commercials with greater frequency than ads for Mondale. Interestingly, the Mondale campaign was more successful than the Reagan team in scheduling ads at times when they would be seen by the most people (Diamond and Bates, 1985). In light of past research on advertising, we might speculate that voters were more aware of the Reagan spots because their high-quality production techniques and their close emmulation of product endorsements resulted in greater entertainment value. Mondale commercials may not have registered as readily because of their more serious tone.

The very small differences in the level of exposure to candidate spots for Bush and Dukakis again favored the Republican side, for reasons similar to those in the 1984 contest. In addition, Dukakis had difficulty getting his ads on their air (Devlin, 1989). Moreover, the Bush ads became a campaign issue in themselves because of their highly controversial negative content. Their notoriety and their prominence in television news reports may have stimulated voter awareness of Bush's spots.

Our study found no apparent evidence of selective exposure to ads in 1984 or 1988. We took into account candidate preference, partisanship, and attitudes toward the candidates, as measured on feeling thermometers. We used the concept of a feeling thermometer, employed traditionally by social scientists, which requires survey respondents to rank how favorably or unfavorably they feel about a candidate. Our scale ranged from a high of 10 (favorable) to a low of 0 (unfavorable). None of these factors related to voters' exposure to ads for particular candidates. Undecided voters were no more likely to report high or low levels of exposure to candidates' spots than were those with a clear voting preference. This finding supports the contention that viewing presidential campaign ads is an unintentional consequence of television watching and that frequent repetition makes them difficult to miss.

There was, however, evidence of selective attention to campaign ads in both election years. In the Fairfax County survey, 12 percent of the respondents reported paying more attention to ads for Reagan, while 19 percent stated that they paid less attention. In total, over 30 percent indicated a tendency to pay attention selectively to candidate advertising. These trends were even more apparent in the Dane County data. Twenty-six percent of the sample reported that they paid more attention to Mondale spots, while 21 percent was more attentive to Reagan ads. Thus, over 45 percent of the Dane County respondents stated that they viewed ads selectively.

In 1988, 25 percent of the Carroll County sample, 27 percent of the Middlesex County sample, and 35 percent of the Fairfax County sample stated that they were selectively attentive to ads. A higher proportion of the Carroll County and Middlesex County respondents reported paying more attention to Dukakis' ads, 16 percent and 17 percent respectively, than to Bush's spots. Almost 25 percent of the Fairfax County voters watched Bush's spots with greater concentration.

Selective attention was significantly related to partisan attachment, candidate preference, and feelings about the candidates in both elections. Respondents reported paying more attention to an ad for a candidate sharing their party affiliation. Voters were also more observant of ads for candidates whom they supported in the election and for whom they held strong positive feelings. There was virtually no evidence to suggest that people desired to learn more about the opposing candidate.

That exposure to advertising in presidential elections is limited to a person's interest in a campaign is more strongly supported in the 1988 data than in 1984. Although the candidates' ads themselves were a campaign issue in both election years, the press made a bigger statement about them in 1988. The controversial Bush ads made a strong contrast with the often confusing, lackluster ads of the Dukakis campaign, thus providing ample grist for the press mill. Thus, in 1988 voters with high levels of interest in the campaign were especially anxious to explore the advertising dimension of the campaign more thoroughly. Correlations (Pearson's r) between exposure to spots and political interest appear in Table 2.1. Attention to political ads was significantly and similarly correlated with political interest in all samples, ranging from .20 to .25.

Time of voting decision was not strongly related to either exposure or attention to commercials, with two exceptions in the 1988 data. Carroll and Middlesex County voters who were late campaign deciders or were still undecided at the time of the study were more likely to be exposed and pay attention to Dukakis' ads. This greater attention to Dukakis' spots may have come about because voters knew less about Dukakis than Bush, an established national politician. The potential to learn something new about Dukakis from his spots was thus enhanced.

Media reliance, the communication channel on which an individual relies most for information about politics, was related to exposure and attention to candidate

Table 2.1
Correlations (Pearson's r) between Exposure to Advertising and Campaign Interest

1984 Presidential Election

| | Reagan Ads | | Mondale Ads | |
	VA	WI	VA	WI
Political Interest	.13*	.00	.12*	.00

1988 Presidential Election

| | Bush Ads | | | Dukakis Ads | | |
	IO	NJ	VA	IO	NJ	VA
Political Interest	.18*	.23*	.30*	.21*	.17*	.30*

*p<.05

ads. Not surprisingly, people who relied on television as their main source of information about politics displayed higher levels of both exposure and attention to campaign spots. The newspaper-reliant followed the television-dependent, while those who relied on other sources, such as magazines and radio, had the lowest levels of advertising exposure and attention. A strong, consistent relationship was found for all samples.

THE CONTENT OF CANDIDATE SPOTS

Exploring the content of political spots has become a significant research endeavor (Bowers, 1972; Humke, Schmitt, and Grupp, 1975; Joslyn, 1980a, 1980b, 1985). These studies often attempt to examine the extent to which ads contain issue, candidate image, and partisan references. More recently, there has been a trend toward examining elements of video style, mythic themes in advertising, and other subtle aspects of content (Kaid and Davidson, 1986; Gronbeck, 1989). While it is difficult to generalize across studies because of variations in the coding schemes applied to categorize content, some consistencies in the findings are evident. The content of campaign advertisements differs depending upon the level of the electoral contest, the party affiliation of the candidate, and whether the spot is for an incumbent or a challenger.

A finding at the presidential level is striking. Contrary to popular belief, election campaign spots contain a great deal of issue, as opposed to purely image, information. One study shows, for example, that in the 1980 presidential contest, issue content was present in about three-quarters of all ads (Shyles, 1983). The use of issue information in spots is central to developing campaign themes and setting the agenda for election debate (Buss and Hofstetter, 1976). Not all ads that mention issues indicate the candidate's position on them, however. Many issue presentations in ads are so vague that they fail to present viewers with concrete information about policies (Joslyn, 1986).

In spite of the careful calculations of media strategists, voters' awareness of issues and perceptions of candidates may differ greatly from what campaign organizations desire to portray in ads. While issue content may be prevalent in ads during presidential elections, it may not be readily digested by the public. A study of advertising during the 1972 presidential election, for example, reveals that there was little correspondence between the issue agendas presented by the candidates and those of voters or news agencies (Bowers, 1977). Television often seems more successful in conveying personality information to voters even when issues are presented.

While there is great concern about whether ads contain sufficient issue information, some scholars have argued that the image content conveyed by ads is equally, if not more, important than issue material. Issues that are prominent during an election may be short-term in duration, of minimal importance in the overall political scheme, or tailored to meet the specific requirements of the campaign to win votes. The 1988 election illustrated this point well, as Bush's organization brought parochial state-level issues to the forefront of the campaign agenda. There is also no guarantee that a campaign issue will be acted upon by a president at all or that a successful candidate will live up to the promises made during an election.

Candidate images can be much more than a superficial portrait or a visual picture of a candidate. Images can represent the personal and professional side of a presidential contender—his character and perceived leadership capacity (Shyles, 1986; Garramone, 1986). Candidate image, therefore, may be a more valid criterion for judging future presidential performance than issue positions. People must assess the ability of the candidates to deal with issues and crises in the long term. Campaign ads that present the candidates' personal statements about themselves may be the more effective form of communication for conveying this type of information.

VOTER PREDISPOSITIONS, SOURCE CREDIBILITY, AND CANDIDATE PERFORMANCE

The propensity of voters to view and attend to ads and to interpret their content is shaped to some extent by predispositions toward candidates and issues, the credibility of the source of the message, and the ability of the candidate to project a positive image on television. In general, individuals form their overall impressions about candidates early, and these images change little over the course of the election campaign (Weitzner, 1975; Nimmo and Savage,

1976). Still, the campaign offers the opportunity for candidates to modify voters' perceptions of specific traits and personal qualities.

When individuals are exposed to televised ads, they view them in light of attitudes that they have already established about the candidates and of their opinions on issues. As we have seen in this study and elsewhere, selective exposure to televised advertising is limited (Comstock, Chaffee, Katzman, McCombs, 1978; Kaid, 1976; O'Keefe and Sheinkopf, 1974), and attention to political spots is tied to voters' attachments to candidates and parties (Atkin, 1980; Hofstetter, Zukin, and Buss, 1978; Patterson and McClure, 1973). It then follows that individuals are likely to evaluate their candidate's spots favorably and to denigrate those of the opponent (Patterson and McClure, 1973). Interpretations of the content of ads for nonpreferred candidates are often critical (Donahue, 1973; Meyer and Donahue, 1973).

Related to voters' attitudes about candidates and their interpretations of ads are their perceptions about the credibility of the message source. Viewers frequently distort the content of political spots on the basis of their willingness to trust the communicator of the message. Individuals tend to agree with views presented in ads that feature highly credible sources and to disagree with those presented by low credibility sources. Politicians are generally considered to be low credibility sources. On highly salient issues, however, voters are likely to agree with their favored candidate's positions as presented in televised ads and to disagree with the opponent's views, although this is not true for low salience issues (Donahue, 1973). Untrustworthy sources of information appear to fare worse on television than in other media. Television highlights the questionable motives of low credibility sources, leading to greater rejection of their positions (Donahue, 1973; Meyer and Donahue, 1973; Andreoli and Worchel, 1980).

In addition to questions of the credibility of the source of an advertised message, candidates must be concerned about the way they come across on television. Some politicians, including Walter Mondale in 1984 and Michael Dukakis in 1988, do not project well in ads. Spots in which they star tend to fail to project positive images (Papert, 1975).

Because of credibility and performance problems, politicians have started to move away from personal appearances in ads. Instead they use celebrities, ordinary citizens, and professional actors in their commercials. Issues of negative advertising and last-minute advertising appeals are closely related to these concerns about source credibility and candidate performances. The success of these strategies hinges on the audience's positive perceptions of the candidates and its willingness to accept the messages that are communicated.

NEGATIVE ADVERTISING

Negative spots comprise a large proportion of the overall number of candidate ads, accounting for approximately half of all the ads broadcast (Sabato, 1982).

In earlier times, candidates were reluctant to use negative ads because they believed that voters preferred positive messages; they feared a backlash effect (Garramone, 1985b; Roddy and Garramone, 1988). The use of negative advertising has risen to new heights in recent years, however, as was clearly shown by the 1984 and 1988 presidential contests. The apparent success of Bush's attack strategy reinforces the fact that negative ads are becoming a political norm.

Negative ads have become more prevalent in campaigns for several reasons. Voters like to know the differences between candidates, and negative spots provide this contrast. Ads using rational cross-pressure techniques, which zero in on the negative characteristics of popular candidates, have been successful in converting voters' perceptions of candidates, especially in congressional races. For example, negative ads run against Culver in Iowa in 1980 were successful in changing voters' beliefs about his ideology, painting him as a liberal when he had previously been considered a moderate. A candidate who relies on attack strategies minimizes the opponent's opportunity for counterattack. There is less focus on his or her own issue positions, and the opponent often finds it necessary to respond to the attack (Tarrance, 1982).

Evidence about the effects of negative advertising is limited and somewhat speculative. Negative ads have the potential to help candidates. Spots attacking the opponent are often evaluated favorably by voters, particularly those from lower socioeconomic backgrounds (Surlin and Gordon, 1977). When negative ads are used against unpopular candidates, especially incumbents, they tend to be successful (Stewart, 1975). Threat appeals that are designed to arouse audience fears by pointing to the policies of the opponent have been shown to influence people's perceptions of issues (Frandsen, 1963).

The most successful negative ads are sponsored independently of the candidates's campaign, as the "Willie Horton" spot demonstrated in 1988. Experimental evidence has demonstrated that viewers are more likely to vote for the candidate on whose behalf the ad has been made when his or her negative ads are produced by an independent sponsor, while backlash effects are diminished (Garramone, 1985).

Still, an entirely negative advertising campaign cannot be successfully sustained unless it is accompanied by tactics that emphasize positive image-building (Tarrance, 1982). Negative ads do not work when the target is perceived to be a nice person. Diamond and Bates (1988) discovered a backlash effect from ads produced against Ford in 1976. A similar type of effect may have resulted from the Mondale campaign's negative spots focusing on a personally popular Ronald Reagan.

LAST-MINUTE ADVERTISING

Last-minute saturation with campaign commercials has become a routine strategy in presidential elections. These ads represent the last-ditch effort of campaign organizations to stimulate voter interest and turnout in the election. Last-minute exposure to campaign communication may increase ticket-splitting, voter turnout, and level of voter information (Hofstetter and Buss, 1980). Exposure to messages late in the campaign is also associated with heightened levels of discussion about the election. Additionally, last-minute exposure to advertising leads to changes in candidate preference among the less involved members of the electorate.

VOTER PERCEPTIONS OF ADVERTISING CONTENT IN THE 1984 AND 1988 PRESIDENTIAL ELECTIONS

Survey respondents were asked about the information they learned from campaign advertisements, as well as about how the spots made them feel about the candidates. Open-ended questions on both surveys requested that respondents list the main point of the two candidates' advertising appeals. The questions were coded into broad categories on the basis of whether the responses reflected mostly issue, image, partisan, or anti-opposition content. A final category included responses from individuals who had seen ads but were unable to recall their content.

While respondents generally stated that they did not pay a great deal of attention to ads, the majority could relate what the spots were about. To a great extent, the themes and agendas stressed by the candidates were processed by the survey participants. For both campaign years, respondents across samples used the same or similar words to describe the content of advertising in many instances, even though they represented a wide range of political outlooks.

When asked to state the main point of Reagan's advertisements in 1984, the most popular response was, "We are better off now than we were four years ago," which was a dominant Reagan campaign theme. The issues that respondents felt his ads stressed most often were defense and the Soviet threat. For Mondale, the survey responses corresponded with the issues that he was attempting to bring to the forefront of the campaign, especially taxes, the federal deficit, the "star wars" defense, and aid to the poor and elderly. People frequently mentioned his tendency to attack Reagan and his administration for their policies. The ads of both candidates appeared to fulfill an agenda-setting function for the election.

In 1988, the respondents reported a far more diverse array of what they saw in the candidates' ads than did our 1984 survey participants. Many respondents recounted Bush's themes of "staying the course"—that status quo leadership represented a "Better America." The issue that they cited most often was crime, especially as represented by Bush's position against prison furloughs. Many people mentioned the highly negative aspects of his campaign and his relentless attacks on Dukakis. The respondents seemed to have a tougher time getting a handle on exactly what Dukakis was trying to get across.

Overall, their descriptions of his ads were not as detailed and exact as their summaries of Bush's ads. The respondents noted that Dukakis was concerned with the future and that he felt he could improve upon the current state of the nation. Survey participants felt that Dukakis demonstrated a concern for the poor and the working class in his ads. They mentioned a wide range of issues that Dukakis dealt with in his spots, including cleaning up the environment, getting drugs off the streets, and health care for all. The Dukakis "packaging" ads were not totally unsuccessful in making their point, at least among our survey respondents.

The respondents in both the Fairfax and Dane County samples perceived the differences in the content of Mondale and Reagan ads in 1984 in similar ways. Their impressions conformed to the predominant content of themes of each candidate's advertising strategy. Respondents found that Mondale ads contained more issue information than did Reagan spots. Overwhelmingly, Reagan's ads were considered to be more image-oriented than were Mondale's. The findings for the 1984 analysis appear in Figure 2.1.

Again in 1988, respondents' perceptions of the content of candidate ads were fairly consistent across samples. However, there were more county-based variations than in the previous election. With the exception of Carroll County, respondents felt that the Bush ads contained far more image than issue information. The trend was less clear for the Dukakis spots. Both Carroll and Fairfax County respondents reported that Dukakis' ads were issue-oriented, but the difference in the proportion who felt that they were predominantly image spots is small. The reverse trend was true for Middlesex County, where far more survey participants cited the high image content of Dukakis' advertising effort. The findings for the 1988 analysis appear in Figure 2.2.

The negative aspect of Mondale's advertising campaign was perceived by individuals in both samples. Thirty-one percent of those interviewed in Fairfax County and 22 percent in Dane County felt that Mondale's ads attacked Reagan. Very few people in either sample believe that Reagan's ads were negative.

Negative campaign appeals were abundant during the 1988 campaign, and respondents felt that they predominated in both candidates' advertising strategies. Bush spots, however, were perceived as being far more negative than Dukakis' spots by respondents in all three samples. There is a marked consistency in the proportion of people in each county—in the middle–30 percent range—who felt that Dukakis ran a primarily negative ad campaign. This compares to proportions in the high 40 to 50 percent range for Bush.

Only a small number of respondents in both 1984 and 1988 reported that the ads contained predominantly partisan information. This finding is in keeping with current trends in presidential political advertising. It is interesting to note that more partisan information was reported for Republican than for Democratic candidates in both years.

The vast majority of survey respondents who had been exposed to ads could recall their content. However, in 1984, more people were unable to relate the

Figure 2.1
Perceived Content of Ads—1984 Election

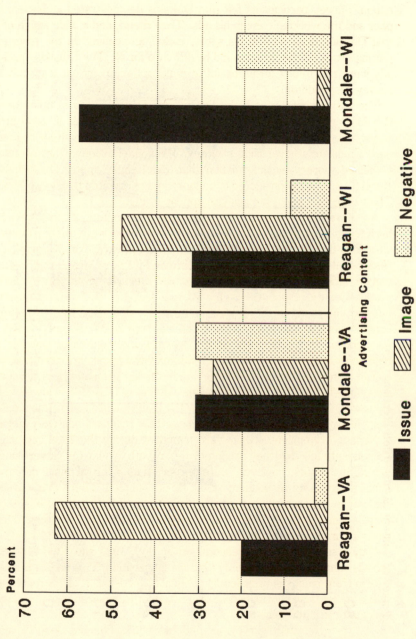

Percent

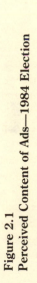

Figure 2.2
Perceived Content of Ads—1988 Election

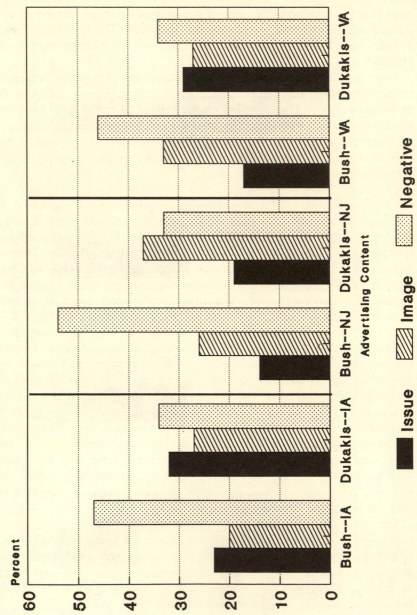

messages from Mondale's ads (approximately 12%), compared with Reagan's spots (6%). A similar pattern appeared in 1988. About 10 percent of the respondents in each county could not recall Dukakis' spots, as compared to approximately 4 percent for Bush. This finding continues to add support to our point that the entertainment value of a spot is an essential component of its effectiveness in attracting voter attention and recall. The Republican formula in both years appears to have had an edge over the strategy used by the Democrats.

There is an interesting proclivity among supporters of particular presidential aspirants to report that their candidate's ads contained issue, as opposed to image, information. These tendencies are related to variations in both partisanship and candidate preference. In addition, partisan and candidate supporters felt disproportionately that the opposition was employing a predominantly negative advertising strategy. This evidence of selective perception is apparent across samples for both election years.

Democrats and Mondale supporters in 1984 were likely to find that Reagan ads were concerned very little with issues and were highly image-based. Republicans and Reagan supporters also perceived that Reagan ads were predominantly image-oriented, but they reported that his ads contained issue information more frequently than did Mondale supporters. A major difference was apparent between the two samples. Reagan supporters in Fairfax County were just as likely to report that Mondale ads contained image as issue information. In Dane County, few Reagan supporters reported that Mondale ads were image-based. Findings for candidate preference appear in Figure 2.3.

In 1988, similar patterns concerning issue and image content perceptions emerged. When we examine those respondents who reported that Bush and Dukakis ads contained predominantly issue information, we find that they are most often supporters of the candidate and his party. The opposite holds true for image content. Candidates' opponents were more likely than supporters to feel that a rival candidate's ads were image-oriented. If we explore the distribution of responses for all aspects of advertising content broken down by candidate preference and partisanship, we find more mixed patterns. Bush supporters found that his ads contained far more image than issue information. With the exception of Carroll County, Dukakis supporters also found Bush's ads were more image-defined as compared to issue-laden. Findings for candidate preference appear in Figure 2.4.

The tendency of respondents to attribute negative themes more often to nonpreferred candidates is apparent in both election years, but especially so in 1988. In 1984, Mondale supporters and Democrats were less likely to believe that his ads focused predominantly on attacks on Reagan than were Reagan supporters. Although very few people felt that Reagan's ads were negative, the relationship here is in the expected direction.

In 1988, the highly negative content of Bush's commercials was clearly perceived by the respondents, even his supporters. The proportion of sup-

Figure 2.3
Ad Content and Candidate Preference—1984 Election

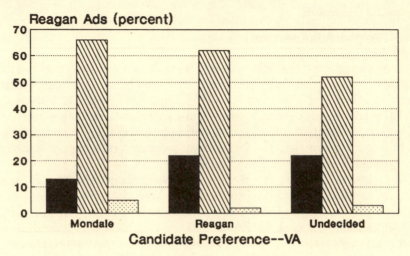

Reagan Ads (percent)

Candidate Preference--VA

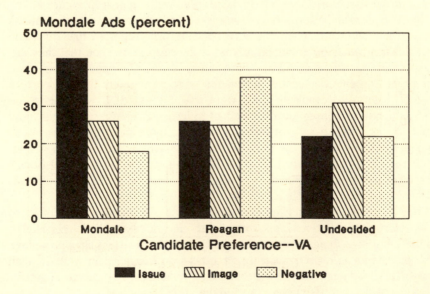

Mondale Ads (percent)

Candidate Preference--VA

■ Issue   ⧄ Image   ⬚ Negative

Figure 2.3 (continued)

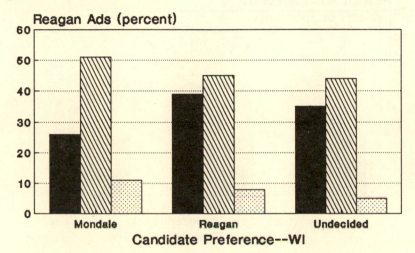

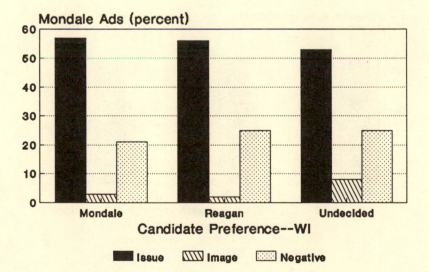

Figure 2.4
Ad Content and Candidate Preference—1988 Election

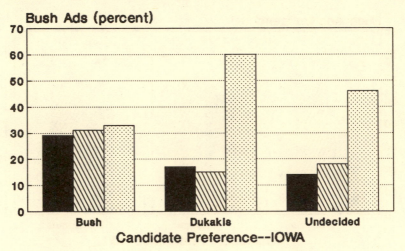

Bush Ads (percent)

Candidate Preference--IOWA

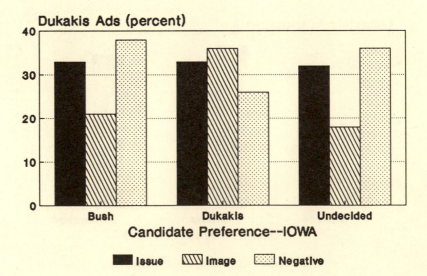

Dukakis Ads (percent)

Candidate Preference--IOWA

■ Issue ▨ Image ▩ Negative

Figure 2.4 (continued)

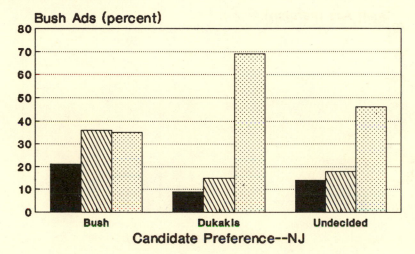

Bush Ads (percent)

Candidate Preference--NJ

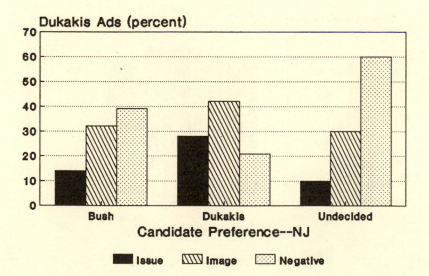

Dukakis Ads (percent)

Candidate Preference--NJ

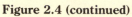

Issue   Image   Negative

Figure 2.4 (continued)

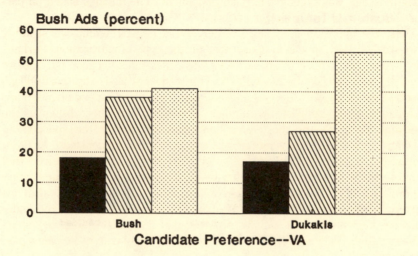

Bush Ads (percent)

Candidate Preference--VA

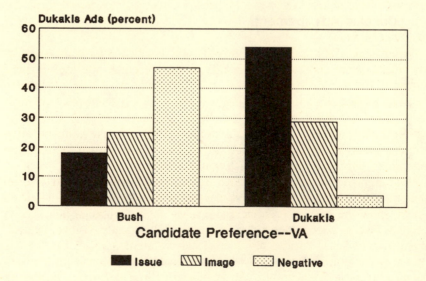

Dukakis Ads (percent)

Candidate Preference--VA

■ Issue ⧄⧄⧄ Image ⋮⋮⋮ Negative

porters who felt Bush's ads were primarily based on attacks on his opponent was far smaller than the proportion of Dukakis supporters who believed that this was the case. Perhaps the most striking finding is that 60 percent, 69 percent, and 53 percent of respondents intending to vote for Dukakis in Carroll, Middlesex, and Fairfax Counties, respectively, perceived that Bush's advertising message was predominantly anti-opponent. The findings based on partisanship illustrate highly similar patterns.

Thus, the oppositions' supporters perceive a negative campaign strategy more readily; they appear to focus more on this type of information. Perhaps they see a special need to attend to negative messages because they desire to defend their candidate against attack. This trend may also indicate a backlash effect, in which supporters of a candidate under attack use these negative ads to reinforce their candidate preference and to increase their dislike of the opponent. Responses to the open-ended questions support this speculation.

Differences were also evident across samples for the undecideds. In 1984, a greater percentage of undecided voters in Fairfax County perceived that Mondale ads were image-based rather than issue-based, while in Dane County the opposite was true. Undecideds in both counties reported that Reagan ads were predominantly image-oriented. Approximately one-quarter of the undecided respondents in both samples reported that they found Mondale's spots to be negative. Very few of them considered this to be true of Reagan's ads. See Figure 2.3.

The undecideds were the least likely to recall the specific content of candidate ads in 1984. Close to one-fifth of the undecideds in the Fairfax County sample who had been exposed to ads for Mondale could not identify their content. In 1988, all of the undecideds in the Middlesex County sample could recall the content of candidate ads, but 14 percent of the undecided voters in Carroll County could not.

This evidence, although limited, provides the foundation for some speculation. First, some undecided voters may in fact resemble the stereotypical portrait of the uninterested and uninformed voter who pays little attention to campaign communication. Interestingly, these voters reacted most often to the negative appeals of both candidates in the elections. We shall see shortly that these negative appeals were translated, more often than not, into negative attitudes about the candidates on both sides. This negativity may increase the undecideds' difficulty in arriving at a voting decision.

We attempted to determine what kind of attitudes the candidates had fostered about themselves based on their advertising appeals. Respondents were asked to state how the ads for each candidate made them feel about him. These responses were coded in categories reflecting predominantly positive, neutral, or negative feelings. Positive attitudes included statements such as, "he has a grasp of the future and knows where he is heading" and "confident, knowing that he is strong and responsible." An example of neutral feelings is, "he doesn't turn me off or inspire me." Finally, negative comments included "annoyed" and "I doubt that he can do all that he promises." (This question was not asked in the 1984 Dane County survey.)

In 1984, almost 50 percent of the respondents reported that Reagan's ads made them feel good about him. Mondale ads generated negative evaluations for an equivalent number of respondents. A slightly higher percentage had neutral reactions to Mondale ads than to Reagan ads.

In 1988, the overall impressions that ads generated about the candidates were negative. In Carroll and Middlesex Counties, half or more of the respondents reported that Bush's ads made them feel negatively about the candidate. Only in Fairfax County did a plurality of respondents (37%) give a favorable response. The reactions to Dukakis' spots were similar, although somewhat less negative, in Carroll and Middlesex Counties.

It is interesting to note that ads elicited positive or negative feelings about candidates far more often than they generated neutral responses. The findings across samples and campaign years are highly similar, averaging about 25 percent neutral responses overall. Both Democratic candidates generated a slightly higher proportion of neutral attitudes from their ads than did their Republican counterparts.

Differences in attitudes that resulted from viewing candidate spots were strongly related to partisan affiliation, candidate preference, and feeling thermometer ratings of the candidates. These findings provide further evidence of selectivity biases in the perception and interpretation of candidate ads.

The 1984 analysis demonstrates that the Mondale ads were not very successful in creating a positive image of the candidate, even among his supporters or Democratic partisans. While 54 percent of those who stated that they would vote for Mondale reported positive reactions, 49 percent had negative comments. Reagan supporters reported predominantly negative attitudes.

As predicted, Reagan voters and Republicans felt good about his image as created through advertising. Mondale supporters had negative comments about the feelings they experienced from Reagan spots. Reagan supporters overwhelmingly reported that Mondale's commercials generated negative feelings.

These findings reflect objections to the attacks on Reagan that featured so prominently in Mondale's strategy. Reagan voters, as well as some Mondale proponents, believed that Mondale's attacks on Reagan were desperate moves that generally were unfair and went too far. A category of comments from Mondale voters indicated that if he were going to criticize Reagan, he should have done so more forcefully. Mondale was frequently characterized as a "wimp" in this regard. In keeping with conventional wisdom, the evidence in 1984 suggests that negative campaign tactics are risky. Negative spots can backfire when the credibility of the attacking candidate is low and the opponent is perceived to be highly personable. Mondale may have moved too quickly to criticize Reagan before he had firmly established a positive image of his own with the electorate. The findings appear in Figure 2.5.

The 1988 election analysis reveals that neither campaign was as successful

Figure 2.5
Advertising Perceptions—1984 Election

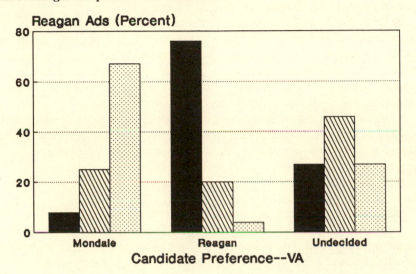

Reagan Ads (Percent)

Candidate Preference--VA

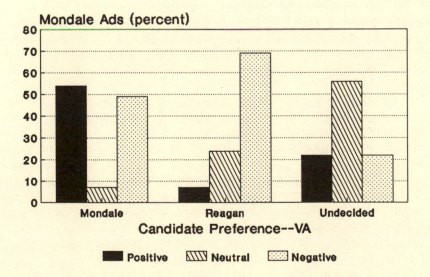

Mondale Ads (percent)

Candidate Preference--VA

■ Positive   ⧄ Neutral   ⬚ Negative

as Reagan's in producing positive attitudes among supporters, nor as unsuccessful as Mondale's in achieving this goal. A slim majority of Bush supporters
in each sample gained positive perceptions of him from his ads. Bush's ads
were most successful in stimulating negative responses from Dukakis voters,
especially in Carroll and Middlesex Counties, where over 80 percent of these
respondents felt this way. Dukakis' ads had far less influence in generating
negative reactions about him from Bush supporters, although negative responses were in the 60 percent range. Dukakis' ads were slightly less successful
than Bush's in generating positive feelings among his supporters and somewhat
more likely to create negative ones. Again, these attitudes were based on the
inability of Dukakis to demonstrate strong leadership qualities through his
advertising. The findings appear in Figure 2.6.

Neither candidate in 1988 had the "likability factor" of a Ronald Reagan.
Dukakis clearly did not distinguish himself among the mass public as a congenial
person. Therefore, Bush's attack strategy had a far better potential for success
than Mondale's in 1984. Still, evidence suggests that an attack strategy alien-
ates a substantial number of voters on both sides. A campaign such as we
experienced in 1988 is more likely to be characterized by voters deciding against
a candidate rather than for one.

A major objective of candidate advertising is to generate voting support
among the undecided. Our analysis in both election years demonstrated that
this goal was not accomplished by the candidates. Neutral or negative feelings
about all the candidates were stimulated by their advertising far more often
than were positive attitudes. Positive attitudes about a candidate are more
likely to bring the undecided to the polls than a choice between the lesser of
two evils.

The undecided voters in 1984 were predominantly neutral in the feelings
that they reported about both Mondale and Reagan ads. In the case of spots
for both candidates, they were evenly split between positive and negative
reactions. Reagan's ads, however, elicited more extreme feelings, split evenly
between positive and negative. Mondale's ads generated more neutral responses overall.

The influence of the ads on the undecideds in 1988 differed between the
Carroll and Middlesex County samples. The one major point of consensus was
that candidate spots were highly ineffective in producing positive responses.
Bush's ads were particularly unsuccessful in this regard. In fact, 35 percent
of Carroll County and 86 percent of Middlesex County respondents reported
that negative feelings about the candidates were generated by their spots.
Very few people in either sample, 10 percent and 5 percent respectively,
derived good feelings from the ads, although a slim majority of respondents in
Carroll County reported neutral sentiments.

Dukakis fared somewhat better among the undecideds, although the positive
feelings generated by his ads were minimal; 16 percent of the Carroll County
and 58 percent of Middlesex County residents reported negative sentiments.

Figure 2.6
Advertising Perceptions—1988 Election

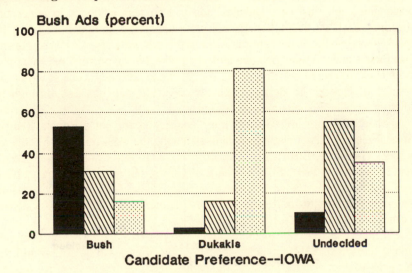

Bush Ads (percent)

Candidate Preference--IOWA

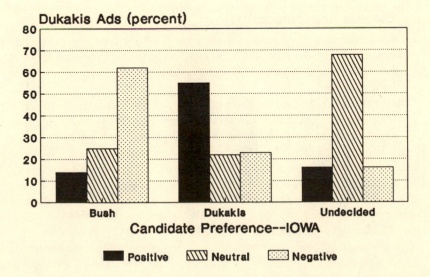

Dukakis Ads (percent)

Candidate Preference--IOWA

■ Positive ▨ Neutral ▧ Negative

Figure 2.6 (continued)

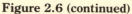

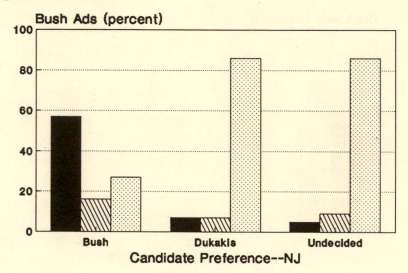

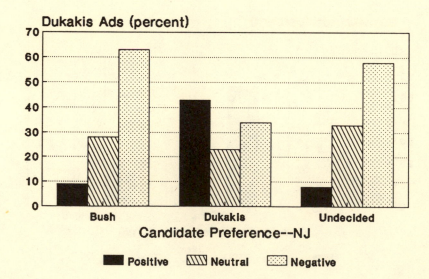

Figure 2.6 (continued)

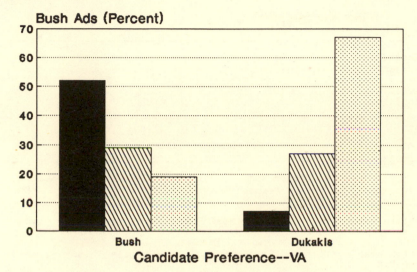

Bush Ads (Percent)

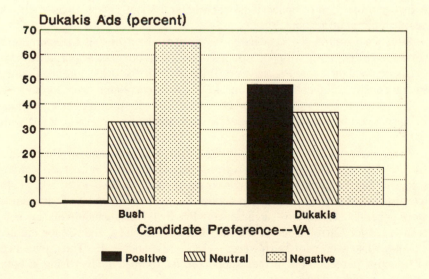

Dukakis Ads (percent)

Table 2.2
Correlations (Pearson's *r*) between Perceptions of Candidates Based on Advertising and Attitudes about Candidates

1984 Presidential Election

	Reagan Ads VA	Mondale Ads VA
Attitudes-Reagan	.54*	.38*
Attitudes-Mondale	-.35*	-.36*

1988 Presidential Election

	Bush Ads			Dukakis Ads		
	IO	NJ	VA	IO	NJ	VA
Attitudes-Bush	.68*	.68*	.55*	-.39*	-.38*	-.46*
Attitudes-Dukakis	-.18*	-.27*	-.45*	.24*	.55*	.62*

* p<.01

A higher proportion of undecideds were neutral about Dukakis based on his ads than felt neutral about Bush.

Attitudes towards the candidates as measured on feeling thermometers correlated significantly with perceptions about the candidates acquired through exposure to their commercials. See Table 2.2. In the 1984 Fairfax County sample, positive perceptions of Mondale ads were correlated (Pearson's *r*) .38 with positive attitudes toward Mondale and −.36 with positive feelings about Reagan. Good feelings in response to Reagan ads were correlated at .54 with positive attitudes toward Reagan and −.35 for Mondale.

There were similar findings in 1988. Positive attitudes about Bush's ads were correlated .68, .63, and .55 with feelings about Bush in Carroll, Middlesex, and Fairfax Counties. Negative correlations of −.39, −.38, and −.46 were recorded for Dukakis. The reaction and correspondence to Dukakis ads were generally slightly lower in intensity. Positive feelings about Dukakis correlated .24 for Carroll County, .55 for Middlesex County, and .62 for Fairfax County, while scores for Bush were −.18, −.27, and −.45. Thus, evidence of selective perception is further supported for campaign advertising in both of these presidential contests.

SUMMARY

The ever-evolving challenges and complexities of campaign advertising were clearly apparent in 1984 and 1988. Campaign strategists must continually anticipate the actions and reactions of their own candidates, their opponents, and the mass public, as they strive to execute a successful advertising effort. Both 1984 and 1988 provided examples of when ad strategies worked and when the strategies, or lack of them, failed to produce the desired results. The bottom line for our study is that voters do take note of campaign spots and that they formulate impressions of candidates based on their advertising.

Respondents were heavily exposed to ads in both election years, but they claimed to pay little attention. There is an apparent paradox at work, however, as the survey participants could recall the content of candidate commercials quite accurately. To a large extent, their accounts reflected the campaign agendas stressed by the candidates.

One of the most interesting contrasts that these two presidential election campaigns allow us to make is of negative advertising strategies. In 1984, Mondale's attacks against the affable Ronald Reagan backfired. His own positive ads were too heavy and issue-laden at the outset to give the public the opportunity to judge Mondale as a person, not as a series of position planks. Reagan's spots were high-quality entertainment. They conformed to television viewers' expectations far more closely than did Mondale's spots and further reinforced the grandfatherly image of Reagan as a man undeserving of the attacks.

The negative strategy used by Bush in 1988 was far more vicious and personally offensive to Dukakis than Mondale's attack on Reagan had been yet it seemed to work. One major difference was the dual advertising strategy employed by the Bush campaign. Positive images of Bush were offered continually, even as the attacks on Dukakis went forward. Since Dukakis neither established a positive image for himself nor fought back effectively until it was too late, Bush's tactics worked far better than the wildest dreams of his handlers.

This study demonstrates, as have others in the past, that political advertising is perceived selectively by the electorate. Voters pay more attention to and have more favorable evaluations of their own candidates' campaign commercials than those of the opponent. Still, a badly botched advertising campaign can promote negative evaluations of candidates, even among their supporters. This point is illustrated by the significant proportion of Mondale supporters who reported being turned off by his advertising campaign. Dukakis voters were not as strongly alienated by his appeals, but they certainly were not inspired by them either.

Still, advertising is not the be-all and end-all of a campaign. It is but one component of the mediated reality of a presidential election contest. The dynamics of campaigns differ widely, as does the influence of candidate ads. The

1988 election seems to demonstrate that, when used skillfully, ads can be an integral part of an effort to reverse a candidate's standing in a campaign. In the final analysis, however, it is difficult to imagine that advertising on Mondale's part, no matter how masterful, could have turned the tide against the extremely popular Reagan in 1984.

NOTES

1. For informative historical accounts of political advertising in American elections, see Diamond and Bates, 1988, and Jamieson, 1984.

2. In recent years, some advertising has been done on behalf of candidates through independent committees that has not been strictly candidate-controlled. One example of this type of advertising was the use of negative spots against liberals running for Congress in the 1988 election by the National Conservative Political Action Committee (NCPAC). Some candidates object to this intrusion on their ability to control campaign communications even when the ads are run for their benefit.

3

Television News and Newspaper News: The Voters' Choice?

NEWS STORIES IN PRESIDENTIAL ELECTIONS

News stories represent by far the largest category of messages in presidential elections. Information about candidates, issues, and the race itself is continually disseminated through newspapers, news magazines, television, and radio. News stories about the other three message types—ads, polls, and debates—feature prominently during campaigns. Election news has the potential to heighten the importance of these other message categories greatly, as we have already witnessed in the case of candidate advertising, especially in 1988.

Officially, news reports about elections are controlled by mass media organizations. It appears, however, that candidates' campaign organizations have an increasingly strong hold over what makes and becomes election news. Charges that campaigns have overstepped their bounds in manufacturing news and manipulating press coverage have gone from rumblings in the 1970s, to stage whispers in the early 1980s, to full-blown accusations in the 1988 campaign.

The success or failure of bids for the presidency hinges more and more on the quality of the campaign operatives rather than on the inherent worth of the candidates themselves. Campaign organizations strive to manage the creation of images through news so that stories complement their own communications, especially their advertising. Political strategists compete to insure that campaign information, such as that derived from polls, is framed contextually to maximize favorable impressions of their candidate and to reflect badly on the opponent.

News coverage during presidential campaigns is abundant, although *what* is covered has been called into question. With the advent of television, candidate behavior has become oriented increasingly toward creating visual imagery, often to the exclusion of conveying substantive messages. Two commentators on recent election coverage have contended that a "problem with TV news is its inability to say, 'Sorry folks, we have no news tonight. Candidate X only did photo opportunities that have no bearing on the race' " (Judy Woodruff and Edward Fouhy in Runkel, 1989: 132). Since newspapers, news magazines, and radio must also rely on candidates to supply much of their news, this statement can be extended to other media. Still, the influence of political operatives falls most heavily on television news because of that medium's heavy dependency on visual presentations.

THE CHARACTERISTICS OF ELECTION NEWS STORIES
IN THE MASS MEDIA AGE

A commentator on the 1988 presidential election made the following observation: "The 1988 campaign will likely go down in the annals of American journalism as the moment when reporters realized that the other side—the newsmakers and their handlers—had taken the upper hand" (Morrison, 1988: 248). This quote, while directed at the 1988 campaign, describes the culmination of a pattern that has been developing throughout the era of mass media politics. Candidates' preoccupation with television coverage has served not only to increase the artificiality of the campaign on television, but has also influenced newspaper reporting of elections (Bogart, 1984; Morrison, 1988).

While journalists complain about the overt manipulation of the media by candidate organizations, they do little to stop it (Nimmo, 1989). In fact, the press may have brought this situation upon themselves inadvertently. The media constitute an "alternative electorate" to which candidates make their appeals. Campaign organizations are highly attentive to the values and beliefs of journalists. Politics in the mass media age involves anticipating news reporting and then accommodating campaign plans to meet journalistic expectations (Arterton, 1984: 29).

A brief overview of the relationship between the press and candidates in this century up to the current mass media election reveals several loosely defined phases. In the pre-television era, candidates and the press had a comfortable, often friendly, alliance. Reporting about the campaign consisted largely of accounts of candidates' speeches, descriptions of scenes of campaign rallies, and estimations of the size of crowds at candidate events. Polling was in its infancy, so it was not a tool used frequently by reporters. At this stage, journalists and politicians seemed to share a general view about what constituted political news.

By the 1950s, television was emerging as a strong force on the campaign front. Television first made its mark through candidates' advertising efforts. News personnel seemed to resent what they felt was an effort to subvert their role in elections. Reporters began to probe more deeply into aspects of the candidates' lives and campaigns than they had previously. An adversarial type of journalism began to emerge by the 1960s. Candidates reacted to the newly assertive mode of reporting by attempting to gain control over the content of news. Assisted by the emerging industry of media specialists, their campaign organizations sought to manipulate campaign news so that coverage would become an integral and coherent part of their overall campaign strategies. More and more, this effort has become a struggle for dominance of the television airwaves (Morrison, 1988).

Candidates have discovered the advantages of presenting the press with planned newsmaking opportunities. Pseudoevents minimize the potential for the tactical errors that are more likely to occur during spontaneous interactions with journalists. The focus on photo opportunities and made-for-TV image-making has become the trademark of American election news.

Reporters covering campaigns are not in a position to force candidates to make more meaningful news, except perhaps by refusing to report the staged events. Journalists are inclined to keep things the way they are in order to deal with the ambiguity and uncertainty that characterize campaigns. To meet their deadlines while confronting the time and space constraints of broadcast and print news formats, journalists have adopted routines for news coverage. Candidates comply by providing news that fits these established patterns. Themes, such as the well-documented "horserace" (Patterson, 1980; Patterson and Davis, 1985), become the norm.

The formulaic nature of news in today's communication environment has been insightfully characterized by Bennett (1988). He identifies four major information biases in television news—personalization, dramatization, fragmentation, and normalization. Personalization is the tendency for news organizations to decontextualize events and issues by focusing predominantly on human interest angles and individual actors. The institutional and political implications of news events are subverted by a concern for private feelings and fantasies. Television news also thrives on stories that feature high drama. Dramatic news stories form a complete narrative, with a beginning, middle, and end in a neat package. These dramatic narratives often play themselves out within the context of stock plot formulas that are among journalists' tools of the trade. A concern for action undermines the political and social realities of the event itself. News stories thus become a combination of fact and fiction. Fragmented news is information disseminated in distinct dramatic capsules. News personnel fail to draw connections between events or to expose their wider significance. Fragmentation results largely from using the story as the basic unit of news reporting. Providing the public with nonintegrated stories in the news makes it difficult to conceptualize politics in a logically consistent manner. Finally, the press deals with difficult and complex dilemmas by normalizing news. Instead of providing more information about an event or issue, journalists attempt to reassure the public by conjuring up familiar and reassuring images. News is filtered through traditional values, beliefs, and visions of society. Often, these normalized messages are delivered to the audience via established political authorities.

While Bennett's analysis describes the status of television news in general, his commentary is highly pertinent to election news coverage in the modern era. By the time the general election arrives, the media audience has already been subjected to a barrage of coverage during the primaries. News coverage about the general election is virtually a daily affair. Reporters must strive not only to cover candidates and issues; they must also present their information in a manner that sustains the interest of widely varying audience sectors for a prolonged period of time. Thus, journalists resort to what they perceive as tried and true tactics for maintaining audience interest.

It may be an understatement to allege that election news has become increasingly dramatic and fragmented, focusing on discrete events and short-lived stories. Personalization and normalization of campaign news has reached new heights in recent elections through the precedent set by Ronald Reagan. Reagan's ability, both as candidate and president, to bring politics into the realm of individual fantasy through the manipulation of symbols and values is unmatched. His successful bids for the presidency used a strategy that played to the press' inherent biases toward the dramatic, the personal, and the normal. He bequeathed a campaign legacy of more of the same. The fact that journalists view elections as contests between candidates vying for personal success and power, rather than as struggles over the direction of national policy (Patterson and Davis, 1985), further fosters these types of news biases.

The foregoing discussion should not leave the impression that personalized, fragmented, dramatized, and normalized news is purely the domain of television. The content of campaign news in print has changed with the introduction of television into the process. Prior to that time, candidates' position papers, newsletters, and speeches provided much of the information that journalists used in reporting about campaigns. Television made it important for news reporters of all types to cover live events (Patterson, 1980, 1982). The campaign itself—an episodic creation of political professionals—became the central component of news accounts.

TELEVISION AND NEWSPAPER COVERAGE OF CAMPAIGNS

The influence of television on the style and content of newspaper news is a relatively recent phenomenon. When television first appeared on the scene, it concentrated primarily on entertainment programming. Television and newspaper content supplemented and complemented each other. When television increased its coverage of news events, however, it began to encroach upon the domain of newspapers. Television news was more accessible and less time-consuming for the audience than newspapers. Television news also lowered people's expectations about how much news they were responsible for as good citizens. Newspapers faced a double challenge of declining readership, exacerbated by the coming of age of the TV generation (Robinson and Jeffres, 1979; Bogart, 1982, 1984).

In an effort to relieve these difficulties, newspapers altered their focus and format. Newspaper reporting of elections has become noticeably more fragmented and personalized. Feature stories about the race, candidate and campaign personalities, and pseudoevents abound. The format of many newspapers has itself become fragmented. Campaign stories no longer appear exclusively in the main section of newspapers. Election-related articles are frequently profiled in "style" sections, magazine supplements, and other parts of newspapers reserved for feature material. Newspaper formats have also changed to highlight dramatic elements in the news. There are bigger and more varied headline styles, more charts and pictures, and greater use of color print.

While there has been a notable convergence in the content and style of news stories on television and in newspapers, the distinctions between these two communication channels remain sizable. These differences derive from technical aspects of the two media forms. At the most basic level, newspaper articles about elections are more detailed and varied because space and format considerations are more liberal than for television. Lacking the capability of providing moving visual imagery, news reporters must furnish detailed descriptive accounts of election events. By contrast, news stories appearing on television are short, generally lasting from 30 to 90 seconds. Visuals are a key component, often filling in details that the accompanying audio does not project (Diamond, 1975; Graber, 1986a; 1986b).

Technological differences strongly influence the ways in which events are portrayed on television and in print. Television derives its power and credibility from its ability to convince audience members that what they are seeing on film is real and important. Advances in television technology have provided news stories with a sense of immediacy not always apparent for newspaper news (Bieder, 1982). Televised news also fosters intimacy between viewers and an event or personality (Henry, 1981). Staged campaign events are thus news because we can see that they happen and we are made to feel that we are a part of them. The case is different for print, as the appearance of black print on a white page does little on its own to persuade the audience of a story's importance or believability. Newspapers make their case through appeals to logic, documentation of information through a varied range of sources, and in-depth analysis.

The established norms of reporters in each medium also have implications for variations in coverage. Television journalists cover several events in a single day. They are rewarded for their ability to simplify the complex. Conversely, newspaper reporters generally cover only one story at a time, hoping to bring details on the topic to light (Henry, 1981; Lichty, 1982). Television reporters have become an integral component of personalized news in their own right. They often become players in the very dramas that they have been dispatched to observe (Henry, 1981; Bennett, 1988). The credibility of the reporter becomes directly linked to the credibility of the news itself. Most newspaper audience members have little feel for the reporter of a story at all. The distance between newspaper reporters and the mass public is maintained by differences in demographic characteristics and attitudinal orientations. The personalized connection that exists for television journalists is lacking, even though newspapers increasingly assign by-lines to articles (Gaziano and McGrath, 1987).

These distinctions in the form of television and newspaper news transcend the emerging similarities in content and style. They have important implications for this research. Individuals develop orientations toward media sources, a situation that determines their propensity to seek out information from a particular channel. Similar messages disseminated in different formats will inspire varying reactions from audience members based on their experience with the medium. These experiences can influence individuals' perceptions and opinions about the nature and credibility of the information that is presented. In election campaigns, the effect of a particular medium combines with campaign stimulae to create pictures of candidates and the electoral process.

THE CONTENT OF CAMPAIGN NEWS

A key issue in discussing news content is bias in press coverage of events. A substantial body of literature focuses on news bias and is relevant to a discussion of voters' orientations toward campaign news stories for several reasons. Bias in the news that favors one candidate over another may influence voters' perceptions of the candidates and can even affect their voting decisions. News coverage that is perceived as being biased may also be ignored or discounted by voters. Voters then may either seek information from other sources or disregard the campaign. In the present study, we attempted to determine the degree to which voters have faith in the accuracy of news reports by examining the attitudes of the respondents to our surveys.

Studies examining the content of campaign news stories have focused either on determining bias in coverage or the extent to which particular categories of information have been reported. There has been little consensus on whether news stories are biased in terms of liberal/conservative or candidate dimensions. A number of observers have found evidence of news stories having a liberal bias and favoring candidates with liberal ideological positions (Efron, 1971; Keely, 1971). They contend that a left-leaning media establishment controls the dissemination of news. Others reach opposite conclusions and provide evidence of the conservative bent of the press. The latter group contend that the mass media are first and foremost a business enterprise; thus, they must cater to monied interests—which are generally controlled by corporate conservatives (Altheide, 1977; Cirino, 1972).

The reasons for such perceived bias in the news run deeper than the ideological predispositions of news personnel. The structure of the journalistic situation and the identity of the candidates are central to the ways in which candidates are covered. Constraints on newscasting cause journalists to pursue strategies of coverage that permit them to meet their deadlines and create newsworthy copy (Bennett, 1988; Berman, 1987; Graber, 1986/1987). Candidates whose campaign strategies fulfill these needs for journalists will be treated better in the press (Hofstetter, 1976; Weaver, 1972). Most members of the press corps are neither liberal nor conservative in their ideological outlooks. Instead, they are trained in a progressive tradition that causes them to seek to expose corruption in the political system. Reporters therefore approach campaigns with a critical eye aimed at the candidates (Ranney, 1983).

Other scholars contend that there is a lack of a consistent bias altogether in news coverage of elections (Hofstetter and Buss, 1978; Frank, 1973). Evidence points to a dearth of explicit editorial comment in either television or newspaper news coverage of the 1968, 1972, and 1976 elections (Graber, 1980). There is similar evidence for the 1980 campaign based on an extensive examination of wire service and network news reports (Robinson and Sheehan, 1983). However, this did not appear to be the case for 1984 (Robinson, 1985; Clancy and Robinson, 1985). These disparities in the detection of bias in the news to some degree reflect inadequate and inconsistent techniques of measurement. In particular, different definitions of bias have been used across studies (Hofstetter and Buss, 1978).

In addition to searching for evidence of bias, scholars have attempted to determine if news stories contain predominantly issue, image, or "horserace" information. The "horserace" component of news coverage (that is, stories that focus upon the election mostly as a game or contest between two opponents) predominates. For example, more than half of television and newspaper coverage of the 1980 election focused on the "horserace" (Patterson, 1980; Robinson, 1981; Robinson and Sheehan, 1983).

The press tends to focus on winning and losing, campaign strategy, personal appearances, and hoopla. Prior to the 1984 campaign, substantive issues comprised a small proportion of election coverage. Candidate image formation was even less apparent. Since 1984, there has been an increase in the image orientation of campaign news because of the appeals of the candidate who were running.

There are differences between television and newspaper coverage of elections. In general, newspapers provide more issue information than does television news, which has a greater orientation toward horserace journalism. Despite such findings, issue information is evident in campaign reporting both on television and in newspapers. Studies indicate that candidates play a role in shaping the issue agenda that is transmitted to voters through the mass media (Williams, Shapiro, and Cutbirth, 1981; Stovall, 1982; Weaver, Graber, McCombs, and Eyal, 1981).

We now explore the specific news strategies and coverage of the candidates in the 1984 and 1988 races in light of our examination of the characteristics and content of television and newspaper news in presidential elections. Some interesting similarities emerge between the two elections. These have prompted some observers to assert that 1988 was a continuation of the prior contest. Yet, the unique personalities of the candidates and the contextual factors surrounding each election figured significantly in each campaign year.

NEWS STORIES IN THE 1984 AND 1988 PRESIDENTIAL ELECTIONS

Campaign strategies become increasingly indistinguishable from campaign news as candidates' organizations play into established news biases. All the candidates we studied attempted to conform to the journalistic expectation that news consists of discrete incidents by orchestrating daily barrages of made-for-TV events. Both Republican candidates specialized in mini-dramas that used effective symbolic props, such as the Statue of Liberty. The Democrats tried, and often failed, to create events centered around issues. Dukakis, for example, used the concept of "theme weeks" to draw attention to specific policy concerns, only to find his focus supplanted by coverage of the tactics of the race itself. A week may in fact be too long to sustain coverage of a single issue theme in the news. For the two Republican candidates, concentrating on the personal seemed to work best, whether it meant creating a warm and friendly feeling about themselves or conjuring up bleak images of the opponent. The Democrats never revealed quite enough of their personal selves to satisfy either the press or the public. Finally, both Reagan and Bush were able to capitalize on their official positions by normalizing news. Both could employ phrases like "Stay the course!" while using the authority of their offices to maximize feelings of security and control. Neither Democratic contender could match this level of normalization.

In presidential elections involving an incumbent, such as 1984, the challenger must generally pursue a vigorous media strategy in order to engage the press and create news. Incumbents, who are newsworthy by virtue of the office of president, do not need to court the press as actively as their opponents must in the campaign context. Presidents are able to use other events associated with running the country to place themselves in the limelight. They can thus limit their confrontations with their opponents on the campaign trail.

In the 1984 presidential contest, the media strategies of the candidates seemed in general to follow this pattern. Adhering to sound campaign practice, the candidates attempted to project through the news media the same information that they desired to disseminate through their campaign advertising. Mondale focused on establishing particular issues as important to his election, while Reagan projected an image of patriotism and positive attitudes about the United States.

By focusing on issues, Mondale appeared to set the agenda for campaign discourse and determined, to a greater extent than Reagan, the content of news coverage. His strategy was to present a highly substantive, policy-oriented agenda to the public against the backdrop of small vignettes of American life. Mondale aimed to create the impression that he was out talking to voters about issues, while Reagan was hiding behind the trappings of his office.

Early on, Mondale campaign organizers sought to have the press, particularly television news personnel, cover the candidate speaking to small groups of supporters while he made his way across the United States. This approach was not entirely successful. On a number of occasions, few people showed up for planned gatherings, and subsequent news analyses stressed the campaign's lack of momentum. Subsequently, the Mondale campaign changed its strategy to focus on the candidate presenting his message in more formal settings. Late in the campaign, Mondale was often shown using charts and graphs to criticize Reagan's policies. He also appeared in front of large rallies of voters (Brownstein, 1984).

In contrast to the mixed results and inconsistent strategy that characterized the Mondale campaign's efforts to attract positive press coverage, Reagan's organization focused on carefully orchestrated and usually large-scale events. This tactic seemed to give Reagan an edge in the competition for campaign news play. Examining news coverage of the campaign on Labor Day, the unofficial "kickoff" date of the election, provides a good illustration.

Mondale and Ferraro marched in the Labor Day parade in New York City which drew no crowd; later in the day, they traveled to Wisconsin, where it was raining. The Reagan organization had staged a massive rally in the president's home state of California, complete with bands and fireworks. Vice-president Bush appeared separately in Illinois, making a speech about economic policy. News commentary emphasized the difference between the tones of the two campaign kickoffs. National television coverage showed footage of the Reagan rally first and then turned to Mondale and Ferraro. NBC, for example, used the following audio commentary to accompany its story about the day's campaign events: "It was an extravaganza—even by Reagan-Bush standards." When depicting Mondale and Ferraro, however, an NBC reporter stated, "They opened their campaign to empty streets; Mondale could only hope that the embarrassingly small turnout at New York's Labor Day Parade wasn't an omen" (Schram, 1984).

The error in campaign strategy illustrated by this example cost the Mondale campaign dearly, as the press began to focus on failed electoral tactics rather than on Mondale's substantive message. To their credit, Mondale and Ferraro, while often missing the mark tactically, appeared to set the issue agenda for the election. The Reagan camp felt strongly enough about Mondale's and Ferraro's attacks on the president's policies that they created opportunities for Reagan and Bush to address their opponents' positions.

In addition to setting the issue agenda of the campaign, Mondale and Ferraro appear to have benefited from better press coverage during the 1984 campaign than did Reagan and Bush. There was generally less time spent on the "horse-race" aspect of coverage in 1984 than in other years, probably because Reagan was substantially ahead throughout the campaign. To fill this void in news reports, campaign issues, as opposed to issues of public policy with which the government was currently dealing, were covered. Mondale and Ferraro received favorable press because of their focus on issues.

Still, good press coverage was not enough to change the tide of the election (Clancy and Robinson, 1985; Robinson, 1985). A fascinating analysis suggests that both the words and pictures on television news favored the Democratic candidates in 1984. News about issues and events that did not focus on the campaign itself worked against the Republican ticket. In spite of this, the traits emphasized most clearly on television news were leadership, a "winner" image, and an ability to communicate. All of these were Reagan's strong points, so this emphasis created an overall impression that Reagan was dominating television coverage of the election—a sentiment echoed by Mondale himself (Graber, 1986a, 1986b, 1986c, 1987a, 1987b).

In 1988, the same basic strategy, or lack thereof, characterized the news component of the candidates' campaigns. Bush's handlers had a more solid game plan and a more compliant candidate to work with than did the Dukakis forces. Thus, Bush's agenda dictated a majority of news coverage of the campaign, often forcing Dukakis into a reactive mode of electioneering.

As with his advertising strategy, the overarching theme of Bush's appeals to the press was that he represented the American mainstream. The basic thrust of Bush's media strategy was to forward a "values agenda." This agenda focused on patriotic, anti-crime, strong defense, and pro-environment topics. The goal was to demonstrate that Bush stood for these positions while Dukakis did not. Little regard was paid to the reality of the candidates' records on these issues.

Bush launched an attack on the ideological front by labeling Dukakis a "Liberal" and simultaneously defining "the L word" in extreme and negative terms. As proof of Dukakis' sinister liberalism, Bush exposed his opponent as a "card-carrying member of the American Civil Liberties Union" and attributed the ACLU's policies to Dukakis personally. Bush created an issues platform based on his opposition to ACLU stands on saluting the flag, the death penalty, the ratings system for movies, and tax exemptions for religious institutions, among others. By foisting the ACLU's policy positions on Dukakis, Bush forced a defensive response from him (Drew, 1989; Germond and Witcover, 1989).

The "flag salute" issue became the major articulation of Bush's patriotic appeals, as well as a cornerstone of his campaign. By embracing the flag as the symbol of his candidacy, Bush could assert his own love of country while calling Dukakis' patriotism into question. Bush based his anti-crime theme more on holding Dukakis accountable for problems with the Massachusetts state furlough program and for his position against the death penalty for drug dealers than on forwarding a positive plan of his own. His anti-crime agenda was bolstered by the "Willie Horton" commercial and other ads that helped him to portray Dukakis as a weak link in the fight against crime. Bush's news agenda on the environment once again closely dovetailed his advertising strategy. "Boston Harbor" came to represent the sum total of the environmental ills facing the nation.

Some of the same people who had managed Reagan's rise to the White House were responsible for choreographing Bush's campaign media effort. His appearances were carefully orchestrated to coordinate the day's agenda item with a flattering and complimentary backdrop. Each day a specific news tidbit with a new twist was slotted for articulation. A "line-of-the-day" was drafted in the hope that it would become the sound-bite that made the evening news (Goldman and Mathews, 1989; Runkel, 1989).

Two occasions stood out for their impressive and strategic use of background visuals. Both occurred in Dukakis' home state. To drive home the anti-crime issue, Bush was positioned at a rally attended by uniformed Boston police cheering him on. To confirm Dukakis' bad record on the environment, Bush took a sail around Boston Harbor in early September and pointed out trash in the wake of the boat. The previous day he had been filmed in California speaking about his love of nature and concern for a clean environment while pictured in front of a crystal clear lake under blue skies (Germond and Witcover, 1989).

There were times, however, when the Bush team organized too much of a good thing and the strategy backfired. The flag had been positioned successfully as the symbolic center of the Bush campaign. Flags were paraded at rallies and waved by supporters all along the campaign trail. To capitalize on this symbolic coup, Bush visited a number of flag factories. In late September, he visited one flag factory too many for even the press to swallow. The nightly network newscasts all noted his overt attempts at symbolic manipulation.

The Bush media campaign experienced two slumps. The first occurred just prior to the presidential debates, the second at the close of the campaign. Throughout the election, Bush walked a fine line between being recast as a "wimp"—a characterization that he had successfully overcome—and creating a backlash effect from his relentless attacks on Dukakis. As Dukakis finally seemed to get on track after the second debate, Bush's strategy faltered somewhat. His overriding concern became not making mistakes. Bush tempered his attacks a bit and grew more evasive with reporters than he had been earlier in the campaign. He focused on issues of national defense and foreign policy, adopting Reagan's theme of "peace through strength." The "Tank" ads were aired during this period to reinforce the message that Dukakis was weak on defense. Bush spent the final days of the campaign dashing from one photo opportunity to another across the country. His finish, however, was not particularly strong (Drew, 1989).

Most of Bush's media campaign was notable for its skillful management and effective execution. The ability of the Bush Team to turn negatives into positives for their candidate is illustrated by their handling of the selection of Dan

Quayle as the vice-presidential contender. Bush was able to use the fact that he stood behind his choice of Quayle under pressure to counter his "wimp" image. He even spoke out in favor of Quayle's service in the National Guard during the Vietnam War, stating that Quayle had served his country instead of fleeing to Canada as many of his generation had. In the meantime, Quayle was kept out of the spotlight, campaigning in small media markets. Bush's own imagery came to encompass Quayle's candidacy as well.

Dukakis' advisors had little experience in general election campaigns. They proved no match for Bush's handlers. Whereas Bush's strategists deftly managed the logistics of a mass media blitz, Dukakis' campaign often could not get even the basics down pat. Problems with site selection and crowd control plagued them. Dukakis' own failure to develop unifying campaign themes was exacerbated by Bush's successful agenda-setting plan. Until the end of the election, Dukakis spent his days practicing reactive politics, following moves plotted by Bush.

From the outset, Dukakis confronted three major obstacles to getting his media campaign off the ground. First, Dukakis had hoped to use the impending trial of Oliver North to question Bush's role in the Iran-contra affair. When the judge in the case postponed the trial, Dukakis' attack lost its bite. Bush simply ignored the issue, and it dropped from the campaign agenda. In addition, the selection of Quayle as Bush's running-mate commanded the bulk of air time early on. Although much of the press coverage was negative, it detracted from Dukakis' ability to command attention and initiate an agenda of his own. Finally, the Bush whom Dukakis faced in the general election had been thoroughly retooled by his campaign strategists. Bush's tough, attacking style took Dukakis by surprise (Goldman and Mathews, 1989; Drew, 1989; Germond and Witcover, 1989).

The strengths of Bush's media strategy mirrored Dukakis' weaknesses. While Bush set the agenda, Dukakis spent much of his time explaining away charges, ranging from attacks on his loyalty to the United States to allegations about his mental health. Dukakis' inability to identify themes to unify his campaign left him continually groping to find a message. The Bush Team had successfully brought out a personal side of their candidate by portraying him as a likeable family man. Dukakis' guarded exterior precluded such personalization, making him a vulnerable target. His situation represented a clear contrast to Reagan's position in 1984.

Dukakis' side was less skillful in crafting photo and sound-bite opportunities than was the opposition. Dukakis himself found it difficult to deliver catchy one-liners, and his advisors often failed to position him with interesting visual backdrops. Many times Dukakis was seen on the evening news speaking in front of closed curtains, juxtaposed with Bush, cloaked in an atmosphere of color and spectacle. Even when Dukakis staged a scene successfully, he was frequently eclipsed by the Republican candidates who managed to get there first. Such was the case with a speaking engagement in front of the Statue of Liberty and a tour of Ellis Island (Drew, 1989; Goldman and Mathews, 1989).

Off to a slow start, Dukakis began to appear in more eye-catching locations and to present a stronger message. One problem was that the messages he chose to project, like Mondale's in 1984, were too complex for presidential politics in the age of the sound-bite. Dukakis attempted to exploit a theme based on the "middle-class squeeze." Abandoning traditional Democratic appeals to the plight of the poor and the elderly, Dukakis elaborated the ways in which Republican administration policies would ultimately hurt the middle class. It was difficult to make a convincing argument on this point when the polls showed that people generally felt that they were faring pretty well under the Reagan administration. Dukakis also made a series of speeches on college campuses; these focused on the topics of drugs, foreign policy, and defense. While these speeches outlined programs in detail, the evening news chose to feature the few sentences in them that attacked Bush and Quayle (Drew, 1989). Once again, television's thirst for the dramatic and personal overwhelmed the articulation of issues. Dukakis' failure to provide *the* sound-bite left it up to the press to define it for him.

Unlike Quayle, vice-presidential nominee Lloyd Bentsen was not a political liability to Dukakis in a direct sense. However, his engaging personal style and flair for politics provided a marked contrast to Dukakis' brooding delivery. Bentsen's appearance in the press served to highlight further Dukakis' failings as a media candidate. (A substantial number of people in our survey—supporters of both candidates—commented that they would have preferred Bentsen to either presidential nominee.)

Dukakis' media campaign actually gained momentum during the final two weeks of the election campaign. His advisors developed "the eighteen-state-strategy," in which Dukakis visited states where he was leading or within striking distance in the polls. The campaign adopted a theme—"on your side"—emphasizing Dukakis' immigrant roots and middle-class values, in contrast with Bush's aristocratic lifestyle. Dukakis warned that Bush was going to "divide America by class" and that he would work to overcome this kind of divisiveness. The new strategy included frequent town meetings and appearances on every television interview program that could possibly be arranged. Dukakis seemed to be highly energized, and his television image improved markedly. Tracking polls indicated that the public perceived the difference. The change, however, came too late.

EFFECTS OF TELEVISION AND NEWSPAPER STORIES

The preceding overview of the media campaigns waged by the presidential candidates in 1984 and 1988 gives a feel for the nature of the mass media experience that characterized these elections. The strategic posturing of candidates dominated the vision of the electoral process at work. We might speculate that such media politics debased the very system it is designed to promote.

Still, the mass public desires campaign news, or at least they feel that election information *should* be reported daily. Election coverage provides Americans with a sense of security in knowing that democracy is alive and kicking. People believe that they can fulfill their duty as citizens by tuning in to election news, if only occasionally. It is not surprising that scholars have reported high levels of exposure to television and newspaper accounts of presidential elections among the populace.

While exposure to campaign news may be high over the course of a campaign, the quality of this exposure and the attention paid to coverage may be less than adequate. Prior research and comments by our survey respondents provide some insights into this phenomenon that harken back to the characteristic biases of campaign news.

The fragmented nature of election news has significant consequences for political learning. Although people report substantial exposure to campaign news, research demonstrates that they gain only a passing knowledge of the issues and candidates. In the 1988 election, for example, Dukakis' campaign research indicated that the public knew very little about his personal qualifications or about his stands on issues right up until the end of the election. Information is recalled best when it has been reinforced through repetition and elaboration. When news organizations, facilitated by candidates, feature episodic coverage to the exclusion of more comprehensive information, people find it difficult to identify even the basic election themes. In addition, many voters do not pay attention to issues during the primaries or the convention period. They wait to see who will be the finalists. Since the news media are hesitant to repeat stories, people who have waited until the general election to make up their minds often suffer from a "knowledge gap." They have missed out on important information that can help their decision-making. Voters realize that they lack information, but feel powerless to do anything about it (Weaver, Graber, McCombs, and Eyal, 1981).

The personalization of news has had several effects on voters' campaign cognitions. First, people know more about the personal characteristics of candidates than about issues. At the same time, they question whether the personal qualities they are reading about or observing on television are truly credible. People are becoming more aware that candidates' images are largely a function of their campaign skills. This impression comes through in news coverage, and it is reinforced through advertising and debates. There is also a blurring of issue and image learning from campaigns, as issues become increasingly personalized. It is difficult for people to sort out one kind of information from the other. The combined effect is an overall hazy picture of the candidates and the campaign as a whole (Graber, 1986b).

The dramatic content of campaigns also influences political learning. Designed to stimulate attention to the news, if often turns voters off. In their search for the dramatic, the media often focus on the negative—on the competing claims fired at one another by candidates. Audience members tire of the insipid dramatic interplays between candidates day after day. They find it difficult to judge who is right or wrong. The news media provide little help on this front, as they frequently report what they hear and see without checking the accuracy. People, including our respondents, find a steady diet of backbiting in the press distasteful.

The normalization of campaign news through the intervention of official spokespersons has reached new heights. "Spin doctors" (political operatives and officeholders from each side) are repeatedly called upon to interpret the day's activities for the voters. The public has grown to resent being told what to think and how to interpret events. They feel that their own role in the political process is being discounted.

Research focusing on audience learning from news stories has produced conflicting results, largely because of difficulties in developing consistent and uniform concepts and measures. News stories have the potential to influence voters in ways similar to candidate advertisements. In theory, news reports should have a greater impact than political spots because they are not generated by candidates. Therefore, they may be perceived as being more legitimate. The credibility of campaign news, however, is more complex, since it is not consistent across media channels. Research indicates that credibility is linked to an individual's reliant medium (Rimmer and Weaver, 1987).

Agenda-setting research demonstrates that people learn which issues are prominent in the campaign from news, although the knowledge acquired and recalled is often shallow. (McCombs and Shaw, 1972; Weaver, Graber, McCombs, and Eyal, 1981). Voter's knowledge of campaign agendas has been linked to reliance on newspaper and television news. Newspapers represent local and state concerns more than television news, which focuses on a national agenda. We might then expect that television news would be a more prominent source of agenda setting for presidential elections. The situation appears to be more complicated, however. A longitudinal study of the 1976 election revealed that newspapers set the long-term agenda for the campaign, while television spotlighted particular events. Television is particularly potent in establishing the agenda for the final stretch of the campaign (Weaver, Graber, McCombs, and Eyal, 1981). Still, individuals learn most about elections from newspapers (Clarke and Fredin, 1978). In fact, voters are more likely to comprehend candidates' issue positions from ads than from television news (Patterson and McClure, 1976).

Exposure and attention to campaign news is largely a matter of prior orientation toward a particular source, lifestyle considerations and habits, a desire to obtain information, and a sense of civic duty. Newspaper- and television-reliant individuals differ in a number of respects. Newspaper use is a more deliberate and time-consuming activity than watching television broadcasts.

Newspaper readers often exhibit a high degree of interest in campaigns. They may use television to supplement their reading or to provide them with an outline of events that they should explore further. Television exposure can be accidental, and it may not be related to an individual's desire to be informed about events at all (Graber, 1986b; Hill, 1983; Miller, Singletary, and Chen, 1988). Almost half of the people who are exposed to television news view it passively and allow it to interfere minimally with other activities (Levy, 1978a). Thus, the probability that newspaper-reliant individuals will be exposed and pay attention to television news is more likely than the reverse. Newspaper-reliant individuals also prefer different types and styles of news than do the television-reliant. Newspaper users will seek out "hard" news presentations in both media, while the television-reliant favor news with entertainment content, such as news magazines (McDonald and Reese, 1987).

Interest in the election is tied to the amount of attention one pays to news, although it is not necessarily linked to exposure. Campaign interest is not constant; it ebbs and flows with specific campaign events, such as conventions and debates. Therefore, patterns of attention and exposure are likely to change during the course of an election (Weaver, Graber, McCombs, and Eyal, 1981; Levy, 1978). Since our study was fielded late in the campaigns, the interest levels of our survey respondents were high.

Regular readers of newspapers have a strong sense of civic duty that is absent in sporadic readers. They are open to a wide range of competing values and ideals. People who view television news often also have a commitment to civic values, although less than newspaper readers have. However, their ideals are more covergent with the mainstream view of political reality (McCombs and Poindexter, 1983; Gernber, Gross, Morgan, and Signorielli, 1984).

Communication and political factors work together to influence candidate selection in a campaign. Mass media use strengthens candidate preference and the decision to turn out to vote (Kennamer, 1987). The perceptual screen of partisanship acts as a filter for candidate choice. Medium effects are becoming increasingly relevant, however. Research has linked the preference for a candidate who comes across best in a particular medium—television or newspapers—to voters who obtain most of their information from that source (Adams, 1982). Undecided and independent voters are also susceptible to these types of medium effects (Lucas and Adams, 1978).

THE EFFECTS OF NEWS STORIES IN THE 1984 AND 1988 ELECTIONS

We questioned our survey respondents about their exposure and attention to campaign news stories. The influence of party identification, candidate preference, and political interest was taken into account. Media reliance and its relationship to attention and exposure to television and newspaper news was explored.

Because of technical constraints on the design of this study, only simple distinctions among types of news stories could be made. Survey participants were asked questions pertaining to their use of television and newspaper news in general. A drawback of this analysis is that it does not probe into the fine distinctions that characterize news stories. Thus, the findings reported here pertain to individuals' basic orientations toward television and newspaper news stories.

Our survey participants in both years reported high levels of exposure to television and newspaper news about the election campaigns. These levels of news exposure are consistent with those reported by the respondents in other studies conducted at this point in an election campaign. We will now make comparisons between usage of television and newspaper news during the two elections under study.

In 1984, Dane County respondents were exposed less frequently to newspaper news than to television news. Sixty-nine percent watched television news reports frequently, while only 55 percent were highly exposed to newspaper news. The opposite was true for Fairfax County, where 65 percent of the respondents were frequently exposed to television reports and 75 percent read the newspaper often—six to seven times per week.

These county-based distinctions may reflect differences in the content of news offerings in each location. Dane County newspapers offer a high proportion of local and state-level news. National news, including information about presidential elections, is less prominent. Fairfax County is served by *The Washington Post*, a newspaper with a high national news profile. Thus, Dane County residents who want to learn about the presidential election would find the national network newscasts more enlightening than people in Fairfax County, who have the option of getting more detailed information from their local newspaper.

Patterns of exposure to television and newspaper news were slightly different in 1988 than they had been in 1984. In our survey, a far smaller proportion of people reported that they viewed television news often than stated that they read the newspaper frequently. The findings are consistent across all three counties. The proportion reporting frequent exposure to television news was 37 percent in Carroll County, 37 percent in Middlesex County, and 36 percent in Fairfax County. By contrast, 69 percent, 73 percent, and 69 percent of respondents in the respective counties read news accounts of the election often.

We can speculate that the preference for newspaper over television news may be linked to the content of televised news that characterized the 1988 campaign. More than in any other election year, the media messages constructed by the candidates' handlers came across on television as largely symbolic fluff or unsubstantiated mudslinging. Perhaps the American public tired of a steady television diet of flags, fanfare, and spitballs. Newspapers could at least provide a modicum of information minus the trite video footage, especially for those interested in the election.

In 1984, exposure to television and newspaper news was related to party identification; although no significant relationships emerged for candidate preference in either sample. The differences between party supporters and exposure to news stories was slight. Republicans tended to be exposed to television news about the election more than Democrats. Independents, while still reporting relatively high levels of exposure to news stories, were less likely than partisan identifiers to view or read news stories frequently.

Party identification did not correspond significantly to news exposure in 1988, although candidate preference was related. In both Middlesex and Fairfax Counties, Dukakis supporters were more likely to be frequent viewers of television news than were Bush voters. The pattern was more mixed for newspaper news. In Middlesex County, Dukakis voters were once again more highly exposed to news stories than Bush supporters, but the opposite held true for Fairfax County. No patterns were discerned for Carroll County for exposure to either type of news.

Undecided voters displayed lower levels of exposure to both television and newspaper news stories in Carroll County than did voters who stated a candidate preference. In Middlesex County, the undecideds fell in between Dukakis and Bush supporters in their level of television news exposure, but they read newspaper stories about the election less often than decided voters.

The overall pattern reveals that Dukakis voters viewed and read more news about the election than did Bush partisans. This finding suggests several differences in the informational needs of the supporters of the two candidates. First, Dukakis was a far less well-known candidate than Bush, who had served two terms as vice president and was already a national political figure. Dukakis supporters had a greater need to find out about their candidate than did Bush voters. In addition, Dukakis supporters were backing a candidate who was trailing far behind in the polls at that point in the campaign. They would therefore have a greater desire to reinforce their decision than supporters of the leader, whose judgment about their candidate was validated statistically.

Interest in the election was an important determinant of news story exposure. In 1984, individuals who were highly exposed to newspaper news were greatly interested in the election, with correlations (Pearson's r) of .25 for Fairfax County and .33 for Dane County. There was no statistically significant relationship for television exposure. The findings were similar in 1988, although television news was significantly correlated with political interest (.23) for Fairfax County only. The relationship was significant, but not strong, for newspaper news in all three counties, with coefficients of .12 for Carroll County, .16 for Middlesex County, and .21 for Fairfax County.

While individuals were highly exposed to television and newspaper news during the 1984 presidential contest, they did not necessarily pay attention to news accounts of the election. There were again county-based differences. In Fairfax County, more people reported paying a great deal of attention to television news (42%), as opposed to newspaper news (35%). There was virtually no difference based on medium for Dane County, with approximately 57 percent paying a lot of attention in each news category.

In 1988, lower proportions of individuals reported paying attention to news stories of both kinds than in 1984. There were slight differences in favor of television news in Carroll and Middlesex Counties. In Carroll County, 26 percent of respondents paid a great deal of attention to television news, as compared to 21 percent for newspaper news. The findings for Middlesex County showed 35 percent for television and 30 percent for newspapers. There were no medium-based differences in attention to news stories for Fairfax County.

Differences in attention to news stories were found on the basis of party identification, as well as candidate preference. In 1984, Mondale supporters and Democrats in Dane County were slightly more attentive to television and newspaper news than were Reagan voters and Republicans. The findings appear in Figure 3.1.

Again, supporters of the underdog paid more attention to television and newspaper news stories about the election than did those backing the winner in 1988. Dukakis voters were more frequent watchers of television news than were Bush backers, especially in Middlesex and Fairfax Counties. Similar findings exist for newspaper news, although the strongest relationships are in Carroll and Fairfax Counties. The findings appear in Figure 3.2.

Undecideds were less likely to pay a great deal of attention to news stories than were those who had made up their minds in the election. This finding is evident in both elections. This probably reflects undecideds' lower level of interest in the campaigns. Campaign interest was determined to be the strongest predictor of attention to both television and newspaper news. (The findings appear in Table 3.1.) The undecideds were among the least interested of the respondents in both campaign years. Independents were less attentive to news stories than were partisan identifiers for both newspaper and television news in all counties.

There was some evidence of selective attention to news stories about the election. In the 1984 Fairfax County sample, about 35 percent reported that they paid selective attention to stories about Mondale; 15 percent indicated that they paid more and 20 percent stated that they paid less attention. Strikingly similar findings emerged in 1988. In each sample, between 30 and 35 percent of the respondents stated that they viewed stories about Dukakis selectively. In Fairfax County, almost exactly the same percentage of people as we calculated in 1984 indicated that they would pay more or less attention to the Democratic contender. The reverse trend was apparent in Carroll and Middlesex Counties. In each county, 10 percent of the respondents stated they paid less attention to stories about Dukakis, while slightly over 20 percent

Figure 3.1
Frequent Attention to News Stories and Party Identification—1984 Election

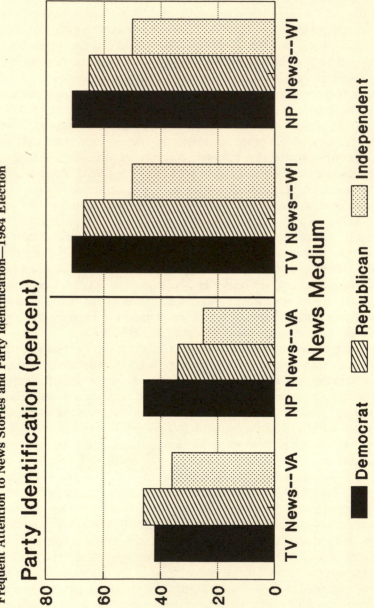

Figure 3.2
Frequent Attention to News Stories and Candidate Preference—1988 Election

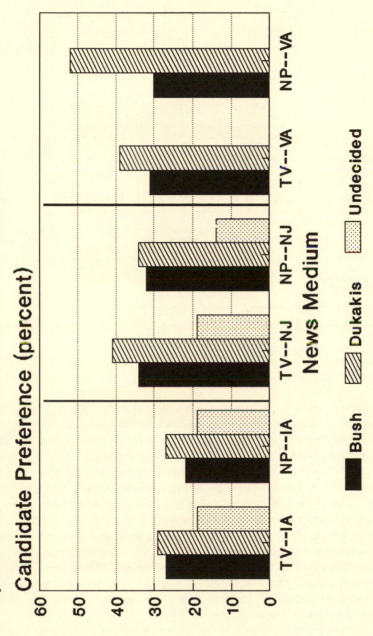

Table 3.1
Correlations (Pearson's *r*) between Attention to Television and Newspaper News and Political Interest

1984 Presidential Election

	Television		Newspaper	
	VA	WI	VA	WI
Political Interest	.27*	.57*	.35*	.54*

Virginia	n=463
Wisconsin	n=702

1988 Presidential Election

	Television			Newspaper		
	IA	NJ	VA	IA	NJ	VA
Political Interest	.39*	.38*	.35*	.44*	.40*	.36*

*p<.01

Iowa	n=234
New Jersey	n=215
Virginia	n=118

said they were more attentive. Not surprisingly, these differences corresponded directly to candidate preference in both elections.

We turn now to investigate the issue of media reliance and its relationship to exposure and attention to television and newspaper news. In general, individuals tended to display higher levels of exposure and were more attentive to news that was disseminated in their reliant medium than that which was not. The trends are highly stable across samples and election years.

Respondents who depended on newspapers as their primary source of information about campaigns were far more likely to be exposed and attentive to newspaper reports about the campaign than were television- or other-reliant individuals. An individual's preferred medium was not as strong a determinant of exposure and attention to television news as it was for newspaper reports. Findings for exposure appear in Figures 3.3 and 3.4; results for attention are found in Figures 3.5 and 3.6.

Our consistent evidence of the greater power of newspaper reliance compared to television reliance to predict high levels of exposure and attention to

Figure 3.3
Media Reliance and Frequent Exposure to News Stories—1984 Election

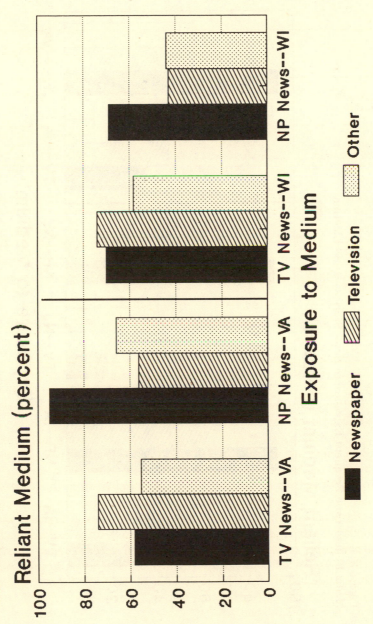

Figure 3.4
Media Reliance and Frequent Exposure to News Stories—1988 Election

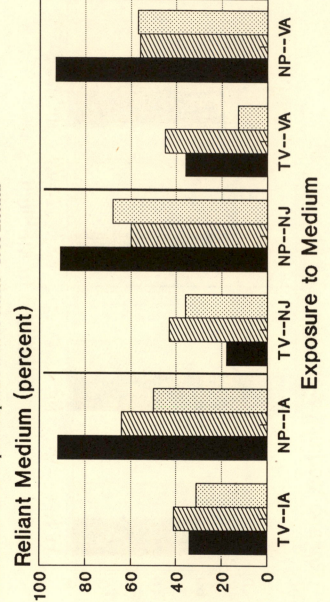

Figure 3.5
Media Reliance and Frequent Attention to News Stories—1984 Election

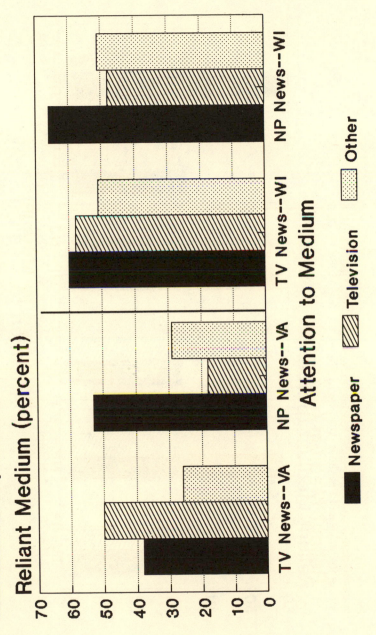

Figure 3.6
Media Reliance and Frequent Attention to News Stories—1988 Election

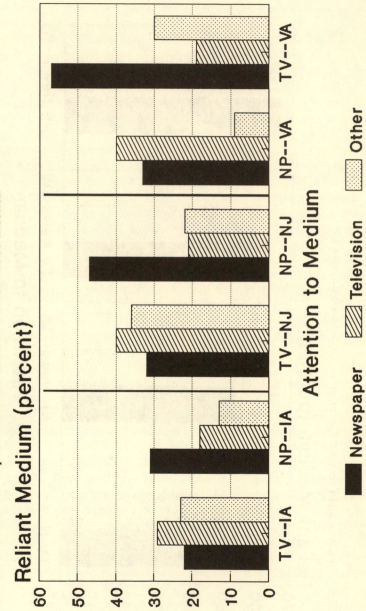

Reliant Medium (percent)

Attention to Medium

Newspaper   Television   Other

news stories in that medium conforms to our expectations. The comparative ease of access to each channel emphasizes that newspaper reading is a more deliberate activity than television viewing. People who are reliant on newspapers are more inclined to watch television news in addition to reading the newspaper. They may even be exposed to television news unintentionally. Television-reliant individuals, however, are less likely to take the extra steps necessary to keep up with events in print. Their news viewing behavior may be haphazard and unfocused as well.

In 1988, we assessed the degree of credibility that the respondents associated with television and newspaper news accounts of the election. Prior research speculates that credibility is linked to differences in the levels of exposure and attention to a particular news source that respondents report. Credibility can also be linked to reliance, as experience with a news source is likely to promote greater trust in that medium. The results of the analysis are inconclusive, although they are consistent across all three samples.

In general, few people trusted campaign news disseminated in either medium much at all. A somewhat higher proportion of respondents in each county reported that they trusted television news a great deal, as compared to those who felt that way about newspaper news. This finding is in keeping with the view that the visual quality of television news fosters greater credibility. At the same time, a slightly higher percentage of people trusted television news very little or not at all than held that opinion of newspaper accounts of the election.

We analyzed the correspondence between levels of exposure and attention with trust in each news source; this yielded insignificant results. It therefore appears that while respondents in our surveys generally did not trust either television or newspaper reports of the campaign very much, this attitude did not influence their tendency to be exposed to, pay attention to, or avoid news stories.

There was a significant difference in the amount of trust that individuals placed in television accounts of the election based on their reliant medium. In Middlesex and Fairfax Counties, the television-reliant were far more likely to trust television news accounts of the election than were the newspaper-reliant. In Middlesex County, 20 percent of the television-reliant trusted television news accounts a great deal, as compared to 6 percent of the newspaper-reliant respondents. In Fairfax County, the figures were 19 percent of the television-reliant compared to 5 percent of the newspaper-reliant. Differences between the two groups in Carroll County were minimal. The relationship is much weaker for trust in newspaper news. Newspaper-reliant individuals were only slightly more likely to trust newspaper news accounts of the election than were the television-reliant.

SUMMARY

The evidence from this study supports the consistent finding that exposure to campaign news stories is high among the mass public. Still, this high level of exposure to news about both the 1984 and 1988 presidential elections did not mean that voters paid a great deal of attention. Neither television nor newspapers were held in high esteem by respondents as trustworthy sources of campaign information.

Voters who supported trailing candidates were more highly exposed and attentive to news stories than were backers of the leaders. In both elections, the leading candidates were national political figures facing lesser-known opponents. Although people knew less about Bush in 1988 than they did about Reagan in 1984, Bush's association with Reagan bred familiarity among voters. In addition to their basic need to find out about their candidate, supporters of the underdog needed to validate their decisions. They had to find reasons to support their candidate in spite of poll results and media coverage of the opposition's momentum. Consistent with prior research, undecided voters, who had the potential to gain the most from news stories in terms of information upon which to base their vote, were the least likely to pay attention.

We discovered differences based on the form of news dissemination. Patterns of exposure and attention to television and newspaper news differed. In 1984, these distinctions were linked to the qualities of the communication media in each county; television's importance as an election news source heightened when newspaper news was focused more directly on local and state news than on national topics. Preference for a particular news source also corresponded to the specific campaign year and the distinctiveness of the coverage in each source. In 1988, respondents reported using newspapers to find out about the election far more often than television. The medium of television highlighted the very superficial and nasty elements of the campaign that were more apparent that year than in any previous election. The coverage became boring, as voters witnessed more of the same tactics packaged slightly differently over the course of an extended campaign season. People tended to tune out and to seek an alternative source of information—print—in which the visual manipulation of the message was not the central component of news presentation.

4

Public Opinion Polls:
A Double-Edged Sword

POLLS IN PRESIDENTIAL ELECTIONS

Public opinion polls are notable for the unique, multifaceted role they play in presidential elections. As a campaign message type, polls are openly disseminated through communication channels and constitute a major category of election news. Polls also perform a covert function in shaping journalists' coverage of campaigns as well as in determining the strategies pursued by candidates. These influences are equally important.

Polls have become a prominent tool for mass media organizations. As a communication form, polls transmit information to voters in a concise, simple, and authoritative manner. They have been used with increasing frequency during presidential election campaigns to predict the relative standing of the candidates. Since the 1970s, they have been accorded a high degree of respect by the mass public. These factors have raised speculation that poll results released through the mass media have an impact on election outcomes—that media-transmitted poll results influence voters' candidate preferences and affect turnout (e.g., Jackson, 1983; Ranney, 1983; DelliCarpini, 1984).

Polls have been a part of the American political scene for many years. Informal public opinion polling dates back to the 1700s. Public opinion polls were first used to measure presidential preference in the election of 1824. Andrew Jackson was correctly predicted as the winner in nonscientific newspaper polls in Pennsylvania and North Carolina. During this same era, members of the traveling class recorded their presidential preferences as they registered at hotels. Sporadic nonscientific polls for state-level candidates also appeared in the 1800s. The first systematic attempt to assess vote choice was made by Tammany Hall, which instituted an early version of a tracking poll. Workers would position themselves in public places and ask people their presidential preference on a daily basis (Roll and Cantril, 1980).

The introduction of scientific public opinion polling into the election process in the 1930s initiated the uneasy alliance between polling and the press. Journalists, not candidates, were the first to make use of presidential preference polls. Early on, few media organizations fielded their own surveys. The press paid to gain access to the polling operations and results of a few leading commercial pollsters. Once it became apparent that polls created a major source of news and that they greatly enhanced journalists' reporting abilities, media organizations began to establish polling operations of their own. In-house polling came to dominate news coverage from the 1970s up to the present.

While scientific opinion polling had been used by congressional candidates as early as 1932, the first polling done by a private firm on behalf of a candidate occurred for Thomas E. Dewey in 1940. When Dewey lost the Republican nomination to Wendell Willkie that year, Willkie continued to engage the services of a pollster, although he was not comfortable with the idea. The Republican pattern of employing pollsters to inform their campaigns continued with Eisenhower. By 1960, the dual role of polls in campaigns was clearly established. Both the Kennedy and Nixon campaigns used pollsters extensively, and the media reported poll results more often than in any prior presidential contest (Roll and Cantril, 1980; Gollin, 1987).

Only in the past two decades has polling become the pervasive presence that it now represents in presidential elections (Rippey, 1980). Prior to this time, the more limited impact of polls could be attributed to several factors. There was only a small number of polling firms in existence; poll results were released infrequently during the course of a campaign. When journalists made their first major foray into reporting election polls in 1936, they suffered a setback. Public regard for the validity of poll results abated as a result of the failure of the *Literary Digest* to predict the election outcome correctly (Squire, 1988). Finally, voters used to rely more heavily on political parties and opinion leaders to provide voting cues in presidential elections than they do today.

In recent years, the mass media's use of poll data has increased, facilitated by the institutionalization of in-house polling operations by television networks, newspapers, and news magazines. Between 1972 and 1980 the networks doubled the frequency with which they mentioned poll results on the evening news during presidential election years (Broh, 1983a, 1983b). This high concentration of polling information in the press continued through the 1984 and 1988 campaigns.

POLLS AS A CAMPAIGN COMMUNICATION FORM

Polling as a management tool in political campaigns and as a reporting tool in journalism have converged to create a major category and source of news (Weaver and McCombs, 1980). As Cantril states:

Public opinion research has had a significant impact on journalism. A kind of "news" is created through polls that would not otherwise exist. This "news" usually has political implications that in turn influence developments later reported. Even the political reporter's work has been affected by the degree to which polls and poll findings penetrate the specific situations that are being covered—and the way they are covered. Further, news organizations now conducting polls of their own are often called upon to defend themselves against the contention that they have a vested interest in reporting their own taking of the public pulse. (Cantril, 1980: 6)

As Cantril points out, the basic identifying trait of polls as a communication message form is that they represent news manufactured by journalists themselves through the production of statistical data that can be reported as fact. News stories that contain polls gain a heightened aura of authenticity by assigning a numerical figure to a political trend. In conducting the current research, we discovered that audience members clearly distinguish news stories that incorporate polling information from other types of campaign messages. Thus, the separate treatment of polls in this analysis is warranted.

Polling has had a dramatic impact on the nature of campaign coverage. Journalists take opinion polls into account when formulating their strategies for campaign coverage. Poll results help to determine how candidates will be covered, how much time will be spent on them, and what aspects of the election will receive attention. In essence, polls play a major role in setting the media's campaign agenda (Ratzan, 1989).

Polls also contribute to the horserace aspect of campaign news, in that they concentrate on the competition between the candidates rather than issues or candidate qualifications for office. News stories of this type are mostly concerned with the size of a candidate's lead, the momentum of the campaign, and the relative popularity of the contestants (Atkin and Gaudino, 1984). In addition, poll results have become a staple of news commentators, who employ them in their analyses.

The increasing proliferation of polls as a campaign news message form has raised concern on several fronts. From a news perspective, there is a fear that the press is compromising objectivity by disseminating the results of presidential preference polls. By their very nature, polls are impossible to report in an absolutely neutral fashion (Roper, 1980). This situation raises the question of whether the press is actually taking sides and determining the fate of one candidate over another. To this end, numerous studies have demonstrated that poll reporting repeatedly favors the front-runner by providing more coverage of that candidate and by labeling her or him a winner (Broh, 1983b; Gollin, 1987; Ratzan, 1989).

The criterion of "newsworthiness" influences the administration and reporting of polls as well. To meet the requirement that news must be current, polls are often conducted hurriedly, creating problems of sample representativeness along with other sloppy side effects (Ladd, 1980). While polls may succeed in being "timely," the type of news that polls represent is in fact time-bound, and misleadingly so. Polls provide a "stop-action" image of politics, a mere snapshot of public views at one particular moment in time (Broh, 1983b; Ratzan, 1989). Journalists, however, do not present polls to their audience with this caveat.

Rarely does a news report provide the contextual picture leading up to the time of the poll. Poll-based reporting has largely supplanted coverage relying on more conventional news-gathering techniques that can provide a richer picture of a campaign (Germond, 1980; Germond and Witcover, 1989). Polls are most often reported as isolated facts, instead of as data for comparison. The press give short shrift to exploring the reasons underlying the findings in the data (Broh, 1983). Poll data are instead related in a way that undermines the dynamics of a campaign. With the reporting of each poll, journalists treat that opinion as a static concept that will not change as the campaign progresses. They leave the impression that people have fully formulated views on the candidates and that they have made their final decisions (Roll and Cantril, 1980).

Voters are made to feel that preelection polls represent a *fait accompli*; this is truly misleading. These polls fail to take into account factors, such as election-day turnout, that can completely mitigate the predictions of any hypothetical contest waged before the balloting takes place. For the public, however, this appearance of finality can have major implications. It can reinforce consonant opinions, call into question dissonant decisions, and alienate those who have not yet made up their minds.

The quality of presidential preference polls released through the news is also at issue. As a whole, press polls are less accurate than private polls (Buchanan, 1986; Gollin, 1987), partly because they use different techniques. In particular, press polls rely heavily on telephone surveys that can be conducted quickly and efficiently. They are thus encumbered with the inherent problems of this technique, including nonrepresentative samples (Sudman, 1983). Although this situation is changing for the better, press polls, especially for newspapers, often are conducted by journalists themselves, many of whom have little formal training or experience in survey methodology (Demers, 1987). Finally, polls are frequently analyzed and reported without the benefit of statistical tests, such as measures of statistical significance and sampling error (Salwen, 1985a, 1985b). Besides tipping off the press to potential problems with a poll, this type of information, provided with an appropriate explanation, can help audience members to become more enlightened consumers of polls. (From a press perspective, however, this might not be the most desirable situation.)

Another major concern centers around the conflation of the news and business aspects of poll reporting. Mass media organizations have a vested interest in reporting news generated by their own polls: it supports their business investment—to the tune of about $20,000 for one decently conducted survey

(Germond and Witcover, 1989). While information from private and academic polls is often available to the press, the vast majority of polling information comes from in-house sources (Demers, 1987). In addition, television and print news sources frequently share the same poll in order to cut costs. All three major network news programs cosponsor polls with prominent news publications. According to some observers, news organizations' factoring of economic concerns into the polling/news reporting equation, coupled with the concentration of identical polling information across media sources, compromises reporters' ability to investigate and challenge potential sources of error in the polls themselves and leads to unsavory journalistic practices (Roll and Cantril, 1980).

The political implications of poll-based reporting are varied and serious. In primary elections especially, polls can single out candidates for success or failure. By identifying early leaders, by selectively including or excluding candidates from poll stories, and by artificially manipulating campaign momentum, the media can thin the field of potential presidential contestants. A candidate who shows poorly in the polls can lose out on funding opportunities from potential backers, as well as on volunteer assistance. Under any circumstances, polls create expectations about candidates. These expectations are then compared to actual campaign results. Election winners can be branded losers if they do not live up to the standards set by the press polls. As we have already mentioned, the front-runners determined by polls receive the greatest amount of election coverage, which almost always helps their cause.

We should not overlook the fact that candidate-sponsored and private polls do make their way into campaign reporting as well. Candidates can "leak" poll findings to the press and place a "spin" on the interpretations of the results. A front-runner, for example, might play down her or his lead in order to head off a sense of complacency among supporters that could result in low turnout. Conversely, a trailing candidate can play the expectations game and try to claim that he or she is doing better than anticipated, in spite of the polls. Once again, important ethical questions arise about the accuracy of the information provided by candidate polls.

THE EFFECTS OF POLLING IN ELECTIONS

A discussion of the influence of media-released polls might begin by asserting that voters readily welcome the encapsulated information that polls provide. Such voters are seeking a means of simplifying campaign complexities, especially in an era when nonmediated voting cues are becoming increasingly scarce. In light of the foregoing discussion, however, we can see that there is nothing simple about polls as campaign messages. With the abundance of often competing polling information available in the press, the situation has instead become complex. While researchers have worked hard to uncover the effects of polls on the media audience, study results remain inconclusive.

That polls can influence the presidential election process more today than in the past is supported empirically. As the number of polling stories in the news has increased, so has their prominence. A nationwide study of newspaper content during the 1980 presidential election revealed that about 15 percent of all news events covered were based on poll data (Stovall and Solomon, 1984). Polling stories are frequently the first or second stories in newscasts during elections (Broh, 1983a, 1983b). In newspapers, poll stories have begun to appear often on the front page— a practice that was not common until recently.

These factors, in turn, have led to a significant increase in public familiarity with polls. In 1944, 44 percent of a national sample had never heard or read about polls, while an additional 28 percent did not follow any of the results of polls. Overall, 72 percent of the sample had virtually no acquaintance with presidential election polls. In contrast, a parallel survey conducted during the 1976 presidential campaign revealed that only 16 percent of the population was not familiar with polls, while 84 percent had some degree of knowledge about them (Gollin, 1980). An update of this study that compared the 1944 data to a comparable sample in 1984 found that almost everyone surveyed had heard of polls and 25 percent followed them regularly (Kohut, 1986).

In general, people seem to be favorably disposed toward polls, and they are willing to trust their results. In a 1975 survey, 71 percent of a national sample expressed confidence in polls, as compared to 57 percent in 1944 (Gollin, 1980). More recently, the public and the press have given greater attention to the reliability and accuracy of poll results, as some pollsters have been well off the mark in predicting election outcomes. In 1984, some major polling organizations were as far as seven points away from Reagan's actual margin of victory. While there was no evidence that this caused a major crisis of confidence in the polls, some members of the mass public became skeptical (Roper, 1986). A study conducted in 1984 found that 68 percent of the mass public felt that polls are right most of the time when predicting elections and that 55 percent believed that polls are accurate on issues. In that same study, however, 21 percent of the sample stated that issue opinion polls are never right. Still, 76 percent asserted that polls are a good thing for the country (Kohut, 1986).

As with political advertising and nonpoll news stories, the credibility of polling information is linked to attitudes about the source and the mode of presentation. Poll information is considered most trustworthy when the source of the poll is reliable. To this end, the mass public often considers candidate polls to be less accurate than media-sponsored polls because campaign sources are not objective (Salwen, 1987).

Most of the speculation about the impact of polling in presidential elections focuses on whether polling can influence candidate preference and voter turnout. Some scholars contend that the continual release of poll results throughout the campaign creates a "bandwagon effect." When news reports early in a campaign reflect uncertainty, so does public sentiment. As poll results and media reports begin to show a solid trend, the public's opinion solidifies in the direction of that trend (Patterson, 1980). Polling reports, therefore, are believed to cause public opinion and to create momentum in favor of the leading candidate.

The bandwagon effect is attributed to the ease with which the press is able to transmit information about winning and losing, as well as to the reasonably accurate perception of the public concerning the impact of that information. A bandwagon is a situation in which large numbers of voters decide to back the candidate who is ahead. In order for a bandwagon effect to occur, voters must be relatively free of other influences and must be convinced that the leading candidate is almost certain to win (Patterson, 1980; Marsh, 1985). That Reagan appeared to be the clear front-runner throughout the campaign created the potential for a bandwagon effect to occur in 1984. A similar pattern can be traced for Bush as he steadily climbed in the polls to take a commanding lead in 1988.

The bandwagon effect is often less prominent during the election than during the primaries. People find it easier to believe that their side can win when they are not continually confronted with primary outcomes and delegate counts. Poll results combine with there other factors to have a drastic impact on public decision-making in primaries (Patterson, 1980).

That polls invariably create a bandwagon effect in any type of election has been challenged, since there is rarely a consistent and sharp change in public support during election campaigns (Gallup, 1948). Recent experience, however anecdotal, contests this point.

A counter-hypothesis to the bandwagon effect—the "reverse bandwagon" or "underdog effect"—has been hypothesized. The underdog effect is produced when poll results lead voters to support the trailing candidate. The backers of the underdog may consider their vote to be useless, while supporters of the winning candidate feel that their vote is unnecessary. Neither group votes, with the net effect of diminishing the winning candidate's electoral margin (Gollin, 1980; Marsh, 1985).

The bandwagon and underdog effects of polling are difficult to test empirically. Experimental evidence has shed the most light on the subject, although the findings are limited, conflicting, and fraught with conceptual and methodological problems (Marsh, 1985). Studies indicate that voters will try to keep the underdog alive in an election (Laponce, 1966; Fleitas, 1971). An experiment supports this finding, discovering a tendency among weakly decided and undecided subjects to react against the candidate favored in poll results in presidential elections (Ceci and Kain, 1982). Another experimental study, however, found that individuals will change their candidate preference in accord with poll results released throughout an election campaign if they are not subject to partisan or ideological voting cues (Owen, 1983).

Nonexperimental evidence is less enlightening and raises even more methodological issues than experimental studies. Polls have been found to have a cumulative influence on presidential preference throughout the campaign period, while the single best predictor of candidates' success is their standing in the first released polls (Beniger, 1976). It is difficult to trace the direction of public opinion poll influences using actual data. People's assessments of candidates based on opinion poll data have been found to be strongly linked to their candidate preference (Marshall, 1983). Yet studies do not shed much light on whether voters' initial opinions were based on polling information or on other sources.

The most substantial evidence about polling effects of this type focuses on the support of political elites, activists, workers, and investors. Studies have shown that when candidates are perceived to have significant support in the polls, their supply of campaign workers and flow of financial resources greatly increases. By contrast, a candidate viewed as losing ground faces a loss in campaign revenues and a defection of workers (Gollin, 1980). This does not occur because elites trust the results of polls, but because they perceive that polls influence the behavior of the mass electorate (Brudney, 1982). As Bogart (1972: 40) contends, "The most significant 'bandwagon effect' of polls is probably on party workers and contributors, rather than on voters flocking to back a sure winner."

A final area in which polls have the potential to influence electoral outcomes is election-night projections. Whether the press should be allowed to report exit polling information and to call elections prior to the close of balloting across the United States has become a heated issue. At its core is a weighing of the First Amendment freedom of the press against allegations that early calls interfere with the conduct of elections. On one side of the debate is the claim that the release of exit poll results that predict presidential race outcomes depresses turnout in states where voting is still in progress. The influence on the outcome of nonpresidential elections can be particularly substantial. Others claim, however, that the influence of early returns on turnout is minimal. Nonvoting has been linked more directly to other problems, such as registration requirements. Thus, violating the press' First Amendment guarantee is clearly unwarranted (Abrams, 1985; Swift, 1985; Milavsky, 1985; Roper, 1985).

There is much controversy over the research on early calls as well. Findings are contradictory and highly speculative (Sudman, 1986). Some scholars have produced evidence that early projections depress turnout in elections because people perceive that their votes will not make a difference (Wolfinger and Linquitti, 1981; Dubois, 1983; DelliCarpini, 1984; Jackson, 1983). These studies make a convincing case that early returns do influence some voters, especially on the West Coast, to abstain from voting. Other researchers contend that the voters have already come to a decision about whether or not to vote on the basis of prior information and are unaffected by early calls (Epstein and Strom, 1981). The early returns issue is particularly difficult to explore in elections in which one candidate registers a landslide victory. In such instances, no consistent effects have been discerned (Mendelson, 1966; Adams, 1985).

POLLS AS NEWS IN THE 1984 AND 1988 PRESIDENTIAL ELECTIONS

In keeping with established trends, polling stories in 1984 and 1988 were of several types. On television news, poll results were often reported in conjunction with the daily coverage of the candidates on the campaign trail. Frequently, vivid graphics accompanied the poll story and depicted trends in voters' candidate preference throughout the nation. At times, poll data were translated into electoral votes, which were then displayed on color-coded maps of the United States. This type of striking graphic accompaniment to poll stories heightened their impact.

Newspaper coverage incorporating poll results was more extensive and somewhat more varied than on television. In *The Washington Post*, for example, stories were generated either from the results of the polls of media organizations, including the *Post*'s own, or from those of the candidates. Headlines frequently stressed the fact that one candidate was either gaining or losing in strength (Taylor and Coleman, 1984; Broder and Sussman, 1984). In addition to stating the results, poll stories tracked the candidates' progress throughout the campaign, compared the results of different pollsters, and reported predictions for specialized groups of voters, such as the residents of particular states and the members of various demographic groups.

As in the past, polling information became even more important to the reporting of the campaign around the time of key events. Poll stories were particularly prominent at the time of the debates. Polls were taken after each debate to determine who had won the debate and how this may have influenced voter preference. The candidates responded to these projections by plotting their strategies for the remainder of the campaign. Poll reporting also became more intensive during the final two weeks of the election period.

Poll stories in 1984 proliferated in the news media, but with slightly fewer stories on network news than in 1980. The frequency of newspaper poll reports remained as high as in prior years, however. Polls were often either the lead or the second story in the newscast. Significantly more poll stories were reported during the weekend broadcasts than during weeknight news, apparently because poll stories are thought to fit in better with the "softer" weekend news formats (Keenan, 1986).

Polls generally demonstrated that Ronald Reagan held the lead throughout the campaign, but pollsters disagreed greatly about the exact margin of his lead. Poll stories became more prominent and prevalent after Mondale made a strong showing in the first debate. This marked the only time during the election campaign that polls seemed to move in his direction, only to swing back shortly thereafter (Dickenson and Broder, 1984).

Pollsters had a sense that the mood of the country was relatively bouyant in 1984. They therefore formulated questions about people's trust in government and their self-satisfaction to guage whether people were voting in favor of Reagan or against Mondale. Polls seemed to demonstrate that the vote in this election was more a positive one for Reagan than a negative one against Mondale (Wattenberg and Ladd, 1985).

Estimates of the number of national polls conducted and released through the mass media during the 1988 general election campaign range from 124 (Germond and Witcover, 1989) to 144 (Ratzan, 1989). More than in any previous election, journalists turned to the pollsters for news. The stories that the polls provided were often devoid of both issue and image information about the candidates—further removing the ability of polls to help the public make informed choices.

In the early days of the campaign, during the convention period, Dukakis was running ahead of Bush in the polls. Dukakis experienced a surge in popularity immediately after the Democratic National Convention that was sparked by his strong showing at that event. Between the two conventions, Dukakis did not campaign much. Instead he retreated to the governor's office. This coincided with the decision by the Bush campaign to emphasize Dukakis' "negatives" by playing up his softness on crime. After the Republican Convention, Dukakis' lead in the polls began to slide, as Bush's negative campaign pressed on and gained force. Once Dukakis lost his lead in the polls, his downward slide continued almost unabated. Although we lack empirical evidence, speculation that a bandwagon effect was at work is not unfounded.

One incident in the 1988 election was a landmark in election coverage and conjured up a vast array of ethical questions about poll reporting. On the night before the second presidential debate, Peter Jennings of ABC news spent approximately thirteen minutes summarizing where the candidates stood in the election campaign to that point. Calling it the "most comprehensive poll of the entire campaign," Jennings proceeded to present presidential preference data on all fifty states, complete with eye-catching visuals. With perhaps the most damaging (for Dukakis) presentation of the entire campaign, a colorful map illustrated Jenning's declaration that Bush had a "lock on the electoral college." Jennings stated that the poll found Bush to be an "overwhelming favorite" for the White House. In reality, the poll was riddled with methodological problems and was proved to be inaccurate in several major respects (see Germond and Witcover, 1989: 417–419; Ratzan, 1989). ABC's polling partner, *The Washington Post*, handled the material with greater caution, pointing out more specifics about the sampling procedures and the timing of what were in actuality numerous polls. The conclusion presented by both television and newspaper coverage was that Dukakis did not have a chance of winning. The graphic presentation, especially coupled with the timing of the poll (just three weeks before the election), made it appear that the election was over.

POLLING EFFECTS IN THE 1984 AND 1988 PRESIDENTIAL ELECTIONS

Given this background of the role of polls in elections and of the specific, pervasive part they played in the 1984 and especially the 1988 general elections, we sought to investigate the audience's relationship to presidential preference polls. We examined respondents' levels of exposure and attention to poll results in our election surveys. We also investigated individuals' faith in the accuracy of polls. Finally, we attempted to assess whether knowing where candidates stood in election polls influenced voters' presidential choice or willingness to turn out to vote.

Awareness of candidate preference polls was high for our respondents in both election years. This is not surprising since the surveys were fielded late in the election cycle. Approximately 95 percent of the respondents in all of the counties under study has been exposed to poll results over the course of the campaign. The vast majority of them had obtained their polling information from more than one source. Most frequently, respondents in all counties acquired their poll data from television, followed closely by newspapers. Far fewer people were exposed to polling information through magazines, while a small number obtained the results of polls from radio and other sources.

In spite of this wide-ranging exposure to polling information, few respondents reported having paid a great deal of attention to polls during the campaign. In 1984, there were some differences between Fairfax and Dane Counties in the proportion of respondents who paid very little or no attention to polls. Approximately half of those interviewed in Dane County reported paying little attention to poll results released either on television or in newspapers. Less than 30 percent in Fairfax County indicated that they had very low levels of attention while about 60 percent said that they paid some attention. For both samples, only 14 percent stated that they were very attentive to poll results.

The findings for the 1988 presidential contest are very similar, including the evidence of greater attentiveness to poll results in Fairfax County when compared to the other samples. Approximately 12 percent in each county reported paying a great deal of attention to media-released poll results. In Carroll and Middlesex Counties, about 37 percent stated that they paid almost no attention to polls, while 50 percent were somewhat attentive. In Fairfax County, 25 percent fell into the low attention category, while 65 percent paid a moderate amount of attention.

Attention to poll results was related to party identification across samples in both campaign years. Republicans paid a lot of attention to poll results, while Democrats were less inclined to do so. Compared to partisans, Independents were least likely to pay attention to poll results. Given these findings, we might speculate that Republican respondents were using polls to reinforce and solidify their vote choice, while Democrats were avoiding polls because they contained dissonant information.

The findings for candidate preference do not strongly support such a hypothesis, however. In 1984, Mondale supporters resembled Reagan voters in that they paid only moderate attention to polls. In fact, in Dane County, a greater proportion of Reagan supporters, than Mondale backers paid very little or no attention to poll results, even though their candidate was well ahead. The results appear in Figure 4.1.

The findings for the relationship between candidate preference and attention to poll results are similar in 1988, with a few exceptions. In Middlesex and Fairfax Counties, Bush and Dukakis supporters were equally unlikely to pay

Figure 4.1
Attention to Polls and Candidate Preference—1984 Election

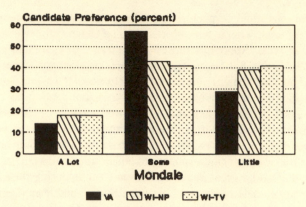

Mondale

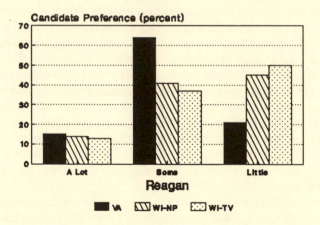

Reagan

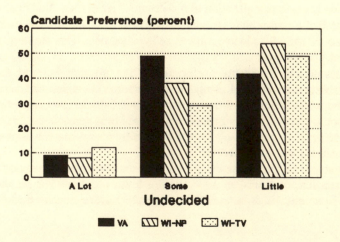

Undecided

much attention to polls, but the data for Carroll County provide evidence of some level of selective attention. There, 34 percent of Bush voters reported paying a lot of attention to poll results, compared to only 11 percent of Dukakis supporters. In addition, 16 percent of Bush followers paid very little or no attention to polls, while almost 30 percent of Dukakis supporters were non-attentive. This greater propensity of Dukakis supporters to pay very little attention to poll results was also found, to a far lesser extent, in Middlesex County. See Figure 4.2 for results.

To explore further the relationship between candidate preference and attention to polls, we computed correlations (Pearson's r) between candidate feeling thermometers and measures of attention to media-released poll results. The findings corroborate the analysis for candidate preference. In 1984, only one statistically significant relationship emerged, for Reagan in Fairfax County, and the coefficient (.13) was small. Similarly, two small but significant relationships emerged in 1988, for feelings toward Bush in Carroll County (.13) and feelings about Dukakis ($-.11$) in Middlesex County. This is hardly overwhelming evidence of a connection between vote choice and attention to polls, at least during the latter stages of an election campaign.

Interestingly, undecided voters paid the least attention to poll results of any respondents during both elections. The findings are strong and consistent across all five counties. These data indicate that the speculation that poll results manipulate the undecideds in presidential campaigns may be inaccurate.

The discrepancy in the findings for party identification and candidate preference warrants explanation. A selective attention hypothesis would lead us to theorize that since the Republican candidates were substantially ahead in the polls by late election, Republican partisans would be more likely to follow the polls. Similarly, supporters of the leading presidential contender would be more attentive to polls than backers of the trailing candidate. While findings for party identification are consistent, the analysis of candidate preference does not support a selective attentiveness explanation. In most instances, supporters of the leading presidential aspirant were no more likely to pay attention to polls than those of the trailing candidate.

A speculative alternative explanation derives from the historical grounding of the use of polls by the two major political parties. The Republican Party employed professional polls long before the Democrats, as the Republicans' grassroots organization was less pervasive. The Republican Party thus has a long-established tradition of using polls, which has been passed on to its partisans and which is less well-developed in their Democratic counterparts. An orientation toward polls may grow out of a traditional partisan familiarity rather than deriving from candidate factors. That Independents are the least attentive to polling fits in well with this explanation.

We next explored the relationships between attention to poll results, interest in the campaign, and time of voting decision. As we would expect those who were very interested in the campaign were also highly attentive to poll results.

Figure 4.2
Attention to Polls and Candidate Preference—1988 Election

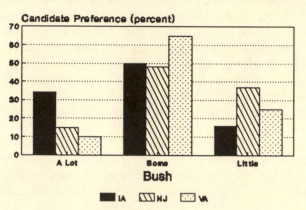

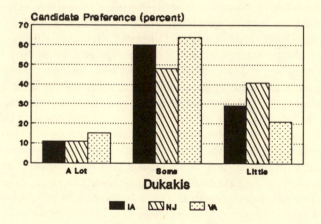

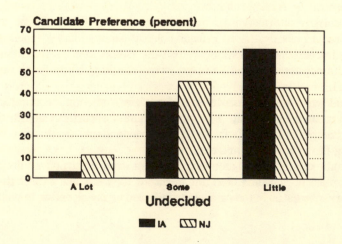

Table 4.1
Correlations (Pearson's *r*) between Attention to and Trust of Polls and
Campaign Interest, Time of Voting Decision

1984 Presidential Election

	Trust			Attention	
	VA	WI		VA	WI
Political Interest	.08	.05		.20*	.27*
Time of Decision	.02	.03		.13*	.00

VA   n=467
WI   n=697

1988 Presidential Election

	Trust			Attention		
	IA	NJ	VA	IA	NJ	VA
Political Interest	.09	.06	.23*	.16*	.20*	.23*
Time of Decision	-.09	.02	.00	-.17*	.02	-.16*

IA   n=232
NJ   n=214
VA   n=117

*   p<.05

The relationship was strong and significant for all five sets of respondents. There was some evidence that late campaign deciders were more attentive to polls than early deciders. This relationship was significant in 1984 in Fairfax County but completely absent in Dane County. During the 1988 campaign, late deciders in Carroll and Fairfax Counties took greater notice of polls than voters who had made their decisions earlier in the campaign. The results appear in Table 4.1.

Our next goal was to examine the respondents' trust in the accuracy of poll results reported through the mass media. A vast majority of people in all five samples believed that poll results were accurate some of the time. When we looked at those who did not take this middling position, the findings indicated that people had little faith in polls. In 1984, substantially more respondents believed that polls were often not accurate than trusted their results. The finding was particularly strong in Fairfax County, where nearly one-quarter of the respondents stated that they trusted poll results rarely or never. Comparable findings emerged in 1988 for all three counties. While approximately 3 percent in each county trusted poll results a great deal, 28 percent in Carroll County, 35 percent in Middlesex County, and 17 percent in Fairfax County had almost no faith at all in their accuracy.

Differences in perceptions of polling accuracy were related to candidate preference and particularly to party identification for our 1984 data. Republicans were more likely to say that they always trusted the results of polls than were Democrats or Independents. Independents, particularly in Fairfax County, were less likely to trust the accuracy of polls than were party identifiers.

Reagan supporters were more apt to believe strongly in the accuracy of poll results than were Mondale voters. A larger proportion of Mondale backers stated that they rarely or never trusted polls than either Reagan supporters or undecideds. See Figure 4.3. There was some additional evidence of the connection between candidate preference and trust in media-released polls. A significant, although not strong, positive Pearson's r correlation (.12) emerged between individuals' ranking of Reagan on a feeling thermometer and their trust in polls. A similar negative relationship ($-.12$) was computed for Mondale.

The findings for 1988 support the notion that voters are somewhat more likely to trust polls reported through the mass media if their candidate is leading, but the results are less noticeable than for 1984. Only a very weak trend in the data suggests that Republicans trusted polls more than did Democrats in each county; the overall lower level of trust for Independents was substantiated. Bush supporters in Carroll and Middlesex Counties were only slightly more likely to say that they trusted polls a great deal than were Dukakis supporters. More striking was the proportion of Dukakis voters in these counties who felt that polls were rarely or never accurate—28 percent in Carroll County and 40 percent in Middlesex County—as compared to Bush partisans—18 percent and 31 percent, respectively. The findings here are strongest in Middlesex County, while these relationships did not hold true for Fairfax County. One finding, however, was highly consistent in both campaign years. Generally speaking, undecided voters had the least amount of trust in polls when compared to those who stated a candidate preference. The results appear in Figure 4.4. Only in Middlesex County did significant correlations between candidate feeling thermometers and trust in poll results emerge. As in 1984, these were quite weak—.13 for Bush and $-.11$ for Dukakis—but in the expected direction.

From these data we might conclude, with some reservations based on the 1988 data, that voters who found that poll results reinforced their decisions were more likely to trust the polls' accuracy than voters who preferred candidates trailing in the polls. Survey respondents who discovered that the polls disagreed with their choice of candidate were not as interested in polls as those who could use them to justify their decision. The evidence presented demonstrates that selectivity bias exists for poll results, as polls are more relevant to supporters of the winning candidate.

Figure 4.3
Trust in Polls and Candidate Preference—1984 Election

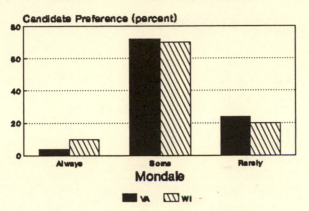

Candidate Preference (percent)

Mondale

■ VA ▨ WI

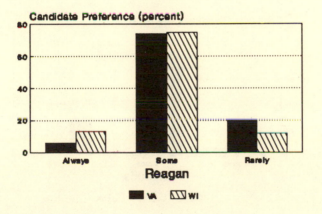

Candidate Preference (percent)

Reagan

■ VA ▨ WI

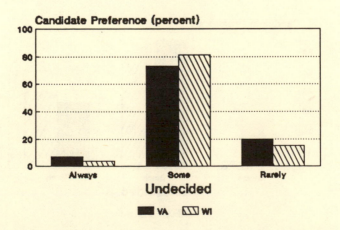

Candidate Preference (percent)

Undecided

■ VA ▨ WI

Figure 4.4
Trust in Polls and Candidate Preference—1988 Election

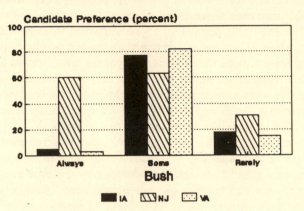

Candidate Preference (percent)

Bush

■ IA ⧄ NJ ⬚ VA

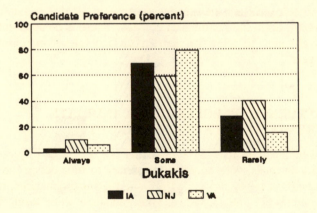

Candidate Preference (percent)

Dukakis

■ IA ⧄ NJ ⬚ VA

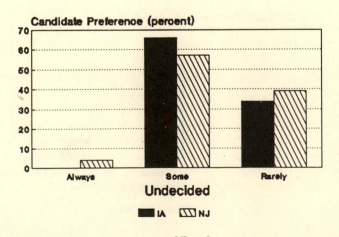

Candidate Preference (percent)

Undecided

■ IA ⧄ NJ

We looked at the issue of individuals' trust in poll results from one additional angle. In an effort to determine if individuals perceived that some sources are more reliable than others, we asked whether the source of polling information mattered. In 1984, 80 percent of those surveyed in Dane County replied negatively, while 20 percent stated that they trusted results released through a particular source more than others. Responses were spread almost evenly between television news, newspaper news, and news magazines. For almost all of these, the source corresponded to the individual's reliant medium. Almost identical responses were reported in 1988 for each county (equivalent information was not available for Dane County that year).

There is an additional, although modest, indication that media reliance is related to individuals' orientations toward election polls. In 1984, media reliance was significantly linked to attention to poll results reported in newspapers in Dane County, but the findings are not impressive. Those who considered newspapers their primary source of political information were likely to pay more attention to polls released through newspapers than were individuals who depended on television or other communications media. Similar findings exist for newspaper polls and newspaper reliance in all three counties in 1988, although once again the relationship is weak. There is no apparent connection between attention to television news polls and television reliance in either election year.

THE INFLUENCE OF POLLING ON CANDIDATE PREFERENCE AND ELECTION TURNOUT

We asked questions to ascertain whether poll results had any self-perceived effect on individuals' vote choice or tendency to turn out in the election. In the 1984 Fairfax County survey and all of the 1988 questionnaires, the questions were hypothetical. They asked: If your candidate were losing in the polls, would you turn out to vote in the election? If your candidate were losing in the polls by a substantial margin, would you most likely vote for him/her or switch to a different candidate? Thus, we asked the individual if she or he personally would be inclined to change candidate preference or abstain from voting if her or his candidate of choice were losing in the election on the basis of poll results.

In retrospect, this was not the best way to ask these questions for two reasons. First, the questions are highly susceptible to response bias. Individuals would be likely to say that they were unaffected by polls to avoid being perceived as easily manipulated by the mass media. These behaviors have to do with matters of civic duty; therefore, people might be hesitant to admit that they are swayed by pollsters. The informed citizen in a democracy is expected to base his or her vote on more substantial information about candidates and issues rather than on the results cf public opinion polls. In addition, the ques-

Table 4.2
Voting Intention and Poll Results—1984 Presidential Election, Wisconsin Sample

"If the poll showed that Walter Mondale or Ronald Reagan was gaining more support, would that make it more likely or less likely that you might vote for him? Or wouldn't it make any difference"

	Mondale (percent)	Reagan (percent)
More Likely	8	2
Less Likely	4	9
No Change	88	89
Total	100	100

tions were phrased in a highly abstract and speculative manner. It might have been more valid to relate them directly to the elections at hand.

Despite these considerations, eight people in the Fairfax sample said that they had switched their candidate preference because of poll results in 1984. Sixteen respondents said that they would not turn out to vote if their candidate were substantially behind in the polls. In 1988, 99 percent of the respondents in all three surveys stated that they would not be swayed in their vote choice by poll results. Still, approximately 5 percent of the respondents in each sample admitted that they would not turn out in an election if their candidate were trailing by a substantial margin.

Because these surveys were conducted by mail, the respondents were to some degree self-selected. As noted earlier, the survey participants overall expressed a higher level of interest in the election than we expect is characteristic of the general public. The fact that anyone in this group answered these questions affirmatively, especially given the potential for response bias noted above, gives rise to speculation that the effects in the population at large might be far greater than they appear here.

In Dane County during the 1984 contest, more striking results were obtained with less conjectural questions. Individuals were asked whether they would be more likely to vote for Mondale or Reagan if the polls showed that one or the other candidate was gaining support. Approximately 12 percent stated that they would move in either direction. This finding held true for situations involving both candidates. See Table 4.2.

In Dane County, the questions were phrased differently to reflect people's perceptions about the influence of poll results on candidate preference and voter turnout. In response to the question; Do you think polls affect which candidates people vote for?, a total of 63 percent of the respondents stated the affirmative. The survey participants who answered yes to that question were queried further: Would the polls have the net effect of increasing the vote for the front-runner, for the underdog, or would there be no overall benefit to either candidate? A vast majority believed that polls helped the front-runner (65%), while only a few felt that the underdog benefited (14%). The remaining 21 percent felt that polls provided no net benefit to either candidate. Moreover, 77 percent of the respondents perceived that publication of the polls affected voter turnout. While more people believed that polls would have the overall effect of depressing turnout, a relatively large percentage of the respondents, 32 percent, asserted that they would cause more people to vote.

SUMMARY

Our survey data reveal some interesting insights, especially in light of the current debates over the propriety of polls in elections. The discovery of a high awareness of polls accompanied by reported low levels of attention deserves noting. This finding is corroborated by our analysis of individuals' trust in presidential preference polls. The exploration yields somewhat less enthusiastic results about people's trust in polling accuracy than is indicated by recent literature. Many of the respondents felt that polls were only somewhat accurate. Those expressing an extreme opinion were more likely to feel negatively about polls than positively. Attention to polls was linked to trust in them, as respondents who felt they trusted polls a great deal were most attentive, and vice versa.

Our finding that attention to polls is linked to party identification, not to candidate preference, works against a plausible explanation that people attend to polls in order to reinforce preexisting opinions. Polling attention may be linked to a familiarity with polls as a communication form; this is more apparent for Republicans than for Democrats. Trust in polls, unlike attention, was linked to candidate preference as well as to party identification, although the findings in this area were not overwhelming.

Media reliance was less important in predicting attention to polls than for either of the other message categories examined thus far. It was only mildly related to attention to newspaper polls. Television polls are so pervasive that reliance effects are mitigated.

In keeping with the results of prior investigations into polling effects, our findings provided mixed evidence for such commonly asserted hypotheses as bandwagon and underdog effects. It should be noted that this research does not constitute a direct test of either theory so the results should be interpreted with reservations.

The evidence that polls influence candidate preferences is the least convincing. Few individuals surveyed were willing to state that they would change

their own candidate preference, although a large number of respondents perceived that other members of the electorate might behave this way. The
consistent reports of low poll attentiveness and trust by Independents and
undecided voters raise further speculation about the influence of polls on vote
choice.

The findings for the influence of polls on turnout are more striking than
those for candidate preference. A consistent finding of approximately 5 percent
in each sample indicated that they would not turn out to vote in an election if
their candidate were trailing in the polls. While 5 percent may not appear to
be a large number on the surface, election outcomes have hinged on far smaller
percentages than this. In actuality, these figures may underestimate the situation, given the tendency for response bias in questions that involve civic
duty. These findings become more compelling when taken in conjunction with
empirical evidence based on systematic studies of real world conditions
(DelliCarpini, 1984).

The findings presented here are of a general nature, taking into account the
audience's overall orientations toward and impressions about polls. Future
research should explore more thoroughly such important relationships as that
between the credibility of specific polling sources and individuals' trust and
interpretation of media-released polling information. We must also keep in mind
that our information about polling was collected late in the campaign, when
perhaps the damage had already been done, in terms of polls influencing vote
choice. It would be enlightening, but extremely difficult, to undertake a longitudinal examination of the impact of polling to determine if and at what time
people were persuaded by presidential preference polls.

5

Televised Presidential Debates:
The Ultimate Pseudoevents

PRESIDENTIAL DEBATES

Televised debates between presidential and vice-presidential candidates have become an institutionalized component of the American electoral process. Until 1976, they were sporadic events. In 1960, the first major televised debate, between candidates Kennedy and Nixon, attracted great public attention. Because of political and legal factors, no subsequent debates occurred in 1964, 1968, or 1972 (Zapple, 1979). Since that time, however, debates have been held in every presidential election.

Presidential debates are a unique communication form because they physically bring the candidates together in the same forum under the same conditions. Thus, the potential for debates to have an impact on elections is strong. In an ideal debate situation, candidates can express their opinions on issues directly to voters without those opinions being filtered through either the eyes and ears of news personnel or the stylistic lenses of political ads. The audience can view the candidates one-on-one and contrast their viewpoints and personal styles.

The audience for debates is large and heterogeneous. It is also substantially an active audience, as viewers make a conscious decision to be exposed to debates. Various societal pressures convince voters that they should tune in to the debates and pay attention to them. Moreover, the aura surrounding presidential debates creates the sense that "history is in the making," and voters may desire to witness it. Therefore, candidates have the opportunity to reach a sizable and diverse cross-section of the American electorate all at once (Meadow, 1983).

On a symbolic level, debates lend legitimacy to the candidates and to the democratic political process. Debates promote the ideal of an open political system. Voters are given the chance to view competition between candidates directly through a nationally televised forum (Meadow, 1983).

Jamieson and Birdsell (1988) identify a variety of ways in which debates can benefit the presidential selection and governing processes. Debates can set themes for a candidate and a presidency. They can increase candidates' responsibility for their claims and positions. Debates can inhibit "credit claiming and blaming" because they force the candidates to confront each other face-to-face. They can highlight presidential leadership qualities and foreshadow the strengths and weaknesses of the candidate if she or he is elected to office. Yet in the United States, this ideal vision of the role of debates has devolved into a hybrid form that still draws large audiences but continually disappoints them.

DEBATES AS A CAMPAIGN COMMUNICATION FORM

The concept of political debate comes out of an oratorical tradition dating to the early days of this nation, when politicians aired their disagreements publicly in direct confrontation guided by rules of conduct. In election campaigns, the 1858 Lincoln–Douglas debates during a race in Illinois for the United States Senate mark the pinnacle of the debate tradition. These debates were characterized by two candidates facing each other and arguing in detail about specifically defined issues in front of live audiences. Debates of this caliber have rarely taken place either prior to or since 1858.

The mass media events that now represent American presidential debates are a far cry from the Lincoln–Douglas tradition. Auer has identified five basic elements of a true debate that have gained wide acceptance among scholars (Martel, 1983; Trent and Friedenberg, 1983; Jamieson and Birdsell, 1988). Auer asserts that, "A debate is (1) a confrontation, (2) in equal and adequate time, (3) of matched contestants, (4) on a stated proposition, (5) to gain an audience decision" (1962: 146). Jamieson and Birdsell add a sixth criterion that "debates are rule governed" (1988: 10).

On the basis of these criteria, our current presidential debates fail to make the grade. Arguably, the contestants are matched and the debates operate under clearly defined rules. Presidential debates, however, do not involve a direct confrontation of the candidates. Instead, they are mediated through journalists who serve as moderators and questioners and who buffer the candidates from each other. While candidates receive equal time to speak, the time allotment can hardly be considered adequate. Debaters speak for a total of approximately thirty minutes on a wide range of foreign and domestic policy issues, with responses about any one issue limited to between one and two-and-a-half minutes (Trent and Friedenberg, 1983). The stated debate topics are overly vague—domestic and foreign policy—and thus, do not permit detailed discussion of particular propositions. Instead, the format encourages questioners to squeeze as many disparate issues as possible into the debate; it also invites questions that relate more to the contesting of the election than to public policy. Finally, this failure to explore issues adequately does not help the audience to reach a decision about the candidates. While much is made of the public's selection of the debate "winner" in post-debate analysis, the evidence is unclear about whether people reach this decision based on the event itself. For these reasons, present-day debates have been characterized as "counterfeit" or "pseudo" debates (Auer, 1962; Bitzer and Reuter, 1980).

Jamieson and Birdsell see today's debates as an amalgamation of a variety of types of discourse, resulting in a form that is neither press conference nor debate. They state:

The common audience, the presence of opposing candidates, the time limits, the right to rebut, and the established rules are vestiges of traditional debate. From the press conferences come the multiple topics, the question-and-answer form, and the use of interrogating reporters. The production techniques and the abbreviated answers are residues of television's grammar, a grammar most evident in the "staged debates." The presence of a studio audience and repeated hints from the panelists suggesting that they see themselves as the deputies of the American people are residues of the telethon. (1988: 118)

Critics, including members of the mass public, find this debased format unsuitable for the conduct of meaningful exchanges between candidates. Comments in response to open-ended questions about presidential debates made by our mail survey respondents summarized these sentiments well. The most frequent lament among the survey participants was that these were "not real debates." They believed that having journalists ask what appeared to be predetermined questions downgraded the quality of the debates. The respondents blamed a format that forces brief responses for permitting candidates to skirt most issues without being held accountable by the journalists.

Issues surrounding the form and content of debates can be explored in relation to the two major sets of actors who play a major role in shaping the debates. Once again, these are the candidates and their campaign organizations on the one hand and the mass media on the other. Presidential debates, as part of both candidate and mass media strategies, do not begin and end with the events themselves. The debate ritual involves extensive pre-and post-event tactics and hype.

The decision to debate or not is still officially the prerogative of the candidates, but pressures on them to debate are powerful. For example, the political parties agreed in advance of the 1988 campaign that presidential debates would be held during the general election (Jamieson and Birdsell, 1988). A candidate, including an incumbent, will face severe political penalties for not debating, given today's political environment. The press portrays candidates who will not debate as evasive and unwilling to confront an opponent on the issues.

In spite of the reality that such debates are almost certain to take place during contemporary elections, candidates continue to engage in a strategic ritual surrounding their decision to participate and under what conditions. Timing the announcement of the decision to debate is an important tactical matter for campaign organizations.

Challengers usually call for debates first in an attempt to force the incumbent into the difficult position of replying. Challengers have the most to gain from debates. They are less well-known than incumbents. They have a greater need to put their positions across to the public. They can hold an incumbent to her or his record. In the recent past, it was possible for the presidential incumbent to pursue a "Rose Garden Strategy" to avoid appearing in public. This strategy has become less successful over time, especially since the Carter presidency. The "Rose Garden Strategy" is viewed less in terms of a president taking care of business at the White House and more as a tactic used by presidents whose political future is in trouble or who have something to hide. In the late 1960s and early 1970s, incumbents could employ such a strategy to avoid debating, but it would be difficult to do so in the current political age.

Once agreement to debate has been reached, the timing, location, topics, format, and participants, including the journalists who will serve as moderators and questioners, become important matters of campaign strategy (Martel, 1983). These pre-debate decisions also become elements of press coverage of the campaign. Candidates must therefore weigh the risks involved in even the minor details surrounding the debates. Tactical errors may cost the campaign momentum, not only during the debate itself, but perhaps more importantly, in the press coverage preceding and following it.

EFFECTS OF DEBATES

Exposure to presidential campaign debates has traditionally been quite high since the Kennedy–Nixon debate in 1960. Studies indicate that from 60 to 90 percent of the population tunes in to at least part of candidate debates during presidential elections, depending upon the particular sample under investigation. Over 35 million homes watched the most recent series of debates in 1988 (Payne, Golden, Marlier, and Ratzan, 1989). Exposure to reports or news analyses after debates is even more widespread (Deutschmann, 1977; Chaffee and Dennis, 1979; Sears and Chaffee, 1980; Robinson, 1980). This high level of debate exposure is fostered by the belief among the mass public that debates at the presidential level are important, even if they are not necessarily informative or influential (Lichtenstein, 1982). Although most members of the electorate appear to be exposed to the debates to some degree, those who are most interested in the election look forward to seeing debates more than do others.

Debates have potentially important cognitive, evaluative, and behavioral effects in an election. They can provide the electorate with information about issues; they can allow for an assessment of candidates' performance under pressure; and they can perhaps influence individuals' vote choice. Evidence concerning these matters is conflicting.

Some studies indicate that people learn something about candidates' positions on issues from debates (Miller and MacKuen, 1980; Chaffee and Dennis, 1979). Debates can also stimulate voters' recall of previously acquired knowledge. They can fulfill an issue agenda-setting function and increase candidate saliency for voters (Miller and MacKuen, 1979; Swanson and Swanson, 1978).

Contrary findings point to a paucity of issue learning from debates. Since debates usually occur late in the election campaign, the information they provide may be redundant in terms of previously disseminated campaign messages. This repetition of information diminishes the effects of debates on political learning (Sears and Chaffee, 1979; Graber and Kim, 1978; Graber, 1984).

There is greater consensus about voters' propensity to learn about candidates' personal qualities rather than issues from debates. Given the fragmented presentation of debate issue topics, viewers are likely to make their assessments based on image-oriented characteristics, such as trust, competence, and personability. Viewers are more likely to see a distinction between candidates premised on their personal attributes rather than on their issue positions (Bowes and Strentz, 1978; Graber and Kim, 1978; Graber, 1984).

There is evidence that debates increase the knowledge gap between informed and uninformed voters rather than help to level it. Those who already know a great deal about the candidates and the campaign tend to learn more from debates, while those who are less aware at the outset gain little. Learning from a debate presupposes a high prior level of political sophistication in order to process the often confusing messages that are disseminated (Bishop, Oldendick, and Tuchfarber, 1978).

There is limited evidence that debates help some people to make up their minds in an election. Those voters who have difficulty in choosing a candidate or who are undecided at the time of the debates are more likely than others to use the debates for campaign decision-making (Davis, 1980). There is also empirical support for the contention that those with lower political interest and knowledge are more likely to be swayed by debates than are the highly sophisticated. Those who come to the debates uninformed are generally less secure about their political decisions. They can be influenced by a candidate's debate performance, but it is more likely that they will be susceptible to the opinions expressed in post-debate analyses (Bishop, Oldendick, and Tuchfarber, 1978; Newton, Masters, McHugo, and Sullivan, 1987; Rouner and Perloff, 1988).

People who are already decided in the campaign use debates for other purposes. They can reinforce their decisions or gather additional information for participation in discussions. One effect of presidential candidate debates is to bond party identification, candidate images, and issue positions to vote choice (Dennis, Chaffee, and Choe, 1980).

The media's preoccupation with determining a debate winner has made this concept important to voters as well. Once again, empirical evidence on this issue is conflicting. This is not surprising since there are no clear criteria for defining "winner" and "loser" in presidential debates (Vancil and Pendell, 1984).

Pre-debate vote choice has been a consistently strong predictor of which candidate a viewer will rate as the winner (Lang and Lang, 1978b; Rosenberg and Elliot, 1987; Davis, 1982; Sigelman and Sigelman, 1984; Rouner and Perloff, 1988). Partisan cues have proved less consistent. While some studies find strong support for a link between partisan predispositions and individuals' perceptions of the debate victor (Wall, Golden, and James, 1988; Payne, Golden, Marlier, and Ratzan,1989), this factor is refuted in other studies (Rouner and Perloff, 1988; Sigelman and Sigelman, 1984). Research focusing on the importance of ideology and gender also yields inconsistent conclusions.

Finally, studies indicate that debate effects tend to be volatile and to have a short life span. Viewers change their opinions about candidates based on debate performance in the period immediately following the debate (Lang and Lang, 1978b), yet these effects generally dissipate after four or five days (Miller and MacKuen, 1979).

DEBATES IN THE 1984 AND 1988 ELECTIONS

A series of three ninety-minute debates were held during both the 1984 and 1988 presidential contests. As has been the case in past presidential debates, all but one of these events were coordinated, at least in part, by the League of Women Voters. The format of the debates consisted of a moderator and a panel of journalists asking questions of the candidates. In what became an issue in itself, the League in 1984 submitted the names of prospective questioners to the candidates' campaign organizations in advance of the debates. Over one-hundred potential panelists were rejected by either Mondale's or Reagan's campaign committees (*Washington Post*, 8 October 1984). When asked their impressions about the debates, a number of respondents to the Fairfax County survey expressed their dissatisfaction with this procedure. They felt that it made the debates appear to be "set up" or "fixed" by the candidates, instead of being a truly impartial test of their abilities. To avoid this kind of negative publicity in 1988, each candidate and the bipartisan Commission on Presidential Debates submitted ten names for consideration. This group of names was reduced to a pool of six from which the Commission selected the final three questioners and the moderator for each debate. There was direct input from the two campaign committees (Germond and Witcover, 1989).

1984 Debates

The first debate between candidates Mondale and Reagan was held in Louisville on 7 October. This was followed by vice-presidential debates between

George Bush and Geraldine Ferraro on 11 October in Philadelphia. The final debate between the presidential candidates took place in Kansas City on 28 October, only nine days before the election.

First Presidential Debate—1984

The first round of debates focused on domestic policy issues. Questions pertained to the federal budget deficit, the economy, abortion, and the relationship between government and religion. In the debate, the candidates presented clearly divergent views on the issues. Much of the time, Mondale had the opportunity to lay out his plans, such as those for budget deficit reduction. Reagan, by contrast, was frequently placed in the position of defending his past policies, including cutting Social Security benefits. The content of the debates was, in fact, highly issue-oriented (Hoffman and Coleman, 1984).

In spite of this concentration on issues, the candidates were greatly concerned about the style with which they handled themselves during the debates. As it turned out, the strategies for handling the questions and the candidates' performances during the debates became a primary focus of media commentary and voter evaluation. The tactic pursued by Mondale and his strategists, particularly Pat Cadell, was to catch Reagan off guard. Mondale was prompted to use physical movements to emphasize his points—to step away from the podium and to lean toward Reagan. These motions were designed to produce an impression of strength. In addition, Mondale's advisors predicted that Reagan would be looking for an opponent who was highly charged and ready for a fight. They suggested that Mondale be friendly and humorous when addressing Reagan, and this surprised the President. Finally, they felt that Mondale could carefully create an issue of the President's age and call into question his ability to lead the country for another four years (Germond and Witcover, 1985).

All of these tactics were employed successfully by Mondale during the first debate. In sharp contrast to his advertising strategy, Mondale showed deference and respect for his opponent. He made a clear distinction between Reagan as a person and the policies of his administration. At one point, Mondale stated, "I like President Reagan" and credited him with raising the morale of the country. This strategy permitted him to focus on the issues and placed Reagan on the defensive. In addition, the age issue was brought into the campaign, prompted by Reagan's failure to respond coherently at several points during the debate (Kastor, 1984).

It appeared as though Reagan's pre-debate briefings had not prepared him adequately for what he was to encounter. First, Reagan was provided with a great deal of statistical information that he was supposed to present throughout the course of the debate. He practiced debating in several tough sessions against Office of Management and Budget Director David Stockman. Campaign aides perceived that Reagan had been the loser. In addition, Reagan had been told to expect a Mondale who would be on the attack. He was directed to steer clear of criticizing Mondale's policies so that his opponent would be perceived as being negative. Finally, Reagan was told to avoid being specific or clear when presenting his views on the issues in order to deflect attacks (Cannon, 1984a).

These tactics did not permit Reagan to utilize his skills fully in front of the television camera. He became confused when presenting statistics, and he disappointed supporters who expected clear, straightforward statements of his policy initiatives. The length of the debate, which was actually one-hundred minutes, seemed to be an adverse factor for Reagan. When his answers became somewhat confused toward the end of the debate, the media and public perceived him as getting tired. These perceptions further served to bring the age issue to the forefront in the coverage that followed.

As has been the case with past presidential debates, the media sought to determine the winner on the basis of public opinion. No network would declare a winner immediately following the performance; they waited until polls could be administered. By the morning following the debate, Mondale had been declared the winner by almost all accounts. Reagan's performance was perceived as worse after the release of these results (Alpern, 1984).

The first debate had changed the dynamics of the campaign, at least temporarily. Mondale's performance in the debate was seen as a sign of new momentum (Coleman and Atkinson, 1984). Reagan was perceived to be struggling to maintain his lead (Cannon, 1984b). A major effect of the debates appeared to be a shift in voter opinions about Mondale and Reagan. Mondale supporters became more satisfied with their candidate, while Reagan voters were troubled by his performance (Broder, 1984a; Schram, 1984). Evidence of selective perception of the debate winner was apparent. Mondale supporters felt overwhelmingly that their candidate had been the victor, while Reagan supporters had mixed reactions (Trebbe and Sutton, 1984). Follow-up polls indicated that Mondale had gained some support among the undecideds and potential switchers (Alpern, 1984). One result of these effects was to place even greater emphasis on the subsequent presidential debate and on the vice-presidential contest that took place next.

Vice-Presidential Debate—1984

The major focus of the vice-presidential debate became the relative merits of the contenders for the top office, rather than the views of Bush and Ferraro themselves. Reports indicated that Ferraro was briefed carefully to present statistical facts in a formalized manner. Bush was told to be himself and to respond to questions matter-of-factly (Morganthau, 1984; Germond and Witcover, 1985).

The vice-presidential debates seemed anticlimactic in media terms, for neither Bush nor Ferraro scored any important points or made any serious errors. Much of the debate focused on Reagan's economic and foreign policies. Bush staunchly defended his running-mate against the attacks of Ferraro. Both camps claimed to be satisfied, although not overwhelmed, with the performances of their candidates. Polls seemed to present mixed views of the winner, with some calling Bush the victor and others considering it a tie. Much of the post-debate media attention focused not on the substantive content of the debate, but on Bush's off-the-cuff comments, which included what many considered to be sexist remarks about his opponent. Once again, the focus turned to the final debate between Reagan and Mondale (Atkinson and Russahoff, 1984; Broder, 1984b).

Second Presidential Debate—1984

The topic of the final debate was foreign policy. Reagan and Mondale clashed over arms control and defense spending. Voters were again presented with candidates who had clearly articulated differences on the issues. Style also proved to be an important factor in the debate. Reagan reverted to the more comfortable posture that had characterized his public career. He was not bogged down with statistical information as he had been in the earlier debate. While making a number of factual errors, he presented his position forcefully and decisively. Mondale also performed well. However, news analyses took the position that Mondale had not overwhelmed Reagan, which would have been necessary to declare victory. While most polls called the debate a draw, commentators interpreted this as a victory for Reagan (Shapiro, 1984). Thus, the strategy of deflating performance expectations worked in Reagan's favor.

1988 Debates

The strategic negotiations over the 1988 presidential debates were full of conflict. The Bush Team, aware that their candidate was leading in the polls and that debating was not his strong suit, sought to minimize the importance of the debates. The Dukakis camp asked for three presidential debates and one vice-presidential debate. They called for direct exchanges between the candidates, no journalists asking questions, topics restricted to issues of foreign and domestic policy, and dates early in the campaign season. In the end, Bush's negotiating team won on all major points. Three debates similar in format to that used in 1984 were arranged. At the last minute, the Dukakis side succeeded in having the candidates stand, rather than sit, during the debate. Dukakis was permitted to stand on a small riser to compensate for the height differential with Bush.

The first presidential debate took place on 25 September in Winston-Salem, North Carolina, during the Olympic Games. The vice-presidential debate between Bentsen and Quayle was held on 5 October in Omaha, followed by the second presidential debate on 17 October in Los Angeles. The final two events were scheduled in the midst of baseball's championship series (Morrison, 1988; Germond and Witcover, 1989).

First Presidential Debate—1988

As had been characteristic of the entire campaign, Bush's organization was more prepared to meet the demands of the pre-debate media onslaught and preparation than was the Dukakis campaign. Bush staffers, as well as the candidate himself, were quick to employ the strategy of lowering media expectations by conceding Dukakis' superior debating ability based on his experience as a political talk-show host. They also sought to set the tone of the debate, appealing to the passion of the press for conflict by billing it the match of "The Ice Man Versus the Nice Man" (Goldman and Mathews, 1988). Bush's briefing books, pre-debate drills, and mock debates were handled with typical political aplomb down to the carefully scripted one-liners that were to be inserted where appropriate during the debate.

The strife-ridden Dukakis campaign continued its course of poor planning and organization. The campaign started planning for the debate too late. They had problems developing a usable briefing book and an unprepared Dukakis performed badly in mock debates. Thus, Dukakis entered the debate without preparation comparable to that of his opponent. The inability of the campaign to find a coherent theme once again plagued Dukakis, lessening his chances to strike a decisive blow even in a medium in which he had experience and command (Goldman and Mathews, 1988).

The topics covered in the first presidential debate ranged widely. They did not even conform to such broad-based constraints as a focus on domestic or foreign policy. The domestic policy issues addressed included drugs, deficit reduction, national health insurance, homelessness, the death penalty, and abortion. Foreign policy, defense, and the "arms for hostages deal" were also covered. Campaign-related topics, such as patriotism and the qualifications of the vice-presidential candidates, were also included in the debate. The vast array of unrelated topics brought the level of fragmentation in debates to a new high.

The performance of the candidates came close to pre-debate expectations. Dukakis demonstrated his superior debating skills by assuming a poised, aggressive position in the debate. He took the offensive most of the time. He was quicker and clearer in his responses and retorts than was Bush. His presentation came off as less practiced than his opponent's. Of course, this was really the case. Bush, on the other hand, stumbled through much of his performance, at times making statements that had little coherence. His scripted one-liners sounded rehearsed, especially when they were misstated. Still, Bush was able to score some points even through his bumbling. After a flustered Bush garbled a response to a question on defense and exclaimed, "It's Christmas!"—an out-of-place joke about his confusion earlier in the campaign about the date of Pearl Harbor Day—he stated, "Wouldn't it be nice to be the Ice Man so you never make a mistake" (Drew, 1989; Germond and Witcover, 1989; Goldman and Mathews, 1989). Here Bush tied his opponent's debate performance to the pre-event media hype planted by his campaign organization. This steely image of Dukakis undercut his performance in the debate.

By most accounts, Dukakis won the debate, but not overwhelmingly. Perhaps because of the closeness of the outcome, the media, with a few exceptions, were slower than usual to comment on "who won" immediately following the debate. Instead, the analyses turned to a procession of "spin doctors" from both sides, who, as expected, proclaimed victory for their candidate. The first polls gave the win to Dukakis. During the next week, as both candidates took to the campaign trail to capitalize on their fortunes and engage in damage control, news accounts told the public that the debate effects had been short-lived. While Dukakis might have won the debate, people still did not like him as a person, the polls reported.

Vice-Presidential Debate—1988

The vice-presidential debate was dreaded by the Republican campaign organizers. This was one debate where claims that the contestants were unmatched could be supported. Quayle had proved difficult to handle during the election campaign. He resented the continuing attacks on his intellect and ethics, and he had rebelled against the tight reins that his campaign had applied to his public appearances. The few times he was left to his own devices, his performances were fraught with embarrassing gaffes. In an effort to prevent such problems from arising during the debate, Quayle received intensive training from his campaign operatives. He underwent a series of pre-event preparatory sessions where he was scripted, given stage instructions, and bombarded with facts.

Democratic contender Bentsen also prepared long and hard for the debate. In the end however, he abandoned much of the prepackaged material in favor of "being himself." The Democratic campaign engaged in the strategy of lowering expectations about Bentsen's performance, fearing that Quayle's youth might upstage the older candidate.

As Drew states, "The two most surprising things about the Vice-Presidential debate were that Bentsen was as good as he was and that Quayle was as bad as he was" (1988: 298). The overprogramming of Quayle resulted in his being a wooden debate performer whose pre-rehearsed speech did not cover all the right questions. Bentsen's easy-going, mature, presidential manner served him well in the debate, especially when he moved in for the attack.

Several questions focused on the candidates' qualifications for the vice-presidency and what each man would do if he had to assume the presidency. Quayle had difficulty answering these questions, leaving himself open to the most memorable sound-bite of all the debates. To emphasize his experience, Quayle strayed from the advice of his handlers. He stated that he had as much experience in Congress as Jack Kennedy did when he ran for president. Bentsen, seizing the opening, replied, "Senator, I served with Jack Kennedy. Jack Kennedy was a friend of mine. Senator, you're no Jack Kennedy." Quayle made the situation worse by retorting, "That was really uncalled for, Senator," to which Bentsen responded, "You're the one making the comparison, Senator" (Goldman and Mathews, 1988: 383).

As in the 1984 vice-presidential debate, much of the time was spent by the candidates articulating and defending the policies of the presidential contenders. Bentsen briefly addressed the points of disagreement that he had with Dukakis. The debaters focused on discrediting their opponents, with Quayle invoking the "Liberal" label and Bentsen stressing that Quayle's right-wing politics had hurt America's underprivileged (Drew, 1988).

The outcome of the debate was clearly in favor of Bentsen. The Republican "spin doctors" could do little to help the situation. In fact, Republican James Baker called Bentsen, "My good friend and fellow Texan" and stated that both men had performed well. Polls demonstrated that Bentsen had been perceived as the decisive victor by the public. For several days following the debate, the Dukakis campaign gained momentum, while the Bush Team tried to minimize the damage. Presidential candidate Bush strove to distance himself from Quayle as much as possible. The debate sparked the Bush organization to strengthen its negative attacks. For the first time in the campaign, Dukakis decided to fight back aggressively.

Second Presidential Debate—1988

The second presidential debate, held in Los Angeles, met with controversy two days prior to the event. The League of Women Voters pulled its sponsorship, alleging "campaign manipulations." The Commission on Presidential Debates took full responsibility for the debate. This required finding a new location at the last minute, as the League denied the candidates the use of the hall.

Both candidates prepared differently for this debate than they had for the first. Until he was stricken with the flu just prior to the debate, Dukakis worked hard on pre-debate preparation. His advisors hoped that he could create a more relaxed, friendlier image. Bush also prepared well, but he refused to memorize as many facts and figures as he had for round one. He wanted to appear more spontaneous.

By most accounts, the first two questions of the debate set the tone for the entire night. Dukakis was asked a hypothetical question about what his position on capital punishment would be if his wife, Kitty, were raped and murdered. Seemingly without a hint of compassion or outrage, he replied that he would maintain his position against the death penalty. This worked against Dukakis. He had failed once again to demonstrate that he was a caring, likable person. Sensing that he had not fielded this question successfully, Dukakis remained off-course for the rest of the debate.

Bush was greeted with a hypothetical question about how he would feel if he were dead and the country were left in the hands of Dan Quayle. He responded that he would have confidence in Quayle, citing the vice-presidential contender's qualifications. Bush proceeded to handle competently the remaining questions about taxes, defense cuts, the deficit, Social Security, abortion, and judicial appointments.

Although the usual "spin doctors" were dispatched to paint a rosy picture of Dukakis' debate performance, the press consensus was that the "Ice Man" had lost the congeniality competition to a personable Bush. "Deprived of realistic road maps as how either candidate would behave in the White House, voters were almost forced to depend on factors of character and personality to predict presidential performance" (Shapiro, 1988: 19), especially when these factors are the ones that the press uses to anchor their reports. With three weeks left to campaign, Dukakis sought to counter his image problems by appearing as often as possible on television talk shows.

DEBATE EFFECTS IN THE 1984 AND 1988 ELECTIONS

Like many studies, the present analysis does not permit conclusive evidence of debate influence as a result of its cross-sectional design. Still, we were able to explore respondents' exposure and attention to debates, the level and breadth of exposure to post-debate analyses, and voter assessments of the candidates' debate performances. Respondents also gave their overall reactions to the debates through their answers to open-ended questions.

In keeping with prior experience, exposure to both the presidential and vice-presidential debates was widespread in both election years. Exposure was consistently highest for the first presidential debate. More people tuned in to the presidential debates than to the vice-presidential event. See Figure 5.1.

In terms of the number of debates to which an individual was exposed, very few people reported that they had seen none of the debates. In 1984, close to 60 percent of the respondents in each sample had viewed at least part of all three debates. With the exception of Fairfax County, whose 1988 figures resemble those of 1984, substantially fewer 1988 respondents were exposed to all three debates. Even more striking is the number of people in Carroll and Middlesex Counties who did not view on television or listen on radio to even a single debate; these groups represented 19 and 17 percent of the samples, respectively. The findings appear in Figure 5.2.

Exposure to debates was related to party identification and candidate preference. During both elections, Democrats tuned in to debates more often than did Republicans. In 1984, Mondale voters were far more likely than Reagan supporters to be exposed to all three debates. These findings suggest that Democrats and Mondale supporters were encouraged by the strong showing of their candidate in the first debate and that they were looking forward to his subsequent performance, perhaps as a means of justifying their voting decision.

While the finding is not as strong as for Mondale in 1984, Dukakis supporters were similarly more likely than Bush backers to be frequent debate watchers. In 1988, Democrats and Dukakis supporters were again given some reason to

Figure 5.1
Exposure to Presidential Debates

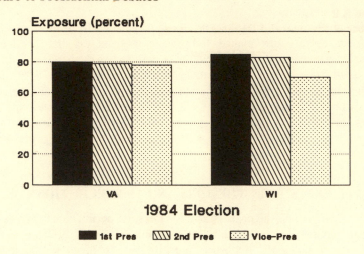

1984 Election

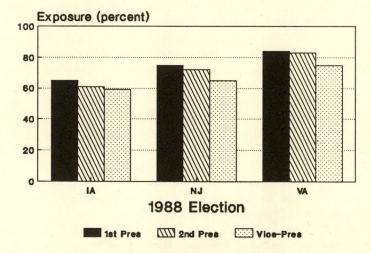

1988 Election

feel good about their candidate based on his performance in the first debate, prompting them to look forward to the second. They may also have anticipated a poor showing by Republican vice-presidential candidate Quayle against his Democratic counterpart, Bentsen. The findings for party identification appear in Figures 5.3 and 5.4; Figures 5.5 and 5.6 contain the results for candidate preference.

Independents watched fewer debates than did partisan supporters, and, with

Figure 5.2
Number of Presidential Debates Viewed

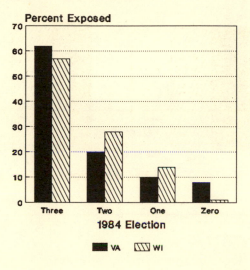

Percent Exposed

1984 Election

VA   WI

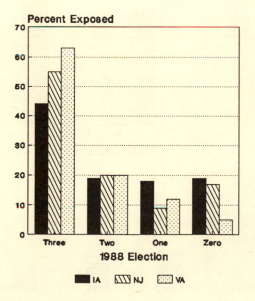

Percent Exposed

1988 Election

IA   NJ   VA

Figure 5.3
Exposure to Debates and Party Identification—1984 Election

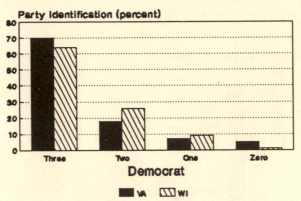

Party Identification (percent)

Democrat

VA WI

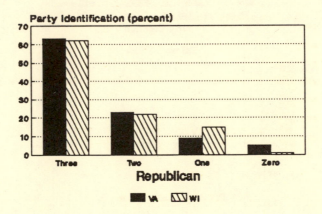

Party Identification (percent)

Republican

VA WI

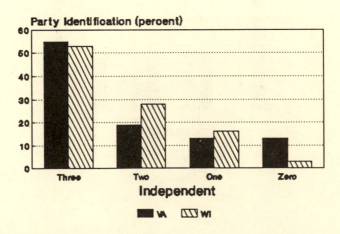

Party Identification (percent)

Independent

VA WI

Figure 5.4
Exposure to Debates and Party Identification—1988 Election

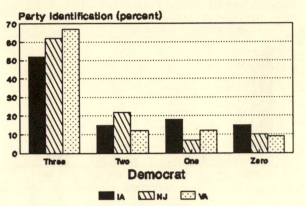

Democrat

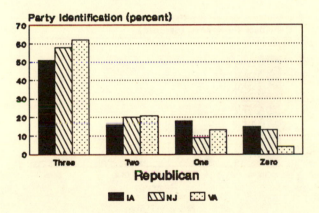

Republican

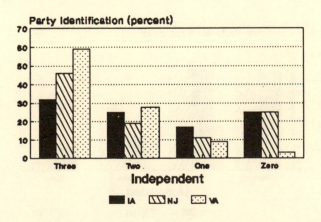

Independent

Figure 5.5
Exposure to Debates and Candidate Preference—1984 Election

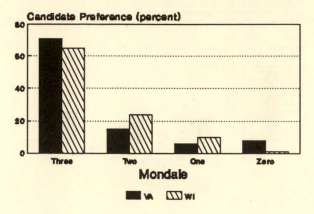

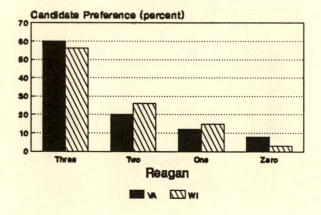

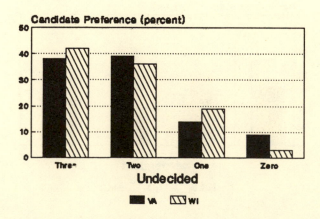

Figure 5.6
Exposure to Debates and Candidate Preference—1988 Election

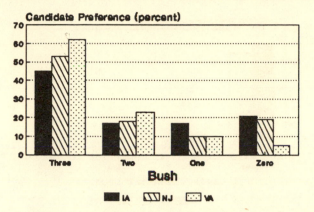

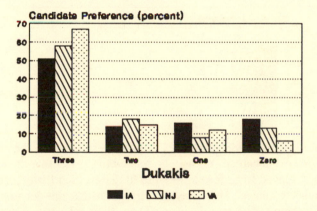

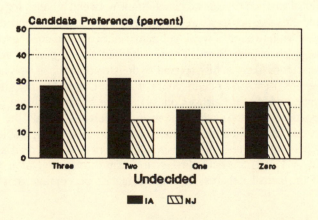

Table 5.1
Correlations (Pearson's *r*) between Debate Exposure and Campaign Interest

1984 Presidential Debates

	Exposure	
	VA	WI
Political Interest	.24*	.18*

VA   n=479
WI   n=707

1988 Presidential Debates

	Exposure		
	IA	NJ	VA
Political Interest	.48*	.43*	.23*

IA   n=234
NJ   n=215
VA   n=118

*p<.01

the exception of the 1988 Middlesex County respondents, the undecideds viewed the fewest debates. This may be related to the fact that the undecideds in our survey tended to be less interested in the election than those who had made a candidate choice. They may also have felt that the debates would do little to help them arrive at a decision. Thus, they did not feel compelled to tune in.

Correlational analysis reveals no connections between feelings for candidates Mondale and Reagan, as measured on thermometer scales, and debate exposure. There is, however, a weak yet significant correspondence for Dukakis in 1988 that is absent for Bush. Those who had strong positive feelings for Dukakis were more likely to be exposed to debates than those who held strong negative feelings (Pearson's *r* coefficients of .16 for Carroll County, .12 for Middlesex County, and .14 for Fairfax County). There was a significant correlation between political interest and exposure to debates in all the samples. The coefficients are substantially higher in 1988 than in 1984; Table 5.1.

Over 90 percent of the survey respondents had heard or read an analysis of the debates. This is a greater proportion than those who had actually seen any one of the actual debates. A slightly higher percentage in all surveys reported that they had received their debate analysis information from television than from newspapers. A majority in each sample stated that they had been exposed to multiple media sources for debate analyses, most often television and newspapers, followed by news magazines, and, least often, radio.

In general, survey respondents reported paying more attention to the debates in 1984 than in 1988. One exception was in Fairfax County, where the findings were similar across elections. In 1984, a greater proportion of individuals in Dane County reported paying a lot of attention to debates than was true in Fairfax County. The 1988 Iowa respondents were significantly less likely to pay attention to debates than were the New Jersey or Virginia survey participants. See Figure 5.7.

As was the case with exposure, Democrats and Republicans paid more attention to debates than did Independents, although it should be noted that Independents in the 1984 Dane County sample were far more attentive to debates than were their counterparts in Fairfax County. Once again, Mondale supporters showed that they were more debate-oriented than Reagan voters or than those who were undecided in the election. The undecideds, particularly in Fairfax, were not attentive to debates. The 1988 findings are consistent with the 1984 observations about undecided voters. Far fewer undecideds were attentive to debates than were those who had already made a candidate selection. Surprisingly, Dukakis supporters were not more attentive than Bush partisans. The findings appear in Figures 5.8 and 5.9.

As with all other campaign messages, attention to debates was strongly correlated with interest in the election for both campaign years. Feelings about Dukakis were positively and significantly related to attention in Fairfax County in 1988 (.16 correlation); this variable was not correlated for any other candidate or county in either election, however. Time of voting decision was also related to attention to debates, as those who decided late in the campaign tended to be somewhat more attentive than those who had decided earlier. This finding was particularly relevant in the 1988 campaign in Carroll and Middlesex Counties, where a substantial number of people in our survey were interested in the election, but did not make up their minds until relatively late in the campaign season. This group should be distinguished from those who were still undecided at the time the survey was fielded. The undecideds were less interested in the election and less likely to use debates to inform their decision-making. See Table 5.2.

Debates were the one message category that had no relevance to mass media reliance. Media reliance was not linked to debate exposure or attention in any of the samples. Since debates are available only on television or radio, exposure is conditioned not by media experience or habit, but rather by a deliberate decision to tune in.

Voter assessments about the winners of the debates corresponded to the calls disseminated by the mass media for the presidential events. Mondale was overwhelmingly declared the winner in the first debate by both the press and

Figure 5.7
Attention to Debates

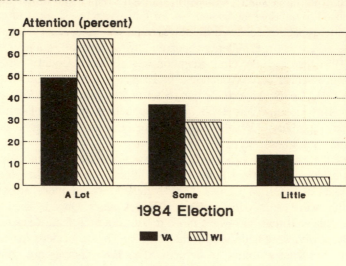

1984 Election

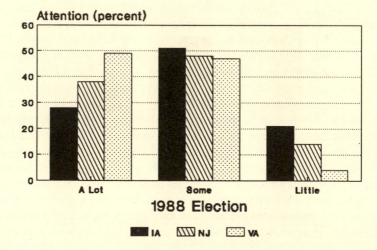

1988 Election

the respondents in Dane County. Only 10 percent of the respondents felt that Reagan had won, and these people were all Reagan supporters. The second presidential debate was called a draw by the greatest proportion of the Dane County sample. Fewer people believed that Mondale had won than felt that Reagan had been the victor. This finding coincides with the attitude that pervaded press accounts after the debate that Reagan had "won a draw." The findings for the 1984 vice-presidential debates were less consistent with mass

Figure 5.8
Attention to Debates and Candidate Preference—1984 Election

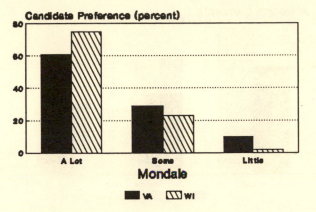

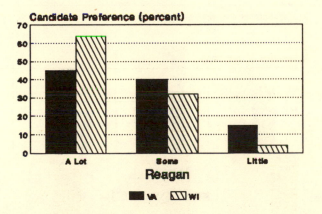

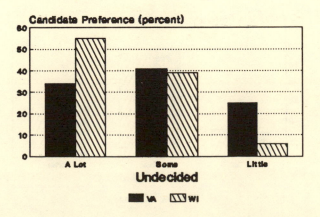

Figure 5.9
Attention to Debates and Candidate Preference—1988 Election

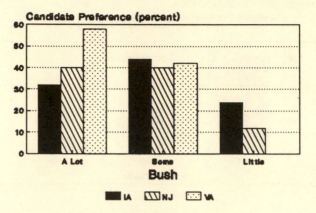

Bush

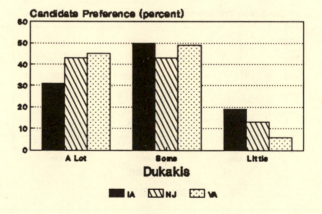

Dukakis

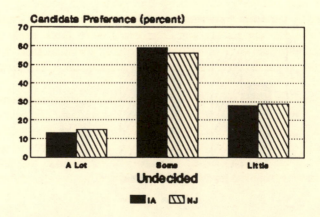

Undecided

Table 5.2
Correlations (Pearson's *r*) between Debate Attention and Campaign Interest, Time of Voting Decision

1984 Presidential Debates

	Attention	
	VA	WI
Political Interest	.39*	.30*
Time of Decision	-.08*	-.07*

VA   n=479
WI   n=707

1988 Presidential Debates

	Attention		
	IA	NJ	VA
Political Interest	.49*	.34*	.20*
Time of Decision	-.23*	-.18*	-.06

IA   n=234
NJ   n=215
VA   n=118

*p<.05

media reports, which seemed to call the debate a draw. In Dane County, almost half of the sample felt that Ferraro had won the debate, with the remainder split between calling Bush the winner and declaring it a toss-up. These results were highly colored by partisan identification and candidate preferences. Mondale supporters and Democrats were more likely to say that Ferraro had won than were other types of voters. This selectivity in perception of the winner in the debates was echoed in Fairfax County. The findings appear in Figure 5.10.

The findings in 1988 similarly reflect mass media interpretations about the candidates' debate performances. The first debate was declared a marginal victory for Dukakis, but it could be perceived as a draw. The vast majority of respondents could not identify a clear winner, although more people gave the victory to Dukakis than to Bush. The opposite occurred in the second presidential debate, in which a majority of the Fairfax County respondents declared

Figure 5.10
Winner of the 1984 Debates

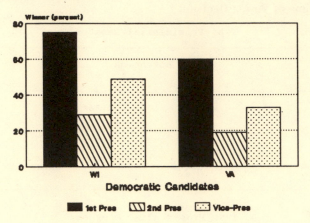

Democratic Candidates

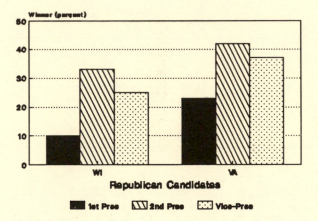

Republican Candidates

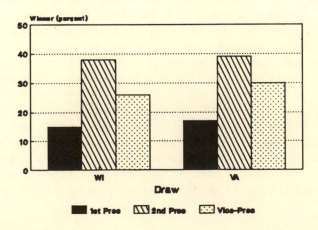

Draw

136

**Figure 5.11
Winner of the 1988 Debates**

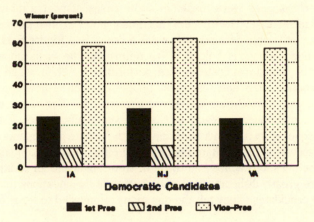

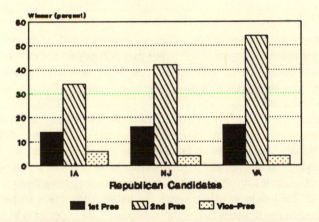

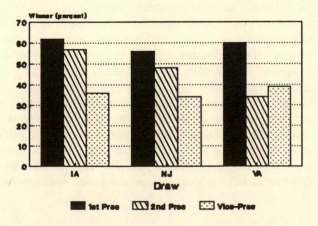

Bush the winner. Bentsen was a distinct favorite in the vice-presidential debate. We should keep in mind, however, that these assessments of the candidates' debate performances were made, in some cases, almost a month after the event had taken place. The effect of this time gap would most probably increase the number of people declaring an event a draw. See Figure 5.11.

Open-ended questions helped us to determine the basis upon which the respondents judged candidate debate performance. When asked to describe their reactions to the debates, most people mentioned how the candidates' performances reflected their images or personalities. Very few comments on the debates mentioned issues at all. Some respondents, in fact, felt that issues were not covered by the candidates and that the debate participants deliberately avoided discussing them. Statements to the effect that the candidates did not answer the questions addressed to them were abundant. In addition, respondents were greatly disheartened by the quality of the questions that journalists asked the candidates. They felt the questions often failed to focus on important issues.

SUMMARY

Recent presidential campaign debates have met with widespread criticism and calls for reform. In spite of the belief that debates do not effectively present the candidates' positions, millions of television sets are turned on for the spectacle. The high degree of exposure to campaign debates was reflected in our 1984 and 1988 data.

The debates in 1984 may have been the most interesting and dynamic aspect of an otherwise monotonous campaign. Mondale's surprising performance in the first debate, the results of opinion polls following it, and the media hype accompanying the subsequent debates may have sparked a renewed interest in the election, at least temporarily. Thus, voters may have been more debate-oriented in 1984 than in other years. Mondale supporters in particular may have looked to the debates to reinforce or justify their decision in the election.

Our findings indicate that interest in the 1988 presidential debates was not as strong as in 1984. The usual pre-debate media coverage was infused with the charges of "candidate manipulation" lodged by the League of Women Voters. These accusations may have reinforced the impression that "these are not real debates." The lackluster first debate, although declared a marginal victory for Dukakis, did not have the same effect of recharging the campaign that was experienced in 1984.

The content of presidential campaign debates much resembles that of campaign news. The information disseminated during debates shares many of the attributes that Bennett (1988) ascribes to television news. Questions and answers focus on the personal and the dramatic. When frightening societal problems are bared, they are quickly normalized. The fragmented nature of debates begins with a format lacking focus on specific topics and is worsened by the candidates' failure to address the questions asked of them. It is not surprising that presidential debates conform to these traits when the power to structure debate content rests with journalists. Candidates are conditioned to give answers that meet the requirements of the medium of television and that will provide good coverage in the post-event media barrage. Thus, presidential debates in the mass media age do not live up to their promise of an open exchange between candidates. They instead offer voters more of the same mass-mediated material packaged differently.

That the package itself makes a difference in voters' orientations toward debates is borne out in this study. In both years, the survey respondents reported a stronger orientation toward debates than toward any of the other message types discussed here. Voters come into contact with ads and news stories on a routine basis, but debates are special events. They offer the prospect of something new and exciting—history in the making. They rarely fulfill this expectation. The consistent finding of high levels of exposure to debates is not matched by correspondingly high levels of attention.

The evidence here supports the position that debates are most important to people who have already made up their minds in the election. Candidate preference and, to a lesser extent, party identification provide perceptual screens through which many people interpret the candidates' debate performances. At best, the debate format provides decided voters with the opportunity to root for their candidate under game-like conditions. Given these hollow rewards, it is unclear how much longer presidential debates, as currently constituted, can continue to entice people to watch.

6

The Uses and Gratifications of Presidential Campaign Messages

The preceding examination provides basic evidence that people distinguish among ads, news stories, poll results, and debates in their orientations toward the campaign media environment. On the whole, there were differences in the amount of exposure and attention that individuals reported across messages categories. Some consistent patterns of media use were observed for specific categories of voters.

General exposure to all four types of campaign messages was high during both presidential elections. Attention was greatest for debates, followed by newspaper and television news. Individuals reported that they paid the least amount of attention to candidate advertisements and poll results.

Some evidence of selective attention was apparent for all four message types. Respondents stated that they were more attentive to news stories and ads about the candidates that they favored. In addition, some limited evidence suggests that Reagan supporters and Republicans were more inclined to believe poll results to be accurate than were other members of the electorate. Finally, perceptions of the winner of campaign debates corresponded to the candidate preference of the respondent.

Interest in the election was consistently related to attention to media messages. This finding corresponds to the fact that undecided voters, and Independents to a somewhat lesser degree, displayed lower levels of exposure and attention to electoral communication. These people tended to be less involved and interested in the two presidential campaigns under study.

Media reliance was related to individuals' orientations toward campaign messages in some instances. Most obviously, television- and newspaper-reliant individuals were most attentive and exposed most often to news stories in their reliant medium. The same held true for reports of poll results. Television-reliant individuals were more likely to be highly exposed to candidate ads than those who depended on newspapers or other sources of information. There was no link between reliance and exposure or attention to presidential debates.

The four previous chapters established the communications context for the 1984 and 1988 presidential elections and examined people's responses to the four message categories. In this chapter, we investigate the processes underlying voter media use in the 1984 and 1988 presidential elections. The analysis constitutes a more direct examination of the communication system outlined in the model of audience media use and outcomes presented in chapter 1 than we have presented thus far. More precisely, this chapter will focus on gratification seeking and satisfaction received from mass media messages. We address two general questions: What types of motivations characterize voter use of the mass media during presidential campaigns? Are these motives satisfied differentially by specific message types? The degree to which ads, news stories, poll results, and debates satisfy voters' needs to acquire campaign information and to feel involved in the elections will be assessed. In addition, we will investigate more thoroughly the nature of audience motivations and use of campaign messages. Specifically, what accounts for differences in levels of media-related satisfaction reported by voters? Variations in these levels will be examined with regard to patterns of election media use and a variety of political factors.

We need to know the degree to which the media are meeting the informational needs of the electorate and providing voters with the sense that they are participating in the campaign in order to understand the democratic process. The present analysis will help us to assess whether or not the mass media are helping to foster an informed and participatory electorate. We will explore what individuals expect to gain from the mass media during elections, such as information about candidates and issues, and to what degree they feel that media messages meet these expectations.

THE MASS MEDIA'S RELATIONSHIP TO VOTERS' CAMPAIGN NEEDS

Every four years, presidential candidates spend vast sums of money producing and airing campaign commercials on television. The presidential election becomes the primary focus of news coverage for several months. News organizations devote ever-increasing amounts of time and effort to campaign reporting. Poll results have come to constitute a major category of campaign news. Televised debates between the candidates are highly publicized campaign events that are watched by a majority of voters. In spite of all of these different types of messages disseminated during campaigns, voters still may not feel that they are being served by mass communication. Voters may in fact tune out particular forms of mass-mediated communication during elections because their experience has been that these message forms do not fulfill their needs and expectations. In addition, people may become alienated from attending to media messages in general when they are confronted with so many of such meager quality in such concentrated doses as they have been during recent election campaigns. In practical terms, this research can help to identify which types of messages are most salient to voters and which might be most successful in contributing to the needs of an informed electorate.

As noted in chapter 1, past studies have produced evidence suggesting that individuals use the mass media to fulfill certain types of needs during election campaigns. The underlying premise of the present analysis is that the types of gratifications sought and received from different message categories can vary greatly. These distinctions cannot be captured in measures of gratification-seeking and reception from the mass media in general. Instead, these differences can be determined only by comparing the degree to which individuals use specific types of communication to satisfy particular needs. This analysis assesses through comparisons how well ads, news stories, poll results, and debates fulfill a general set of media-oriented needs in elections.

Most studies to date have concentrated on examining gratifications as exogenous variables in research that attempts to explain other effects, such as level of political knowledge or attention to specific events portrayed through the media (McLeod, Bybee, and Durall, 1979; McLeod, Glynn, and McDonald, 1983). In this sense, analysis has proceeded without a thorough understanding of the nature of campaign-related motivation measures, particularly of how they are related directly to other media and political variables. The present research addresses this question by treating the gratification measures as dependent variables.

METHOD AND MEASUREMENT

A series of questions designed to measure voters' motivations for using the mass media in elections has been developed by political communications researchers and employed in a number of studies. An early version of what is measured here was constructed by Blumler and McQuail (1969) for their study of television and British elections. Blumler and McQuail identified several types of gratifications sought from the media and placed them into three basic categories. The first consisted of "political decision motives" and included reinforcement of decision and vote-guidance. "Surveillance" was associated with such motives as judging candidates and keeping up with issues and political parties. "Excitement" referred to items relating to campaign involvement and predicting the winner. These measures were adapted to fit the American political context by McLeod and Becker (1981). They placed campaign uses and gratification measures into the categories of surveillance, vote guidance, anticipated communication (giving the individual something to discuss with others), excitement, and reinforcement. The questions used in this analysis are derived from those used by McLeod and Becker. Before proceeding with a discussion of the specific measures used in each of the surveys, it is necessary to examine some of the problems of measuring and conceptualizing uses and gratifications in relation to the analytical questions at hand.

Measurement Issues in Uses and Gratifications Research

Prior research demonstrates that individuals differentiate between media gratifications sought and received (Lometti, Reeves, and Bybee, 1977; Palmgreen, Wenner, and Rayburn, 1981). McLeod, Bybee, and Durall (1979) compared gratifications sought from media use in the 1976 presidential election to how well these gratification were satisfied by candidate debates. They discovered definite conceptual distinctions between the two motivational dimensions. Therefore, a clear distinction must be made as to whether the measure actually accounts for the gratifications sought versus those received by the audience.

There is a basic problem with conceptualizing and measuring gratifications sought and received. The possibility exists, particularly when individuals are reporting motives for using a particular medium or message, that they will combine the gratifications that they seek with those that they expect to receive based on their prior experience or knowledge of the channel or type of communication. Some evidence supports the contention that measures of gratifications sought may be confounded with the gratifications that individuals perceive they will obtain from particular programs (Palmgreen, Wenner, and Rayburn, 1981; Rayburn and Palmgreen, 1984).

A further difficulty in using these types of measures is the inability to arrive at consistent schemes for categorizing the variety of motivations. There appears to be a general lack of consensus in the political communication field about how to classify groups of motivations theoretically. In addition, statistical techniques have tended to identify different patterns of gratifications for different data sets (Becker, 1979; Weaver, 1980). One possible reason for this lack of conceptual clarity is that researchers tend to use extremely specific categories when examining audience gratifications. Scholars have suggested that more basic categories of audience orientations may be better able to predict and explain media effects than more complex ones (Blumler, 1979; Weaver, 1980). We employ this tactic in the analysis that follows.

Measurement of Uses and Gratifications in the Current Research

The difficulties associated with using two data sets collected by different researchers are especially apparent for this portion of the analysis for the 1984 election. Because the Dane County survey was conducted over the telephone and quite extensive, it was possible to gather data on both gratifications sought and received from the mass media in the 1984 presidential contest. This could not be done in the Fairfax County questionnaire because of its more limited

Figure 6.1
Scale Content and Question Wording for Gratifications Sought from the Mass Media—Dane County, WI, 1984 Election

<u>Surveillance</u>

Gratifications sought from the mass media in presidential campaigns:

--to see how the candidates stand on issues
--to judge the personal qualities of the candidates
--to help you make up your mind how to vote
--to remind you of your candidate's strong points
--to judge the candidate's weak points
--to see what the candidates would do if elected

<u>Campaign Involvement</u>

Gratifications sought from the mass media in presidential campaigns:

--to give you something to talk about with others
--to enjoy the excitement of the election race
--to judge which candidate is likely to win

scope, so the Fairfax County survey contains measures for gratifications received only. These factors limit our ability to make direct comparisons between the two samples. Still, it is possible to note consistent trends in the data, as long as they are interpreted with caution and an awareness of the differences between the two sets of measures. The 1988 data use questions identical to those in the 1984 Fairfax County questionnaire.

Nine separate measures of gratification-seeking were employed in the Dane County survey in 1984. These measures represented gratifications sought from the mass media in a general sense and were not asked for each individual message category. For each of these variables, respondents used a three-point scale to report the degree to which they sought that particular item from the mass media. From these measures, two distinct gratification dimensions were created. The first represents a surveillance dimension of gratification-seeking. This variable is an additive index of items concerned with the voter's acquisition and use of knowledge about the campaign, such as finding out where the candidates stand on issues and assessing their personal qualities. The second, labeled the campaign involvement dimension, consists of items related to an individual's orientation toward the campaign as an event. This measure consists of anticipated communication, vote-guidance, and excitement items. The question wordings for each dimension appear in Figure 6.1.

Measures of gratifications received from specific types of messages were also employed in the Dane County Survey. These questions asked how helpful ads, television news, newspaper news, and debates had been to the respondents during the campaign in judging where the candidates stood on issues and finding out about the personal qualities of the candidates; note that poll results were not included as a separate category in the Dane County survey. The respondents used a ten-point scale, ranging from not at all to extremely helpful to rank their feelings.

In an effort to create greater comparability in the scale variances and to facilitate the use of statistical techniques (such as regression), additive indices that reflect general modes of gratification-seeking were constructed. These indices represent the degree to which individuals seek to satisfy basic surveillance/information-seeking and campaign involvement needs through the mass media.

Problems arise in comparing gratifications sought with gratifications received using the Dane County data because the basic measures are not directly comparable. The survey contained measures of gratifications received for the surveillance dimension only. The specific measures of gratifications received from media messages were finding out particular information about issues and candidate qualities. These measures were not combined into an index in an effort to determine if there are any significant differences between gratifications received for issue compared to candidate quality information.

For the 1984 Fairfax County data and all of the 1988 data, the gratification measures represent to what extent a particular type of message fulfilled a certain need for an individual during the two presidential campaigns under study and to what degree the message was used for that purpose. Eleven separate measures of media gratifications for each kind of message—ads, news stories, poll results, and debates—were employed.

The same two dimensions that we specified for gratifications sought in the Dane County data set were used here as well. The first is the surveillance/information-seeking dimension and the second is the campaign involvement dimension. Additive indices were constructed to represent gratifications received from specific messages for surveillance and campaign involvement. Information about scale content appears in Figure 6.2.

Measures of Mass Media Factors

Three different types of media factors are examined in this analysis. They are exposure, attention, and mass media reliance. Evidence suggests that exposure and attention to the mass media are linked to a variety of effects, such as learning and image formation. The channel through which an individual receives mediated communication can be a salient factor in determining the ways in which voters process campaign messages. Media exposure, attention, and reliance can be related to audience gratifications as well.

The measures of exposure employed in the analysis represent how often an individual reported coming into contact with each type of campaign message. In the Dane County data set, exposure to ads, television news, and newspaper

Figure 6.2
Scale Content and Question Wording for Uses and Gratifications
Measures—Fairfax County, VA, 1984 Election; All Surveys, 1988
Election

Surveillance

Gratifications received from each of ads, news stories, poll
results, and debates in presidential campaigns:

--to help me make up my mind about how to vote in the election
--to assess the personal qualities of the candidates
--to reinforce my opinions about the candidates
--to gain information about the candidates' stands on issues
--to evaluate the candidates' qualifications for office
--to see what the candidates would do if elected
--to find out the candidates' strong and weak points
--to determine the differences between candidates

Campaign Involvement

Gratifications received from each of ads, news stories, poll
results, and debates in presidential campaigns:

--to give me something to talk about with others
--to keep me interested in the campaign
--to determine which candidate will win the election

news was based on respondents' rankings on a scale ranging from frequent exposure to none at all. Similar measures were used in the 1984 and 1988 mail surveys for news stories and poll results. Exposure to ads was a combined measure taking into account the frequency of viewing spots for both candidates running in an election. Debate exposure in all surveys was based on the total number of debates that a respondent had watched on television or heard on the radio; the measure ranged from zero to three, for people who had watched both presidential and the vice-presidential debates.

Attention to election communication was measured on scales ranging from a great deal to little or no attention. Separate measures were obtained for ads, television news, newspaper news, and debates in Dane County, and for ads, news stories, poll results, and debates in all other instances.

Media reliance was a measure of the degree to which an individual used a particular channel for information about the election. Separate scales were computed for television and newspaper reliance, based on the respondents' rank ordering of the sources that they used for campaign information. These measures were employed in the present analysis, as opposed to discrete categories based on the source used most often. The vast majority of respondents reported relying on either television or newspapers as their main source of information about politics. Individuals often use both to some degree, however. This type of measure of media reliance allows this fact to be taken into account.

Measures of Political Factors

Individuals' political orientations may influence the ways in which they view and make use of campaign communication. Basic measures of partisanship, candidate preference, and decidedness in the election were examined. In addition, partisan strength, interest in the election, feelings about the Democratic and Republican presidential candidates, and time of voting decision were considered.

Comparable measures of partisanship, candidate preference, partisan strength, and interest in the presidential election existed for all surveys. Feelings about the Democratic and Republican candidates were obtained through the use of feeling thermometers for the individual candidates in both the Fairfax County and the 1988 data sets. For Dane County, indices were constructed on the basis of responses to specific questions about the candidates' personal qualities. These measures ranged from extremely good to extremely bad feelings about the Democratic and Republican tickets.

Time of voting decision was originally measured differently in the two surveys. On the Dane County questionnaire, time of decision was broken down into seven discrete categories, ranging from haven't decided to decided before the primaries. This question was left open-ended on the mail questionnaires. For purposes of this analysis, the item was coded into categories equivalent to those in the Dane County data set.

Control Variables

Age and education are related to certain aspects of mass media use, such as television dependency and levels of political knowledge and value-holding (McLeod and McDonald, 1985). Therefore, we introduce these two variables as controls in our multivariate analyses.

ANALYSIS OF MASS MEDIA USES AND GRATIFICATIONS

Gratifications Sought and Received—Dane County, WI, 1984 Election

To reiterate, the basic questions addressed here are: What do individuals desire from campaign communications and to what extent are these needs satisfied by different types of messages disseminated during an election? The overarching goal of the analysis is to determine if members of the audience make distinctions in how they orient themselves toward specific forms of campaign communication during presidential contests. We anticipate that differences in the levels of gratifications received from media use during presidential elections will be evident across message categories. As messages differ in both form and content, ads, news stories, and debates are expected to fulfill needs to varying degrees during a campaign.

The study that most directly addresses these issues was conducted by McLeod, Bybee, and Durall (1979). In their research, the authors defined three categories of gratifications sought from the mass media during the 1976 presidential contest. These included surveillance/vote-guidance, contest/excitement, and communication utility. They contrasted two motivational models and used the example of debate-watching as a means of satisfying these needs. They concluded that elements of both models are useful in explaining the media gratification process. The drive-reduction model predicts that individuals will use the mass media directly to satisfy the gratifications that they seek, while the exposure-learning model proposes that the gratifications received are largely the result of accidental media exposure. Perhaps more importantly, they discovered that gratifications sought and received are two distinct conceptual dimensions.

Prior to undertaking a more complex examination of the relationship between gratifications sought and received, we made a basic comparison of the degree to which individuals seek to satisfy their surveillance and campaign involvement needs. We examined the means and standard deviations of the gratification-seeking measures, which were recorded on a three-point scale. Individuals in the 1984 Dane County sample sought to satisfy needs associated with the surveillance dimension more than those connected with campaign involvement, particularly in terms of their desire to find out where the candidates stood on issues; this had the highest mean score (2.8), as well as the lowest standard deviation (.5) of all the measures. The need to feel involved in the election was less important to the respondents, especially for items dealing with anticipated communication and contest excitement.

The Dane County data allow for a comparison of the gratifications received from ads, television news, newspaper news, and debates in terms of judging where the candidates stood on issues and finding out about their personal qualities. Again, we examined items means and standard deviations. These measures were based on scales ranging from one to ten. All four message types performed about equally well in providing information about candidate qualities. The means hovered around 6.5, and the standard deviations were approximately 2.5. Television news satisfied this need to a slightly greater extent than did other communication forms, while newspaper news was the least successful in this regard. There was more variation in the degree to which these four message categories satisfied issue information-seeking needs. Newspaper news appeared to satisfy this need more than the other message types, with a mean of 7.1 and a standard deviation of 2.1. It was followed by debates, with a mean of 6.6 and a standard deviation of 2.9. Television news was perceived as significantly less helpful in providing issue information (mean 3.0, standard deviation 2.4), ranking lower on this dimension than advertising (mean 4.2, standard deviation 2.9).

A comparison of the general need to find out about candidates' stands on issues and personal qualities with the gratifications received from ads, television news, newspaper news, and debates appears in Table 6.1. Overall, people sought information about candidates' stands on issues more than they desired to learn about their personal qualities. Television news, newspaper news, and debates were almost equal in their ability to satisfy the need for issue information. Approximately 50 percent out of the 77 percent of the sample respondents who reported seeking issue information a lot were gratified by television and newspaper news a great deal. Ads were the least successful in providing this need gratification. Most people indicated that candidate advertisements were of little or no help.

Television news and debates were the best sources of gratification for learning about the personal qualities of the candidates. These findings coincide with the perception that television, as a visual medium, is more satisfactory in conveying image-related information than are print media. Surprisingly, newspaper news was better than ads in satisfying this need. Ads are often designed with the specific intent of conveying positive signals about candidate qualities, yet the respondents in this sample did not use them for this information. In general, gratification-seeking was more nearly satisfied through mediated messages for information-seeking about personal qualities than about candidates' stands on issues. A substantial number of respondents did not find that the media met the need to acquire issue knowledge.

The next portion of the analysis considers the gratification-seeking measures in conjunction with media use variables, in order to determine their relationship to gratifications received from the various message types. We predict that the degree to which individuals feel that a particular type of campaign message satisfies an election-related need is linked to their patterns of electoral communication use and their more general orientations toward the mass media. Gratification-seeking, we assume, is an important determinant of an individual's tendency to use the mass media during the campaign. In addition, we hypothesize that the level of exposure and the amount of attention paid to a specific message type are related to gratifications received. Specifically, the greater the desire to satisfy a particular need, the more likely that an individual will be highly exposed and attentive to mediated messages. In addition, a high degree of exposure and attention will correspond to high levels of gratifications received. Finally, differences in need gratification will be related to the particular communication channel toward which a person is oriented. Those who rely more heavily on television for their campaign information tend to receive greater satisfaction from messages that are television-oriented, such as ads, television news, and debates. Those who depend more on newspapers will be more likely to find that news stories satisfied their needs.

Regression analysis was used to examine these relationships. A hierarchical least-squares regression procedure was employed. The controls were entered

Table 6.1
Comparison of Gratifications Sought and Received for Judging Where the Candidates Stand on Issues and Finding Out about Candidates' Personal Qualities—Dane County, WI, 1984 Election

	Issues			Qualities		
	A Lot	Some	None	A Lot	Some	None
Sought Gratification	77% (569)	20% (144)	3% (23)	53% (388)	40% (298)	7% (40)
Gratification Received From:						
Ads	13% (91)	44% (312)	43% (308)	13% (92)	43% (300)	44% (308)
TV News	50% (362)	40% (293)	10% (70)	45% (324)	43% (381)	12% (84)
NP News	50% (363)	44% (319)	6% (46)	35% (255)	53% (381)	12% (87)
Debates	50% (353)	32% (227)	18% (131)	46% (322)	37% (264)	17% (121)

into the equation first, as they may be a source of a spurious relationship between the independent and dependent measures. The remaining variables were entered into the equation in a temporal sequence (Cohen and Cohen, 1975). The goal of hierarchical regression is to examine the increase in the variance explained by the regression equation after each step. The zero-order correlation coefficients were reported to determine the relationship between each of the independent variables and the dependent variable. The partial correlation coefficients demonstrate the effect of particular independent variables on the dependent variable, controlling for the effects of all other variables in the equation. In most cases, the partial correlation coefficient is almost identical to the standardized regression coefficients.[1]

The dependent variables in the regression analyses are measures of gratifications received from ads, television news, newspaper news, and debates to gain information about issues and candidate qualities. A general measure of gratification-seeking for the surveillance/information-seeking dimension was constructed. It consists of items assessing the individuals' use of the media for judging where candidates stand on issues and finding out about their personal qualities.

The independent variables were entered in a hierarchical fashion, guided by the assumptions of the model of mass media uses and outcomes. Controls for age and education were entered first, followed by exposure to the specific message category, mass media reliance, gratification-seeking, and attention to the particular message type.

The results of the regression analysis appear in Table 6.2 for issues and Table 6.3 for candidate qualities. Information-seeking was an important predictor of gratifications received from ads, television news, newspaper news, and debates on both the issue and candidate quality items. As anticipated, the greater the desire to obtain information during the campaign, the higher the level of gratifications received from media messages about the election. The findings were most impressive for debates.

Exposure and attention also were related significantly to the dependent variables. These factors were generally more important for finding out about issues than for discovering candidate qualities. The evidence also suggests that the channel through which the communication is disseminated influences how it is received and processed by the individual. As predicted, the television-reliant reported higher levels of gratifications received from ads for issue information-seeking and from television news for both items. Newspaper reliance was strongly related to gratifications received from newspaper news.

Examining the controls, we found that the older our respondents were, the less gratification they received from ads and debates for the personal qualities item. Lower educational attainment was associated with higher levels of need gratification for ads and television news. Otherwise, the controls were not significant.

Table 6.2
Multiple Regression Analysis of Media Uses and Gratification-Seeking Variables as Predictors of Information-Seeking about Issues from Specific Types of Media Messages—Dane County, WI, 1984 Election

	Ads		TV News		NP News		Debates	
	Corr.	Part.	Corr.	Part.	Corr.	Part.	Corr.	Part.
Age	-.04	-.09	.05	-.02	.02	-.04	-.03	-.08
Education	-.14*	-.16*	-.10	-.12*	.06	-.01	.12*	.06
Exposure	.13*	.12*	.21*	.17*	.25*	.14*	.18*	.13*
TV Reliance	.11*	.07	.17*	.13*	-.08	-.09	.01	.03
NP Reliance	-.07	-.03	-.08	-.01	.29*	.24*	.02	.01
Info-Seeking	.19*	.16*	.17*	.11*	.18*	.10	.27*	.25*
Attention	.21*	.11*	.19*	.13*	.23*	.09	.24*	.16*
Total R²		.12*		.12*		.15*		.13*

*p<.05

Table 6.3
Multiple Regression Analysis of Media Uses and Gratification-Seeking Variables as Predictors of Information-Seeking about Candidate Qualities from Specific Types of Media Messages—Dane County, WI, 1984 Election

	Ads		TV News		NP News		Debates	
	Corr.	Part.	Corr.	Part.	Corr.	Part.	Corr.	Part.
Age	-.10*	-.14*	.01	-.05	.09*	.03	-.08	-.13*
Education	-.13*	-.17*	-.12*	-.13*	-.08	-.11*	.08	.02
Exposure	.10*	.08	.21*	.17*	.25*	.14*	.16*	.11*
TV Reliance	.07	.02	.13*	.03	-.03	.04	-.01	.00
NP Reliance	-.08	-.07	-.14*	-.11*	.14*	.10*	.02	.00
Info-Seeking	.17*	.14*	.15*	.15*	.19*	.13*	.21*	.19*
Attention	.22*	.14*	.10*	.06	.17*	.07	.23*	.17*
Total R^2	.12*		.08*		.08*		.11*	

*p<.05

Uses and Gratifications—Fairfax County, VA, 1984 Election; 1988 Election

The mail questionnaires did not include questions on gratification-seeking. Analyses similar to the preceding one were performed for Fairfax County in 1984 and for all three samples in 1988. These analyses also differ from those for Dane County in that they include poll results as an additional message category.

We examined the means and standard deviations for the gratification measures for the four campaign message categories. The scales used to measure gratifications ranged from a high of 4, indicating that an individual used the message a lot for the particular purpose, to a low of 1, meaning that the message was not used at all. In all categories, the respondents reported that news stories satisfied their campaign information and involvement needs to the greatest extent. In almost every instance across both election years, the mean value was 3.0 or greater and the standard deviation was lower than for any other message category. Debates were used almost as often, with the average mean value of 2.9 for each sample. For the surveillance items, a consistent pattern emerged, with news stories and debates satisfying needs often, followed by ads and poll results. The pattern changed somewhat for the campaign involvement dimension. News stories still scored the highest, followed by debates for the anticipated communication and excitement items. However, on both of these measures, polls outranked ads in the degree to which they satisfied voters' needs. On the vote-guidance dimension, polls were rated second to news stories, followed by debates and ads. Thus, polls scored lowest on the surveillance items, while ads were least effective on the campaign involvement dimension. These findings, which are strikingly consistent across campaign years and samples, indicate that individuals differentiate between specific categories of campaign communication based on the degree of satisfaction that they receive from them.

Multiple regression analysis was performed to predict the degree to which voters' felt that a specific type of message satisfied their surveillance and campaign involvement needs. Controls for age and education were entered into the equation first, followed by exposure to the message type, mass media reliance, and message attention.

The results of the analysis of the surveillance dimension appear in Table 6.4 for 1984 and Table 6.5 for 1988. Examining the control variables, we found a consistent relationship between age and gratifications from poll results. Older respondents used polls more often than younger survey participants. There was also some evidence of a negative connection between age and satisfaction from candidate ads. Political spots were used most often by younger people. The consistent finding in Virginia in both election years was that individuals with higher levels of education were less gratified by poll results for information-

Table 6.4
Multiple Regression Analysis of Media Use Variables as Predictors of Surveillance Gratifications from Media Messages—Fairfax County, VA, 1984 Election

	Ads		TV News		NP News		Polls		Debates	
	Corr.	Part.	Corr.	Part.	Corr.	Part.	Corr.	Part.	Corr.	Part.
Age	-.21*	-.12*	-.12*	-.21*	-.12*	-.21*	.09	.17*	-.19*	-.23*
Education	-.17*	-.08	.07	.04	.07	.04	-.21*	-.19*	-.17*	-.08
Exposure	.03	-.04	.06	.05	.16*	.02	-.01	-.04	.31*	.13*
TV Reliance	.26*	.13*	-.10*	.01	-.10*	.01	.18*	.11*	.19*	.13*
NP Reliance	-.21*	-.07	.21*	.11*	.21*	.11*	-.13*	-.04	-.10*	-.04
Attention	.34*	.33*	.18*	.10*	.32*	.21*	.26*	.29*	.41*	.31*
Total R²		.21*		.14*		.16*		.16*		.25*

*p<.05

Table 6.5
Multiple Regression Analysis of Media Use Variables as Predictors of Surveillance Gratifications from Media Messages—All Counties, 1988 Election

		Ads		TV News		NP News		Polls		Debates	
		Corr.	Part.	Corr.	Part.	Corr.	Part.	Corr.	Part.	Corr.	Part.
Age	-IA	-.24*	-.21*	-.04	-.05	.12	.09	-.11	-.06	-.22*	-.37*
	-NJ	-.05	.00	.00	.00	.00	-.01	.18*	.21*	-.10	-.20*
	-VA	-.15*	-.10	-.06	-.05	-.05	-.09	.22*	.26*	-.23*	-.25*
Education	-IA	-.11	-.16*	.14*	.14*	-.03	-.06	.19*	.19*	.12	.02
	-NJ	-.01	.00	.11	.06	.10	.06	.00	.07	.13*	.03
	-VA	-.08	.00	.04	.00	.04	.00	-.19*	-.23*	.00	-.04
Exposure	-IA	-.02	-.02	.01	-.08	.19*	.12	-.10	-.10	.48*	.40*
	-NJ	.23*	.11	.00	.01	.11	-.05	.00	-.06	.50*	.43*
	-VA	.23*	.05	-.03	-.16*	.04	-.06	-.05	-.03	.43*	.41*
TV Reliant	-IA	.15	.10	.03	-.04	.01	-.01	.13*	.12	.05	.04
	-NJ	.18*	.19*	.15*	.14*	-.14*	-.06	.00	.10	.00	-.02
	-VA	.23*	.08	.17*	.13*	-.05	.00	.16*	.18*	.01	.03
NP Reliant	-IA	.01	.07	.04	.00	.04	-.12	-.07	-.04	.07	.07
	-NJ	.06	.16*	-.14*	-.06	.14*	.00	.10	.11	-.08	-.02
	-VA	-.03	-.02	-.05	-.10	.18*	.08	.13*	.22*	.00	.02
Attention	-IA	.35*	.31*	.41*	.43*	.34*	.31*	.25*	.26*	.41*	.21*
	-NJ	.29*	.24*	.17*	.21*	.33*	.30*	.34*	.37*	.32*	.09
	-VA	.47*	.40*	.19*	.28*	.38*	.35*	.06	.04	.17*	.06
Total R^2	-IA		.20*		.21*		.14*		.14*		.36*
	-NJ		.14*		.08		.12*		.17*		.29*
	-VA		.24*		.11*		.16*		.16*		.28*

*$p < .05$

157

seeking than were those with fewer years of formal schooling. The opposite was true for Iowa in 1988.

Exposure was related significantly only to information-seeking gratifications derived from debates. A positive relationship existed for exposure to news stories and debates. Being exposed to ads or poll results had little or no effect on the level of surveillance gratification that an individual reported. Attention, however, was the strongest predictor of the degree to which individuals reported that campaign messages satisfied their surveillance needs in all samples across both elections.

In 1984, the relationship between attention and surveillance gratification was strongest for debates. The finding was related less clearly to any particular message category in 1988, although it seems to have been least prominent for poll results.

As expected, media reliance was linked to individuals' processing of campaign media messages. Television reliance was related to the use of ads, television news, and debates for seeking information about the campaign. In the Virginia samples, television reliance was also positively linked to using poll results on this dimension. This finding may result from the differences in presentation of poll results on television and in print. Poll results often led off an election story on television, and they were accompanied by visuals to make them more salient. The vast majority of the Fairfax County respondents who reported using a newspaper for election information read *The Washington Post*. Frequently, stories involving poll results were not front page news and instead were buried deeper in the paper. This factor made poll results less prominent than they were on television. Newspaper news stories were more gratifying for the newspaper-reliant, but only in the 1984 sample.

The results of the regression analysis for the campaign involvement dimension appear in Table 6.6 and Table 6.7. We found that the control for age had a consistently negative relationship for each of the message categories, although the coefficients were not always statistically significant. Older respondents were less inclined to use media messages for gratification of this kind that were younger people. Educational attainment was significant in terms of poll results in 1988. Those who were highly educated used poll results to keep involved in the election more often than did those with fewer years of formal education.

For the campaign involvement dimension, greater exposure had little or no effect in terms of individuals being gratified by ads, news stories, and poll results in 1984. Exposure to advertising remained significant after multivariate controls were introduced in New Jersey in 1988, as did exposure to newspaper news in Iowa. Yet these findings were isolated. The strongest and most consistent finding was that exposure was positively related to campaign involvement for debates. Since the surveys were conducted after all of the debates had taken place, individuals who reported a high level of exposure to debates received some level of satisfaction from the debates' ability to keep them

Table 6.6
Multiple Regression Analysis of Media Use Variables as Predictors of Campaign Involvement from Media Messages—Fairfax County, VA, 1984 Election

	Ads		TV News		NP News		Polls		Debates	
	Corr.	Part.	Corr.	Part.	Corr.	Part.	Corr.	Part.	Corr.	Part.
Age	-.21*	-.15*	-.14*	-.17*	-.14*	-.17*	-.14	-.12	-.17*	-.23*
Education	-.17*	-.08	-.05	-.06	-.05	-.06	-.06	-.02	-.08	-.05
Exposure	.09	.03	.05	.02	.04	-.06	.11*	.08	.35*	.21*
TV Reliance	.23*	.15*	-.05	.00	-.05	.00	.11*	-.02	.15*	.11*
NP Reliance	-.13*	.02	.14*	.11*	.14*	.11*	-.10*	.08	-.04	.07
Attention	.35*	.31*	.21*	.15*	.25*	.18*	.42*	.42*	.38*	.23*
Total R²		.19*		.13*		.14*		.21*		.24*

*p<.05

Table 6.7
Multiple Regression Analysis of Media Use Variables as Predictors of Campaign Involvement Gratifications from Media Messages—All Counties, 1988 Election

		Ads		TV News		NP News		Polls		Debates	
		Corr.	Part.	Corr.	Part.	Corr.	Part.	Corr.	Part.	Corr.	Part.
Age	-IA	-.13*	-.08	.00	-.02	.00	-.03	.01	.08	-.07	-.17*
	-NJ	.00	.00	.11	.11	.11	.05	-.12	-.02	-.02	-.09
	-VA	-.20*	-.16*	-.01	-.05	-.02	-.06	-.10	.02	-.12	-.12
Education	-IA	-.06	-.07	.07	.07	.08	.05	.17*	.20*	.03	-.02
	-NJ	-.08	-.04	-.01	.00	-.01	.02	.29*	.23*	.11	.01
	-VA	-.03	.11	.16*	.14	.16*	.15*	-.02	-.07	.06	.05
Exposure	-IA	.05	.00	.04	-.03	.17*	.14*	.09	.03	.42*	.25*
	-NJ	.28*	.16*	.07	-.04	.17*	.01	.25*	.11	.48*	.36*
	-VA	.05	-.13	.09	-.04	.07	-.07	.15*	.08	.26*	.20*
TV Rely	-IA	.10	.09	.01	-.03	.01	-.11	.13*	.09	.05	.05
	-NJ	.14	.15*	.03	.08	-.01	.04	-.07	-.04	.10	.12
	-VA	.20*	.15*	.21*	.14	-.01	-.10	-.10	-.04	.12	.14*
NP Rely	-IA	.05	.06	.01	-.02	.00	.00	-.06	-.10	.01	.00
	-NJ	.10	.19*	-.08	-.02	.07	.05	-.04	-.03	-.09	.00
	-VA	.00	.02	-.01	-.07	.21*	.10	.24*	.19*	.05	.05
Attention	-IA	.37*	.33*	.26*	.27*	.19*	.15*	.39*	.39*	.39*	.11
	-NJ	.35*	.29*	.32*	.35*	.34*	.31*	.48*	.45*	.33*	.06
	-VA	.41*	.39*	.25*	.26*	.41*	.37*	.22*	.19*	.15*	.03
Total R^2	-IA	.16*		.08		.06		.21*		.22*	
	-NJ	.20*		.13*		.13*		.30*		.23*	
	-VA	.23*		.13*		.20*		.10*		.11*	

*p<.05

engrossed in the campaign. As exposure was measured by how many debates an individual watched or listened to, there may have been a conditioning effect at work. In other words, those who found that the first debate satisfied a need to feel involved in the campaign may have taken the time to be exposed to subsequent debates. In addition, debates are scheduled more formally than most other types of campaign messages. The decision to be exposed constitutes a more conscious behavior in the case of debates than for other forms of communication.

Attention once again was the strongest predictor that needs were being satisfied by a particular message type. This finding was especially true for poll results in both presidential election years. Individuals who paid attention to polls found them a satisfactory means for keeping involved or interested in the election.

Examining the coefficients for mass media reliance revealed that television dependence was related to campaign involvement for ads and debates in 1984. Newspaper reliance was associated with the use of news stories. The 1988 analyses show almost no connection between media reliance and campaign involvement gratifications. While reliance had no effect for polls in 1984, it was significantly related to satisfying involvement needs in Fairfax County in 1988.

The foregoing analysis lends support to the contention that voters' patterns of mass media use during elections are related to their own personal ability to satisfy particular needs through specific types of messages disseminated during a campaign. Mass media gratifications from particular election messages can be predicted, to differing degrees, by levels of exposure and attention. Attention is more important for voters' processing of campaign messages than is exposure. In addition, individuals who have experience with a particular media channel expect that certain needs will be gratified by the messages disseminated through it. Ads and debates, as predominantly televised messages, were more salient to television-reliant respondents than to other types of voters.

Political Orientations and Mass Media Gratifications

The model of mass media use and outcomes stresses that the audience is not simply an undifferentiated mass. Instead, it is composed of individuals with widely differing orientations toward the social and political world. In order to tap even a very small aspect of this diversity, we examine information-seeking/surveillance and campaign involvement gratifications in relation to a variety of political variables. The assumption is that individuals who differ in their orientations toward the political system and to presidential elections will vary in the level of gratifications that they receive from particular types of media messages.

Strength of partisanship is one factor that can be related to voter gratifications from media use. Studies indicate that more stable partisan behavior is evident for voters who are politically interested and attentive to campaign information.

A group of "floating voters," consisting of individuals who are less politically active, informed, and partisan, has become the focus of a number of studies. Findings, however, have been inconsistent on this point. Converse (1962) contended that uninvolved voters, who are likely to be weak partisans, have the potential to be greatly influenced by short-term electoral forces, particularly information flow, provided that the messages reach them. If information is not widely disseminated, these voters demonstrate a high level of partisan stability.

Converse's findings have been challenged by scholars who have found that information gained through the mass media tends to reinforce partisan stability, even among less involved voters (Dryer, 1971; Zukin, 1971). Researchers have been unable to find a connection between higher levels of media use and partisanship (Todd and Brody, 1980). Furthermore, strength of partisanship and likelihood for partisan defection in elections have not been related to the level of political information-holding displayed by voters (Macaluso, 1977). We seek here to add a new dimension to this debate by examining the relationship of partisan strength to media gratifications.

Interest in the election is another political variable that has a connection to media gratifications. Individuals displaying higher levels of political interest are more likely to seek information about the campaign and to become involved.

Another factor we explore is attitudes toward candidates. Early voting studies suggested that media messages had little influence on the actual voting behavior of decided voters. People who had made up their minds for the election tended to use the media to learn more about their particular candidate and to reinforce their position. Attitudes toward candidates can be linked to the gratifications that voters receive from campaign media. Individuals are likely to be more strongly oriented toward messages that portray their favored candidate positively. For example, Mondale supporters would be more likely than Reagan backers to feel that debates gratified their information and involvement needs.

Time of voting decision has been shown to be related to voter media use. Such pioneering scholars as Key and Munger (1959) noted that the time at which voters make their decision to support a candidate is important to our understanding of voting behavior. The time dimension is even more pertinent today than in earlier periods because of the increasing numbers of people who are undecided until late into the campaign.

Research has revealed that those who make their decisions early in the campaign are most interested in and attentive to the election (Mendelson and O'Keefe, 1976). They experience the greatest amount of exposure to media messages about the election, tend to be television-reliant, and enjoy discussing politics with others. Voters who switch their candidate preferences during the campaign are moderate users of the media for campaign information and are most dependent upon newspapers. Finally, late deciders are inattentive to the campaign and media reports; they depend on neither television nor newspapers for political information. Strong partisans make up their minds early and are subject only marginally to media influence. Those not precommitted to candidates use information presented during the campaign to decide which candidate to support. Individuals not exposed to the campaign turn to partisan ties, however weak, in making their decision (Chaffee and Choe, 1980).

We again use hierarchical regression analysis to explore a number of hypotheses about political factors and media gratifications. First, voters who are less attached to political parties will find media messages less gratifying, as these individuals generally display lower levels of interest, attention, and involvement during elections. Interest in the election will be positively related to gratifications received from media messages. Next, individuals will find that media messages that present their candidate favorably will be more gratifying on both surveillance/information-seeking and campaign involvement dimensions. Finally, individuals who make up their minds later in the election campaign will be more likely to receive gratifications from the mass media for surveillance/information-seeking. Voters who have decided early, by contrast, will be more likely to find that the media satisfy their campaign involvement needs.

In the 1984 presidential election, it was possible to identify message types that were more favorable to one candidate than to the other. Reagan ads were generally perceived as upbeat and as presenting a positive view of both the candidate and the future of the nation. By contrast, Mondale ads were frequently aimed at attacking his opponent rather than developing a favorable image for the Democratic ticket. As demonstrated earlier, the ads tended to be more gratifying for Republicans and Reagan supporters. News stories could be perceived as more supportive of Mondale, particularly for the Fairfax County sample. *The Washington Post* is regarded by many as representative of the liberal press, and it was the primary source of print information for those surveyed in Fairfax County. In fact, *The Washington Post*, as well as *The Milwaukee Journal* and *The Capital Times* that were read by many of the Dane County respondents, endorsed Mondale during the election (*Washington Post*, 19 October 1984). Poll results should be more gratifying for Reagan supporters, since his lead was substantial throughout the course of the entire election campaign. Finally, the debates appeared to mark the high point of the campaign for voters backing the Democratic ticket. Mondale was considered to have performed quite well against his opponent, particularly during the first debate.

It is far more difficult to make judgments about what messages favored which candidates in 1988. Even if we were to use skill and competence as guidelines to make this determination, the negativity of the campaign tended to counterbalance much of the advantage that Bush had in the area of advertising. News stories were also influenced by this factor. Clearly, polls were more favorable to Bush than to Dukakis. Debates can be considered overall to have favored the Democrats because of Dukakis' first round performance and Bentsen's clear superiority over Quayle.

Identical regression analyses were performed for all five counties. Once again, controls for age and education were entered into the analysis first. These were followed by the strength of partisanship measure, which represented a general orientation toward the political system. Interest in the election was put into the model next, followed by measures of candidate affection, and, finally, by time of voting decision.

In general, the political variables were not as successful as the media use measures in predicting gratifications from information-seeking/surveillance and campaign involvement, especially for the 1984 data. In fact, no tables are presented for the Dane County analysis because so few coefficients are significant. The results for information-seeking appear in Table 6.8 for Fairfax County in 1984 and in Table 6.9 for all counties in 1988. The campaign involvement findings are located in Table 6.10 and Table 6.11.

Strength of attachment to political parties was not a good predictor of surveillance gratifications from any type of message in 1984. The variable was significant in the 1988 analysis for information-seeking from debates. The negative coefficients in Middlesex and Fairfax Counties indicate that respondents who were less attached to political parties were more likely to use debates to satisfy their information needs than were the strongly partisan.

In terms of campaign involvement gratifications, by contrast, significant findings were revealed for news stories, poll results, and debates in Fairfax County during the 1984 contest. Voters who were more strongly partisan exhibited higher levels of need gratification for these message varieties. These findings were anticipated based on prior research, as strong partisans tend to be more politically active and attentive to the campaign. Similar findings did not appear in the 1988 analysis, however.

In both election years, political interest was significantly, and in several instances, very strongly related to gratifications received from both news stories and debates. As expected, those who were most interested in the campaign were likely to use news stories and debates to find out about the election and to keep interested and involved. The other types of messages were not used to fulfill these needs as consistently or intensively.

Political interest was not related to surveillance for either ads or poll results in 1984, but it was a significant factor in predicting campaign involvement from polls that year. In 1988, interest was significantly related to information-seeking and campaign involvement for ads and polls in Middlesex and Fairfax Counties.

The regression analysis provides support for the hypothesis that audience selectivity tends to shape the gratifications received from using media messages. Individuals in Fairfax County who had strong positive feelings for the Republican candidates reported that ads and poll results satisfied their surveillance and campaign involvement needs. Interestingly, the results were significant only for the surveillance dimension. Democratic supporters demonstrated higher levels of need gratification from news stories and debates in terms of surveillance and campaign involvement. This finding was one of the few significant relationships in the Dane County sample for information-seeking about candidates and issues.

The results for 1988 were less conclusive for the candidate attitude variables

Table 6.8
Multiple Regression Analysis of Political Orientation Variables as Predictors of Information-Seeking from Specific Types of Media Messages—Fairfax County, VA, 1984 Election

	Ads		News		Polls		Debates	
	Corr.	Part.	Corr.	Part.	Corr.	Part.	Corr.	Part.
Age	-.18*	-.18*	-.11	-.15*	.08	.08	-.22*	-.24*
Education	-.18*	-.15*	.06	.05	-.20*	-.20*	-.03	-.06
Party Strength	-.03	-.03	.05	.00	.07	.08	.03	.00
Interest	.02	.07	.15*	.17*	.08	.06	.11*	.20*
Feel-Dems	-.06	.00	.13*	.10*	-.05	.03	.27*	.22*
Feel-Reps	.14*	.13*	-.06	.10*	.18*	.16*	-.17*	-.05
Time	.05	.08	-.03	.01	.04	.12*	.10*	.13*
Total R^2	.09*		.06		.09*		.16*	

*$p < .05$

Table 6.9
Multiple Regression Analysis of Political Variables as Predictors of Information-Seeking from Specific Types of Media Messages—All Counties, 1988 Election

	Ads		News		Polls		Debates	
	Corr.	Part.	Corr.	Part.	Corr.	Part.	Corr.	Part.
Age -IA	-.24*	-.30*	-.14*	-.16*	.23*	.22*	-.30*	-.30*
-NJ	.00	-.04	-.11	-.04	.12	.12	-.22*	-.19*
-VA	-.15*	-.15	-.03	-.06	.22*	.18*	-.20*	-.24*
Education -IA	-.10	-.20*	.10	.02	-.11	-.02	.13*	.03
-NJ	-.03	-.09	.18*	.10	-.08	.00	.16*	.03
-VA	-.08	-.11	.12	.07	-.21*	-.28*	.01	.00
Party Str. -IA	.02	.08	.21*	.13	-.05	.05	.00	.04
-NJ	.23*	.11	.10	-.06	.06	-.01	-.22*	-.18*
-VA	.06	-.06	.12	-.01	-.06	-.04	-.05	-.24*
Interest -IA	.00	.01	.28*	.21*	-.23*	-.23*	.26*	.29*
-NJ	.31*	.22*	.38*	.31*	.11	.08	.47*	.39*
-VA	.24*	.23*	.33*	.26*	-.13	-.17*	.29*	.29*
Feel-Dems -IA	-.06	-.01	.06	.05	-.01*	-.13*	.10	.10
-NJ	.14*	.16*	.22*	.20*	-.10	-.01	.22*	.12
-VA	.14*	.08	.01	.00	-.07	-.41*	.33*	.24*
Feel-Reps -IA	.06	.06	.03	.00	.29*	.31*	-.18*	-.13
-NJ	.19*	.19*	.13	.21*	.32*	.31*	.02	.07
-VA	-.12	-.04	-.19*	-.06	.44*	.53*	-.29*	-.12
Time -IA	.05	.06	-.08	.01	-.04	.07	.23*	.29*
-NJ	.08	.15*	-.01	.02	.07	.12	.07	.12
-VA	-.09	-.12	-.01	.00	-.02	.05	.00	-.09
Total R² -IA		.11*		.12*		.21*		.26*
-NJ		.12*		.21*		.14*		.30*--
-VA		.12*		.15*		.39*		.26*

*p<.05

Table 6.10

Multiple Regression Analysis of Political Orientation Variables as Predictors of Campaign Involvement from Specific Types of Media Messages—Fairfax County, VA, 1984 Election

	Ads		News		Polls		Debates	
	Corr.	Part.	Corr.	Part.	Corr.	Part.	Corr.	Part.
Age	-.19*	-.19*	-.13*	-.15*	-.14*	-.18*	-.18*	-.21*
Education	-.19*	-.16*	-.04	-.03	-.06	-.05	-.03	-.04
Party Strength	.06	.05	.11*	.06	.18*	.12*	.10*	.06
Interest	.03	.06	.15*	.15*	.18*	.15*	.15*	.18*
Feel-Dems	-.06	-.02	.10*	.11*	.02*	.04	-.23*	-.21*
Feel-Reps	-.10*	.07	.05	.08	.11*	.08	-.06	.03
Time	.00	.04	-.01	.06	-.12*	-.02*	.01	.07
Total R^2	.08*		.07		.09*		.13*	

*$p < .05$

Table 6.11
Multiple Regression Analysis of Political Variables as Predictors of Campaign Involvement from Specific Types of Media Messages—All Counties, 1988 Election

		Ads		News		Polls		Debates	
		Corr.	Part.	Corr.	Part.	Corr.	Part.	Corr.	Part.
Age	-IA	-.09	-.13	-.05*	-.06*	.04	.09	-.12	-.13
	-NJ	-.03	-.05	.00	.04	-.24*	-.18*	-.16	-.12
	-VA	-.16	-.18*	-.03	-.06	.02	-.01	-.13	-.16
Education	-IA	-.06	-.11	.06	.01	.19*	.21*	.19*	.04
	-NJ	-.13	-.18*	.04	-.04	.29*	.26*	.21*	.07
	-VA	.05	.03	.12	.07	.06	.00	.01	.00
Party Str.	-IA	.08	.10	.07	.00	.09	.13	.03	.04
	-NJ	.31*	.20*	.10	-.10	.11	.13	.15	.02
	-VA	.12	.00	.12	-.02	.17*	.08	-.04	-.20*
Interest	-IA	.00	.01	.17*	.14	-.01	-.07	.20*	.20*
	-NJ	.29*	.19*	.37*	.32*	.19*	.06	.41*	.31*
	-VA	.25*	.21*	.33*	.26*	.29*	.22*	.26*	.25*
Feel-Dems	-IA	-.06	-.01	.07	.12	-.06	-.06	.05	.09
	-NJ	.13	.14	.25*	.29*	-.01	.02	.22*	.26*
	-VA	-.11	.00	.27*	.14	-.04	.02	.25*	.19*
Feel-Reps	-IA	.10	.13	-.19*	.21*	.26*	.25*	.00	.01
	-NJ	.11	.10	.15	.24*	.22*	.28*	-.04	.05
	-VA	.19*	.11	-.19*	-.07	.27*	.20*	-.20*	-.07
Time	-IA	-.06	.01	-.06	-.01	.06	.14	.16*	.20*
	-NJ	.01	-.10	.02	.08	.12	.20*	.07	.14
	-VA	-.06	-.07	.01	.00	.07	.11	-.04	-.11
Total R²	-IA		.05		.06		.13*		.10*
	-NJ		.18*		.23*		.14*		.26*
	-VA		.02		.15*		.39*		.16*

*p < .05

than they were for the 1984 analysis. As noted earlier, with the exception of poll results, it was difficult to identify messages that consistently favored one candidate over the other. Because polls so completely endorsed the Republican ticket, respondents with strong positive feelings toward that party's candidates were likely to gain both surveillance and involvement gratifications from them. While few of the relationships were statistically significant, polls were frequently related negatively to gratifications for respondents who favored the Democratic candidates. Some less impressive evidence indicated that people who felt positively about the Democratic candidates were more likely to be gratified by debates, while the opposite proved true for those who preferred the Republicans. In the 1988 New Jersey sample, gratifications from news stories were consistently linked to favorable attitudes toward the Democratic contenders.

Among Fairfax County voters in 1984, there was no support for the hypothesis that voters who decided later in the election would score higher on the information-seeking/surveillance dimension than those who made up their minds earlier in the campaign. Evidence suggests that late deciders instead found their campaign-involvement needs were met by poll results and debates, contrary to expectations. In Dane County, the later that respondents made up their minds, the more likely they were to be gratified by debates in terms of providing both issue and candidate quality information. This evidence across samples suggests that debates are a salient type of campaign communication for those deciding later in the campaign. It was found for both dimensions in the 1988 Iowa data set as well. There is no other convincing evidence that time of voting decision made a difference in campaign gratifications for any other message type in the 1988 campaign.

SUMMARY

This chapter constitutes an empirical exploration of the uses and gratifications of mass media messages during presidential elections. Guided by the model of mass media use and outcomes, the analysis demonstrates that individuals make distinctions among types of media messages in elections on the basis of their orientations toward the mass media and the political realm. Voters' needs to receive information about the campaign and to feel involved in the electoral process are served differently by the message categories of ads, news stories, poll results, and debates explored in this study.

The level of gratification exhibited by voters on the gratification dimensions of information-seeking and campaign involvement can be predicted by patterns of media use, and to a lesser degree, by political variables. Generally speaking, respondents reported that the media satisfy their information-seeking/surveillance needs more than their campaign involvement requirements. Attention and exposure were consistent predictors of gratifications received from the mass media. In addition, distinct patterns were discerned for the relationship between media reliance and gratifications. People who relied heavily on newspapers were more gratified by news stories. The television-dependent were satisfied to a greater extent by debates.

There is also evidence that voters' ability to be gratified by media messages was shaped by their political orientations, especially their feelings about the candidates. One striking example is the greater orientation toward debates for Mondale supporters in 1984. Another is the strong and significant relationship between supporters of the Republican candidates and gratifications from poll results that existed for both campaign years.

In a broad sense, these findings indicate that the influence of the mass media may not be as limited as is often portrayed in a substantial amount of communication effects research. Voters look to the media to fulfill important needs during an election campaign. It appears from the findings of this analysis that different types of campaign messages fulfill these needs to varying degrees. Moreover, different types of voters are gratified by some messages more than by others. Thus, the form that campaign messages take is relevant to their acceptance by voters. Some segments of the mass audience respond more to televised communication, while others display a greater inclination toward messages disseminated in print. Even though the content of various types of campaign messages may be quite similar, the form is important.

NOTE

1. In circumstances that involve direct comparisons across samples, it is optimal to report unstandardized coefficients. Standardized coefficients are a function of the sample variances. Thus, it is impossible to make meaningful contrasts across samples using correlation coefficients (Achen, 1982; Hanushek and Jackson, 1977). In this research, the measures in the Dane and Fairfax County samples were not directly comparable at the outset, in terms of either substance or measurement. Therefore, strict comparisons across the two samples could not be made. The standardized coefficients are reported to facilitate examination of the relationships within each sample.

7

Conclusion

Voters are presented with a vast and continual stream of mediated messages about presidential campaigns over the course of several months during election years. The purpose of this project was to make a comparative assessment of the degree to which individuals were oriented toward specific categories of messages. Prior research in political communication has tended to examine the influence of particular types of mass media messages separately rather than to compare their relative importance to voters. This study takes into account four basic types of campaign messages—ads, news stories, poll results, and debates—that can be readily distinguished by voters.

The evidence presented here demonstrates that particular election messages are used by voters to different degrees to achieve a variety of outcomes. The basic distinctions that members of the electorate make among message types are important for how individuals receive and process campaign information. Voters are exposed and pay attention to some messages more readily than they do others. People find that some messages fulfill information-gathering and campaign involvement needs during elections more successfully than other message types do.

Individuals' views of the usefulness, quality, and reliability of messages form a perceptual screen that they employ to help them to filter the thick soup of mediated communication during elections. This screening process facilitates voters' ability to make sense of what is presented to them through the mass media. The process also allows people to seek out the forms of campaign communication that are most relevant to them and to ignore other messages. Individuals are thus able to cope better with the flood of campaign messages with which they are confronted during presidential elections.

PLACE OF THIS STUDY IN THE CONTEXT OF COMMUNICATION RESEARCH

Political communication research has gone through a number of phases. Early work sought to uncover evidence of a strong, direct media influence manifested in changes in individuals' behavior. When voting studies of the 1940s and 1950s failed to produce substantial evidence of persuasive influence, the "limited effects" tradition in mass media research emerged and dominated the field for several decades. Upon reevaluating the role of the mass media in politics and reassessing the findings of earlier work, mass communications researchers focused on understanding more about the nature of media effects and the more subtle aspects of the mass media's influence. The present research works from the perspective of this increasingly dominant theoretical tradition.

The general theoretical premises underlying the model of mass media use and outcomes presented in chapter 1 derive from the uses and gratifications approach in mass communications research. The approach is based on the assumption that individuals have certain needs that they seek to gratify through use of the mass media. In this study, we explored the particular assumption that a variety of forms of presidential campaign messages differentially satisfy voters' needs to gain information about the campaign and to foster a sense of involvement in the political process.

The findings presented here provide encouragement for scholars engaged in revitalizing the uses and gratifications perspective in communication research. Audience motives for using the mass media guide individuals in their propensity to be exposed to messages, to pay attention to communication, and to be affected by the media. Peoples' experience with the mass media influences their choice of communication channel, as well as how they process information received from the media. These orientations shape the ways in which audience members learn from the media and formulate images about people, issues, and political processes. They also serve to condition individuals' future expectations about communications.

Not all aspects of the model could be tested directly in this research. The nonconscious processes underlying individuals' motivations for media use could not be considered in a study that employed survey research. This study did not deal directly with the content of political communication or with what voters learned specifically about candidates and issues, for example. Such important research requires an extensive content analysis of campaign communication in conjunction with reports from members of the electorate about what they learned from the mass media.

This study also highlights the desirability of exploring the diversity of the communications audience, rather than treating it as an undifferentiated mass. This research barely scratches the surface when exploring the complex make-up of the mass media audience. It demonstrates, however, that when the characteristics and orientations of the audience are taken into account, they point to different patterns of media gratification and use on the part of specific subsegments of the population. The study establishes a foundation upon which further research studies about individuals' experience with communicated messages can be based.

The importance of the historical context within which election communication takes place is all too often disregarded in quantitative research. All presidential elections have unique characteristics that set them apart from others. To a large extent, these traits structure the nature of the communication and the reactions of the audience. The media environment during the 1984 and 1988 presidential elections provided the context within which the present analysis should be interpreted. Yet, taking into account the specific differences in context, the fact that many of our findings are consistent with research on past elections increases our ability to generalize. For example, the finding that individuals who were undecided in the election are the least likely to pay attention to campaign communication is an important one that persists over time.

Finally, the use of county-wide data is a lesson learned from the research of early communications scholars. One major benefit of using different samples from discretely defined geographic locations is that we could identify differences that exist for respondents with experiences in varied media environments. Many studies in the mass communication field attempt to generalize from small samples to the population at large. Others make generalizations from national samples with no apparent awareness of important distinctions that affect how people are oriented toward the media; these distinctions are shaped by access to specific forms and channels of communication. The present study demonstrates the necessity of taking into account the characteristics of the sample and the media environment that exists for the respondents when studying media processes and effects. Once again, this procedure strengthens our ability to generalize when consistent patterns are discovered under diverse conditions.

IMPLICATIONS OF THE FINDINGS FOR OUR UNDERSTANDING OF DEMOCRATIC POLITICS

One of the reasons for undertaking this study was to determine how large a role the mass media have assumed in American elections, given recent changes in the nature of the political process and the campaign-media environment. The results suggest that media now serve a greatly enhanced function in politics, as the importance of electoral institutions, such as political parties, has declined.

The present study does not provide a direct test of these assumptions. The research indicates that the power of the mass media in elections depends partially on the attitudinal predispositions of the electorate. The mass media provide substantive informational inputs that work in conjunction with individuals' preexisting political orientations to create images of candidates and issues.

Voters who do not have strong political inclinations, who are not interested in politics, or who do not affiliate with a political party are less inclined to be exposed and attentive to mediated political communication than are other members of the electorate. This study confirms the findings of other scholars that media influence appears to be least apparent for segments of the electorate that one might expect to be most susceptible to its messages.

The findings here highlight a number of points about voters' orientations toward campaign media. First, simple maximizing the level of exposure to campaign messages clearly will not have the effect of meeting voters' campaign needs for information and involvement. We found that individuals' exposure to all forms of campaign communication is high, while their levels of attention are consistently low. The analysis of gratifications received from media messages indicates that, with the possible exception of debates, mere exposure does not predict information-seeking or campaign involvement satisfaction. Experience with a particular mass communication channel, operationalized here as media reliance, has some influence in determining campaign-related gratifications from particular message varieties. These effects are modest when they are compared to the relationship between attention and gratifications received.

Voters are frequently overwhelmed by media messages in campaigns. Some respondents to our survey characterized campaign media as highly intrusive. While people receive highly concentrated doses of election media, our analysis indicates that the content of material presented is far from meaningful. Media content does not help voters to learn about the candidates and the electoral process, nor do the media encourage voters to feel involved in the campaign or to take an active role in politics. In fact, the trivial, vapid, packaged plethora of ads and news may well have the opposite effect.

Political professionals have gotten media management down to such a science that the form of the message is often all that distinguishes one information fragment from another. All campaign messages, whether emanating directly from a candidate's organization or not, have come to look and sound suspiciously like political advertisements. Staging, scripting, and directing have become the order of the day. The real and momentous political consequences of the electoral process are masked and subverted by the staged drama of the campaign.

Perhaps even worse is that the *quantity* of campaign media is being offered as evidence of the health of our political process. Foresaking quality, we are asked to accept the campaign charade that we witness every four years during presidential elections as a vast and open display of information dissemination— of democracy in action. What we actually experience is an exercise in information control forced on voters by the careful packaging of candidates. The condition has worsened with each recent electoral contest. Morrow sums up this situation in a reaction to the 1988 presidential campaign:

The year represents something close to a dismantling of the American presidential campaign. The candidates perform simulations of encounters with the real world, but the exercise is principally a series of television visuals of staged events created for TV cameras. The issues have become as weightless as clouds of electrons, and the candidates mere actors in commercials. (1988: 21)

Journalists and candidates justify their behavior by alleging that they are giving the voters what they want, but to place the blame with the electorate is deceptive. The low levels of gratifications that our respondents received from the four types of campaign messages in this study indicate the opposite. American voters are not satisfied by what candidates and the mass media have to offer as they engage in the portentous task of selecting their president. Still, the electorate feels helpless to effect a change.

Bennett argues that people have a choice about the kinds of information media they must live with and that they can take steps to change the current situation. First, members of the mass media audience must become informed consumers of what is presented to them. Second, people must register resistance to the steady flow of personalized, fragmented, dramatized, and normalized media fare they endure. He writes, "Each individual has a personal stake in thinking critically about events in the news and in forming an independent perspective on the political world" (1988: 208). Unless the electorate carries this responsibility into the realm of presidential campaign politics and demands something better, the future promises even more elaborately packaged presidents.

References

Abrams, Floyd. "Press Practices, Polling Restrictions, Public Opinion, and First Amendment Guarantees." *Public Opinion Quarterly* (1985): 15–18.

Achen, Christopher H. *Interpreting and Using Regression.* Beverly Hills, CA: Sage Publications, 1982.

Adams, William C. "Media Power in Presidential Elections: An Exploratory Analysis, 1960–1980." In *The President and the Public*, ed. Doris Graber, 111–144. Philadelphia: Institute for the Study of Human Issues, 1982.

Adams, William C. "Early TV Calls in 1984: How Western Voters Deplored by Ignoring Them." Paper presented at the Annual Conference, American Association for Public Opinion Research, Princeton, NJ, 1985.

Alpern, David M. "Fritz Sways the 'Switchables,' " *Newsweek*, 15 October 1984: 33.

Altheide, David L. *Creating Reality: How TV News Distorts Events.* Beverly Hills, CA: Sage Publications, 1977.

Andreoli, Virginia, and Stephen Worchel. "Effects of Media Communicator and Message Position on Attitude Change." *Public Opinion Quarterly* (1980): 59–80.

Arterton, F. Christopher. "Campaign Organizations Confront the Media-Political Environment." In *Race for the Presidency*, ed. James David Barber, 3–25. Englewood Cliffs, NJ: Prentice-Hall, 1978.

Arterton, F. Christopher. *Media Politics.* Lexington, MA: Lexington Books, 1984.

Atkin, Charles K. "Political Campaigns: Mass Communication and Persuasion." In *Persuasion: New Directions in Theory and Research*, eds. Michael E. Roloff and Gerald R. Miller, 285–308. Beverly Hills, CA: Sage Publications, 1980.

Atkin, Charles K., and James Gaudino. "The Impact of Polling on the Mass Media." In *The Annals of the American Academy of Political and Social Science: Polling and the Democratic Consensus*, ed. John L. Martin (1984): 119–128.

Atkin, Charles K., and Gary Heald. "Effects of Political Advertising." *Public Opinion Quarterly* (1976): 216–228.

Atkin, Charles K., Lawrence Bowen, Oguz B. Nayman, and Kenneth G. Sheinkopf.

"Quality Versus Quantity in Televised Political Ads." *Public Opinion Quarterly* (1973): 611–617.

Atkinson, Rick, and Dale Russakoff. "Bush, Ferraro Clash in Debate." *The Washington Post*, 12 October 1984: A1, A14.

Auer, J. Jeffrey. "The Counterfeit Debates." In *The Great Debates: Kennedy vs. Nixon, 1960*, ed. Sidney Kraus, 142–160. Bloomington, IN: Indiana University Press, 1962.

Babrow, Austin S. "Theory and Method in Research on Audience Motives." *Journal of Broadcasting and Electronic Media* (1980): 471–487.

Baer, Donald, et al. "The Making of a President." *U.S. News and World Report*, 17 October 1988: 22–36.

Ball-Rokeach, Sandra, Milton Rokeach, and Joel W. Grube. *The Great American Values Test: Influencing Behavior and Belief through Television*. New York: Free Press, 1984.

Barlett, Dorothy L., Pamela B. Drew, Eleanor G. Fahle, and William A. Watts, "Selective Exposure to a Presidential Campaign Appeal." *Public Opinion Quarterly* (1974): 264–270.

Bauer, Raymond A. "The Communicator and the Audience." In *People, Society and Mass Communications*, eds. Lewis Anthony Dexter and David Manning White, 125–140. Glencoe, IL: Free Press, 1964.

Bauer, Raymond A. "The Audience." In *Handbook of Communication*, eds. Ithiel de Sola Pool, Frederick W. Frey, Wilbur Schramm, Nathan Maccoby, and Edwin B. Parker, 141–152. Chicago: Rand McNally College Publishing, 1973.

Becker, Lee B. "Measurement of Gratifications." *Communication Research* (1979): 54–73.

Becker, Lee B., and John C. Doolittle. "How Repetition Affects Evaluations of and Information Seeking about Candidates." *Journalism Quarterly* (1975): 611–617.

Becker, Lee B., and Klaus Schoenbach. "When Media Content Diversifies: Anticipating Audience Behaviors." In *Audience Responses to Media Diversification: Coping with Plenty*, eds. Lee B. Becker and Klaus Schoenbach, 1–28. Hillsdale, NJ: Lawrence Erlbaum Associates, 1989.

Becker, Lee B., and Charles D. Whitney. "Effects of Media Dependencies: Audience Assessment of Government." *Communication Research* (1980): 95–120.

Becker, Lee B., Maxwell E. McCombs, and Jack M. McLeod. "The Development of Political Cognitions." In *Political Communications*, ed. Steven H. Chaffee, 21–64. Beverly Hills, CA: Sage Publications, 1975.

Beniger, James R. "Winning the Presidential Nomination: National Polls and State Primary Elections, 1937–1972." *Public Opinion Quarterly* (1976): 22–38.

Bennett, W. Lance. "The Ritualistic and Pragmatic Bases of Political Campaign Discourse." *Quarterly Journal of Speech* (1977): 219–238.

Bennett, W. Lance. *News: The Politics of Illusion*. New York: Longman, 1988.

Berelson, Bernard R., Paul F. Lazarsfeld, and William N. McPhee. *Voting*. Chicago: University of Chicago Press, 1954.

Berman, Ronald. *How Television Sees Its Audience*. Newbury Park, CA: Sage Publications, 1987.

Bieder, Joan. "Television Reporting." In *The Communications Revolution in Politics*, ed. Gerald Benjamin, 36–48. New York: Academy of Political Science, 1982.

Bishop, George F., Robert W. Oldendick, and Alfred J. Tuchfarber. "Debate-Watching and the Acquisition of Political Knowledge." *Journal of Communication* (1978): 99–113.

Bitzer, Lloyd, and Theodore Reuter. *Carter vs. Ford: The Counterfeit Debates of 1976.* Madison, WI: University of Wisconsin Press, 1980.

"Blackballing of Prospective Debate Panelists." *The Washington Post*, 8 October 1984: A14.

Blumler, Jay G. "The Role of Theory in Uses and Gratifications Studies." *Communication Research* (1979): 9–36.

Blumler, Jay G. "The Social Character of Media Gratifications." In *Media Gratifications Research: Current Perspectives*, eds. Karl Erik Rosengren, Lawrence A. Wenner, and Philip Palmgreen, 41–59. Beverly Hills, CA: Sage Publications, 1985.

Blumler, Jay G., and Michael Gurevitch. "The Political Effects of Mass Communication." In *Culture, Society, and the Media*, eds. Michael Gurevitch, Tony Bennett, James Curran, and Janet Woolacott, 236–268. London: Methuen, 1980.

Blumler, Jay G., and Denis McQuail. *Television in Politics*. Chicago: University of Chicago Press, 1969.

Blumler, Jay G., Michael Gurevitch, and Elihu Katz. "Reaching Out: A Future for Gratifications Research." In *Media Gratifications Research: Current Perspectives*, eds. Karl Erik Rosengren, Lawrence A. Wenner, and Philip Palmgreen, 255–273. Beverly Hills, CA: Sage Publications, 1985.

Bogart, Leo. *Silent Politics*. New York: Free Press, 1972.

Bogart, Leo. "Newspapers in Transition." *Wilson Quarterly* (1982): 58–70.

Bogart, Leo. "The Public's Use and Perception of Newspapers." *Public Opinion Quarterly* (1984): 709–719.

Bowers, Thomas A. "Issue and Personality Information in Newspaper Political Advertising." *Journalism Quarterly* (1972): 446–452.

Bowers, Thomas A. "Candidate Advertising: The Agenda Is the Message." In *The Emergence of American Political Issues*, eds. Donald L. Shaw and Maxwell E. McCombs, 53–68. New York: West Publishing, 1977.

Bowes, John E., and Herbert Strentz. "Candidate Images: Stereotyping and the 1976 Debates." In *Communication Yearbook 2*, ed. Brent D. Rubin, 391–406. New Brunswick, NJ: Transaction Books, 1978.

Broder, David S. "Mondale Campaign Feels Spirits Revive." *The Washington Post*, 10 October 1984a: A4.

Broder, David S. "Both Camps Satisfied with Debate." *The Washington Post*, 12 October 1984b: A1, A20.

Broder, David S., and Barry Sussman. "Reagan's Lead in Poll Cut to 12 Points: Mondale Trails 54 to 42 Percent in Latest Post-ABC Survey." *The Washington Post*, 18 October 1984: A1, A6.

Broh, C. Anthony. "Horse-Race Journalism: Reporting the Polls in the 1976 Election." *Public Opinion Quarterly* (1980): 514–529.

Broh, C. Anthony. "Polls, Pols, and the Parties." *Journal of Politics* (1983a): 736–737.

Broh, C. Anthony. "Presidential Preference Polls and Network News." In *Television Coverage of the 1980 Presidential Campaign*, ed. William C. Adams, 29–47. Norwood, NJ: Ablex Publishing, 1983b.

Brownstein, Ronald. "Public Seeing Campaign through the Eye of the TV Camera." *National Journal*, 22 September 1984: 1752–1757.

Brudney, Jeffrey L. "An Elite View of the Polls." *Public Opinion Quarterly* (1982): 503–509.

Buchanan, William. "Election Predictions: An Empirical Assessment." *Public Opinion Quarterly* (1986): 222–227.

Bumiller, Elisabeth. "Reagan's Ad Aces." *The Washington Post*, 18 October 1984: D1.

Bumiller, Elisabeth, and Thomas Headley. "The Spot That Got Yanked." *The Washington Post*, 18 October 1984: D1.

Burnham, Walter Dean. *The Current Crisis in American Politics*. New York: Oxford University Press, 1982.

Buss, Terry F., and C. Richard Hofstetter. "An Analysis of the Logic of Televised Campaign Advertisements: The 1972 Presidential Campaign." *Communication Research* (1976): 367–389.

Bybee, Carl R., Jack M. McLeod, William D. Luetscher, and Gina Garramone. "Mass Communication and Voter Volatility." *Public Opinion Quarterly* (1981): 69–90.

Campbell, Angus, Philip E. Converse, Warren E. Miller, and Donald E. Stokes. *The American Voter*. New York: John Wiley and Sons, 1960.

Cannon, Lou. "Reagan After Debate: Incumbent Struggles to Regain Stride." *The Washington Post*, 9 October 1984a: A1, A12.

Cannon, Lou. "The Problem Was Reagan." *The Washington Post*, 15 October 1984b: A2.

Cantril, Albert H. "Introduction." In *Polling on the Issues*, ed. Albert H. Cantril, 3–12. Cabin John, MD: Seven Locks Press, 1980.

Ceasar, James W. *Presidential Selection*. Princeton, NJ: Princeton University Press, 1979.

Ceci, Stephen J., and Edward L. Kain. "Jumping on the Bandwagon with the Underdog: The Impact of Attitude Polls on Voting Behavior." *Public Opinion Quarterly* (1982): 228–242.

Chaffee, Steven E., and Sun Yuel Choe. "Time of Decision and Media Use during the Ford-Carter Campaign." *Public Opinion Quarterly* (1980): 53–69.

Chaffee, Steven E., and Jack Dennis. "Presidential Debates: An Empirical Assessment." In *The Past and Future of Presidential Debates*, ed. Austin Ranney, 75–106. Washington: American Enterprise Institute, 1979.

Chebat, Jean-Charles, and Pierre Filiatrault. "Credibility, Source Identification and Message Acceptance: The Case of Political Persuasion." *Political Communication and Persuasion* (1987): 153–160.

Cirino, Robert. *Don't Blame the People*. New York: Random House, 1972.

Clancey, Maura, and Michael J. Robinson. "General Election Coverage, Part I." In *The Mass Media in Campaign '84*, eds. Michael J. Robinson and Austin Ranney, 27–33. Washington: American Enterprise Institute, 1985.

Clarke, Peter, and Susan H. Evans. *Covering Campaigns*. Stanford, CA: Stanford University Press, 1983.

Clarke, Peter, and Eric Fredin, "Newspapers, Television, and Political Reasoning." *Public Opinion Quarterly* (1978): 143–160.

Cohen, Akiba. "Attention to the Mass Media among Straight and Split Ticket Voters: A Research Note." *Human Communication Research* (1975): 75–78.

Cohen, Jacob, and Patricia Cohen. *Applied Multiple Regression/Correlational Analysis for the Behavioral Sciences*. New York: John Wiley, 1975.

Coleman, Milton, and Rick Atkinson. "Mondale: Challenger Declares Campaign Is 'Brand-New Race,' " *The Washington Post*, 9 October 1984: A1, A2.

Comstock, George. *Television in America*. Beverly Hills, CA: Sage Publications, 1980.

Comstock, George, Steven Chaffee, Natan Katzman, and Maxwell McCombs, eds. *Television and Human Behavior*. New York: Columbia University Press, 1978.

Converse, Philip E. "Information Flow and the Stability of Partisan Attitudes." *Public Opinion Quarterly* (1962): 578–599.

Cundy, Donald T. "Political Commercials and Candidate Image: The Effect Can Be Substantial." In *New Perspectives on Political Advertising*, eds. Lynda Lee Kaid, Dan Nimmo, and Keith R. Sanders, 210–234. Carbondale, IL: Southern Illinois University Press, 1986.

"Dailies Make Endorsements: Foreign Economic Policy of Candidates Weighed." *The Washington Post*, 29 October 1984: A4.

Davis, Denis. "Influence on Voting Decisions." In *The Great Debates*, ed. Sidney Kraus, 331–348. Bloomington, IN: Indiana University Press, 1980.

Davis, Mark H. "Voting Intentions and the 1980 Carter-Reagan Debate." *Journal of Applied Psychology* (1982): 481–492.

DeFleur, Melvin L., and Sandra Ball-Rokeach. *Theories of Mass Communication*. New York: Longman, 1982.

DelliCarpini, Michael X. "Scooping the Voters? The Consequences of the Network's Early Call of the 1980 Presidential Race." *Journal of Politics* (1984): 866–885.

Demers, David Pearce. "Use of Polls in Reporting Changes Slightly Since 1978." *Journalism Quarterly* (1987): 839–842.

Dennis, Jack, Steven E. Chaffee, and Sun Yuel Choe. "Impact on Partisan, Image, and Issue Voting." In *The Great Debates*, ed. Sidney Kraus, 314–330. Bloomington, IN: Indiana University Press, 1979.

Dervin, Brenda. "Mass Communicating: Changing Conceptions of the Audience." In *Public Communication Campaigns*, eds. Ronald E. Rice and William J. Paisley, 71–87. Beverly Hills, CA: Sage Publications, 1981.

Deutschmann, Paul J. "Viewing, Conversation, and Voting Intentions." In *The Great Debates*, ed. Sidney Kraus, 232–252. Bloomington, IN: Indiana University Press, 1962.

Devlin, L. Patrick. "Contrasts in Presidential Campaign Commercials of 1988." *American Behavioral Scientist* (1989): 389–414.

DeVries, Walter, and V. Lance Tarrance. *The Ticket-Splitters*. Grand Rapids, MI: William B. Erdmans, 1972.

Diamond, Edwin. *The Tin Kazoo*. Cambridge, MA: MIT Press, 1975.

Diamond, Edwin, and Stephen Bates. "The Ads." In *The Mass Media in Campaign '84*, eds. Michael J. Robinson and Austin Ranney, 49–52. Washington: American Enterprise Institute, 1985.

Diamond, Edwin, and Stephen Bates. *The Spot*. Cambridge, MA: MIT Press, 1988.

Diamond, Edwin, and Adrian Marin. "Spots." *American Behavioral Scientist* (1989): 382–388.

Dickenson, James R., and David S. Broder. "Poll Results Indicate Democrat Did Best: Republicans Say 'Knockout' Bid Failed." *The Washington Post*, 9 October 1984: A12.

Donahue, Thomas R. "Impact of Viewer Predispositions on Political TV Commercials." *Journal of Broadcasting* (1973): 3–14.

Drew, Elizabeth. *Election Journal: Political Events of 1987–1988*. New York: William Morrow, 1989.

Dryer, Edward C. "Media Use and Electoral Choices: Some Political Consequences of Information Exposure." *Public Opinion Quarterly* (1971): 244–253.

Dubois, Philip L. "Election Night Projections and Voter Turnout in the West." *American Politics Quarterly* (1983): 349–363.

Efron, Edith. *The News Twisters*. Los Angeles: Nash Publishing, 1971.

Elliot, William R., and Cynthia P. Quattlebaum. "Similarities in Patterns of Media Use: A Cluster Analysis of Media Gratifications." *Western Journal of Speech Communication* (1979): 61–72.

Epstein, Laurily K., and Gerald Strom. "Election Night Projections and West Coast Turnout." *American Politics Quarterly* (1981): 470–492.

Escarpit, Robert. "The Concept of 'Mass,' " *Journal of Communication* (1977): 44–47.

Fleitas, Daniel W. "Bandwagon and Underdog Effects in Minimal Information Elections." *American Political Science Review* (1971): 434–438.

Frandsen, Kenneth D. "Effects of Threat Appeals and Media of Transmission." *Speech Monographs* (1963): 101–104.

Frank, Robert. *Message Dimensions of Television News*. Lexington, MA: Lexington Books, 1973.

Friedson, Elliot. "Communications Research and the Concept of the Mass." In *The Process and Effects of Mass Communication*, eds. Wilbur Schramm and Donald F. Roberts, 197–208. Urbana, IL: University of Illinois Press, 1974.

Gallup, George. *A Guide to Public Opinion Polls*. Princeton, NJ: Gallup, 1948.

Garramone, Gina M. "Audience Motivation Effects: More Evidence." *Communication Research* (1984): 79–96.

Garramone, Gina M. "Motivation and Political Information-Processing: Extending the Gratifications Approach." In *Mass Media and Political Thought: An Information-Processing Approach*, eds. Sidney Kraus and Richard M. Perloff, 201–219. Beverly Hills, CA: Sage Publications, 1985a.

Garramone, Gina M. "Effects of Negative Political Advertising: The Role of Sponsor and Rebuttal." *Journal of Broadcasting and Electronic Media* (1985b): 147–159.

Garramone, Gina M. "Candidate Image Formation: The Role of Information Processing." In *New Perspectives on Political Advertising*, eds. Lynda Lee Kaid, Dan Nimmo, and Keith R. Sanders, 235–247. Carbondale, IL: Southern Illinois University Press, 1986.

Gaziano, Cecilie, and Kristin McGrath. "Newspaper Credibility and Relationships of Newspaper Journalists to Communities." *Journalism Quarterly* (1987): 317–328.

Gerbner, George, Larry Gross, Michael Morgan, and Nancy Signorielli. "Political Correlates of Television Viewing." *Public Opinion Quarterly* (1984): 283–300.

Germond, Jack. "The Impact of Polling on Journalism." In *Polling on the Issues*, ed. Albert H. Cantril, 20–27. Cabin John, MD: Seven Locks Press, 1980.

Germond, Jack, and Jules Witcover. *Wake Us When It's Over*. New York: Macmillan, 1985.

Germond, Jack, and Jules Witcover. *Whose Broad Stripes and Bright Stars: The Trivial Pursuit of the Presidency 1988*. New York: Warner Books, 1989.

Glass, David P. "Evaluating Presidential Candidates: Who Focuses on Their Personal Attributes?" *Public Opinion Quarterly* (1988): 517–534.

Goldenberg, Edie N., and Michael W. Traugott. *Campaigning for Congress.* Washington: Congressional Quarterly Press, 1984.

Goldman, Eric F. "Poll on the Polls." *Public Opinion Quarterly* (1944–45): 461–467.

Goldman, Peter, Tom Mathews, and the *Newsweek* Special Election Team. *The Quest for the Presidency: The 1988 Campaign.* New York: Simon and Schuster, 1989.

Gollin, Albert E. "Exploring the Liaison between Polling and the Press." *Public Opinion Quarterly* (1980): 445–461.

Gollin, Albert E. "Polling and the News Media." *Public Opinion Quarterly* (1987): S86–S94.

Graber, Doris. *Mass Media and American Politics.* Washington: Congressional Quarterly Press, 1980.

Graber, Doris. *Processing the News: How People Tame the Information Tide.* New York: Longman, 1984.

Graber, Doris. "Mass Media and Political Images in Elections." In *Research in Micropolitics.* Volume 1. *Voting Behavior*, ed. Samuel Long, 127–159. Greenwich, CT: JAI Press, 1986a.

Graber, Doris. "Media Images and Status Quo Enforcement—Summing up the Evidence." Paper presented at the Annual Meeting of the American Political Science Association, Washington, 1986b.

Graber, Doris, "Creating Candidate Imagery, Part II: An Audio-Visual Analysis." *Campaigns and Elections* (1986c): 14–21.

Graber, Doris. "Framing Election News Broadcasts: News Context and Its Impact on the 1984 Presidential Election." *Social Science Quarterly* (1987a): 552–568.

Graber, Doris. "Kind Pictures and Harsh Words: How Television Presents the Candidates." In *Elections in America*, ed. Kay Lehman Schlozman, 115–141. Boston: Allen and Unwin, 1987b.

Graber, Doris, and Young Yun Kim. "Why John Q Voter Did Not Learn Much from the 1976 Presidential Debates." In *Communication Yearbook 2*, ed. Brent D. Rubin, 407–421. New Brunswick, NJ: Transaction Books, 1978.

Gronbeck, Bruce E. "Mythic Portraiture in the 1988 Iowa Presidential Caucus Bio-Ads." *American Behavioral Scientist* (1989): 351–364.

Hanushek, Eric A., and John E. Jackson. *Statistical Methods for Social Scientists.* New York: Academic Press, 1977.

Henry, William A., III. "News as Entertainment: The Search for Dramatic Unity." In *What's News: The Media in American Society*, ed. Elie Abel, 133–158. San Francisco: Institute for Contemporary Studies, 1981.

Hewes, Dean E., and Sally Planalp. "The Individual's Place in Communication Science." In *Handbook of Communication Science*, eds. Charles R. Berger and Steven H. Chaffee, 146–183. Newbury Park, CA: Sage Publications, 1987.

Hill, David B. "Qualitative Dimensions of Exposure to Political Television." *Social Science Quarterly* (1983): 614–623.

Hoffman, David, and Milton Coleman. "Debaters Clash on Economy." *The Washington Post*, 8 October 1984: A1, A14.

Hofstetter, C. Richard. *Bias in the News.* Columbus: Ohio State University Press, 1976.

Hofstetter, C. Richard, and Terry F. Buss. "Bias in Television News Coverage of Political Events: A Methodological Analysis." *Journal of Broadcasting* (1978): 517–530.

Hofstetter, C. Richard, and Terry F. Buss. "Politics and Last-Minute Political Television." *Journalism Quarterly* (1980): 24–37.

Hofstetter, C. Richard, and Paul J. Strand. "Mass Media and Political Issue Perceptions." *Journal of Broadcasting* (1983): 345–358.

Hofstetter, C. Richard, Cliff Zukin, and Terry F. Buss. "Political Imagery and Information in an Age of Television: The 1972 Campaign." Paper presented to the annual meeting of the American Political Science Association, Washington, D.C., 1976.

Hofstetter, C. Richard, Cliff Zukin, and Terry F. Buss. "Political Imagery and Information in an Age of Television." *Journalism Quarterly* (1978): 562–569.

Humke, Ronald, Raymond L. Schmitt, and Stanley E. Grupp. "Candidates, Issues, and Party in Newspaper Political Advertisements." *Journalism Quarterly* (1975): 499–504.

Iyengar, Shanto. "Television News and Citizens' Explanations of National Affairs." *American Political Science Review* (1987): 815–831.

Iyengar, Shanto, and Donald R. Kinder. *News That Matters: Television and American Opinion*. Chicago: University of Chicago Press, 1987.

Iyengar, Shanto, Mark D. Peters, and Donald R. Kinder. "Experimental Demonstrations of the 'Not-So-Minimal' Consequences of Television News Programs." *American Political Science Review* (1982): 848–858.

Jackson, John. "Election Reporting and Voter Turnout." *American Journal of Political Science* (1983): 615–635.

Jackson-Beeck, Marilyn, and Robert G. Meadow. "The Triple Agenda of Presidential Debates." *Public Opinion Quarterly* (1979): 173–180.

Jamieson, Kathleen Hall. *Packaging the Presidency*. New York: Oxford University Press, 1984.

Jamieson, Kathleen Hall. "Context and the Creation of Meaning in the Advertising of the 1988 Presidential Campaign." *American Behavioral Scientist* (1989): 415–424.

Jamieson, Kathleen Hall, and David S. Birdsell. *Presidential Debates: The Challenge of Creating an Informed Electorate*. New York: Oxford University Press, 1988.

Joslyn, Richard A. "The Content of Political Spot Ads." *Journalism Quarterly* (1980a): 92–98.

Joslyn, Richard A. "Manifestations of Elazar's Political Subcultures: State Public Opinion and the Content of Political Advertising." *Publius* (1980b): 37–58.

Joslyn, Richard A. "The Impact of Campaign Spot Advertising on Voting Defections." *Human Communication Research* (1981): 347–360.

Joslyn, Richard A. *Mass Media and Elections*. Reading, MA: Addison-Wesley Publishing, 1984.

Joslyn, Richard A. "Television Spot Ads and the Origins of Candidate Appeals." Paper presented to the annual meeting of the American Political Science Association, New Orleans, LA, 1985.

Joslyn, Richard A. "Political Advertising and the Meaning of Elections." In *New Perspectives on Political Advertising*, eds. Lynda Lee Kaid, Dan Nimmo, and Keith R. Sanders, 139–183. Carbondale, IL: Southern Illinois University Press, 1986.

Kaid, Lynda Lee. "Measures of Political Advertising." *Journal of Advertising Research* (1976): 49–53.

Kaid, Lynda Lee. "Political Advertising." In *Handbook of Political Communication*, ed.

Dan D. Nimmo and Keith R. Sanders, 249–267. Beverly Hills, CA: Sage Publications, 1981.

Kaid, Lynda Lee, and John Boydston. "An Experimental Study of the Effectiveness of Negative Political Advertisements." *Communication Quarterly* (1987): 193–201.

Kaid, Lynda Lee, and Dorothy K. Davidson. "Elements of Videostyle: Candidate Presentation through Television Advertising." In *New Perspectives on Political Advertising*, eds. Lynda Lee Kaid, Dan Nimmo, and Keith R. Sanders, 184–209. Carbondale, IL: Southern Illinois University Press, 1986.

Kaid, Lynda Lee, and Keith R. Sanders, "Political Television Commercials: An Experimental Study of Type and Length." *Communication Research* (1978): 57–69.

Kastor, Elisabeth. "The Great Face-Off." *The Washington Post*, 11 October 1984: B1.

Katz, Elihu, and Paul F. Lazarsfeld. *Personal Influence*. New York: Free Press, 1955.

Katz, Elihu, Jay G. Blumler, and Michael Gurevitch. "Utilization of Mass Communication by the Individual." In *The Uses of Mass Communication*, eds. Jay G. Blumler and Elihu Katz, 19–32. Beverly Hills, CA: Sage Publications, 1974.

Katz, Elihu, Michael Gurevitch, and Hadasah Haas. "On the Use of Mass Media for Important Things." *American Sociological Review* (1973): 164–181.

Kebbel, Gary. "The Importance of Political Activity in Explaining Multiple News Media Use." *Journalism Quarterly* (1985): 559–566.

Keely, Joseph. *The Left-Leaning Antenna: Political Bias in Television*. New Rochelle, NY: Arlington House, 1971.

Keenan, Kevin. "Polls in Network Newscasts in 1984 Presidential Race." *Journalism Quarterly* (1986): 616–618.

Kennamer, J. David. "How Media Use During Campaigns Affects the Intent to Vote." *Journalism Quarterly* (1987): 291–300.

Kessel, John H. *Presidential Campaign Politics*. Homewood, IL: Dorsey Press, 1984.

Key, V. O., and Frank Munger. "Social Determinism and Electoral Decision: The Case of Indiana." In *American Voting Behavior*, eds. Eugene Burdick and Arthur J. Brodbeck, 281–299. Glencoe, IL: Free Press, 1959.

Kippax, Susan, and John P. Murray. "Using the Mass Media: Need Gratification and Perceived Utility." *Communication Research* (1980): 335–360.

Klapper, Joseph T. *The Effects of Mass Communication*. Glencoe, IL: Free Press, 1960.

Kohut, Andrew. "Rating the Polls: The Views of Media Elites and the General Public." *Public Opinion Quarterly* (1986): 1–10.

Ladd, Everett Carll. "Polling and the Press: The Clash of Institutional Imperatives." *Public Opinion Quarterly* (1980): 574–584.

Ladd, Everett Carll, Jr., and Charles D. Hadley. *Transformations of the American Party System*. New York: W. W. Norton, 1975.

Lang, Gladys Engel, and Kurt Lang. "The First Debate and the Coverage Gap." *Journal of Communication* (1978a): 93–98.

Lang, Gladys Engel, and Kurt Lang. "Immediate and Delayed Responses to a Carter-Ford Debate: Assessing Public Opinion." *Public Opinion Quarterly* (1978b): 322–341.

Lang, Kurt, and Gladys Engel Lang. "The Mass Media and Voting." In *American Voting Behavior*, eds. Eugene Burdick and Arthur S. Brodbeck, 217–235. Glencoe, IL: Free Press, 1959.

Lang, Kurt, and Gladys Engel Lang. *Voting and Nonvoting: Implications of Broadcasting Returns before the Polls Are Closed*. Waltham, MA: Blaisdell, 1968.

Laponce, J. A. "An Experimental Method to Measure the Tendency to Equibalance in a Political System." *American Political Science Review* (1966): 982–993.

Lasswell, Harold D. "The Structure and Function of Communication in Society." In *The Communication of Ideas*, ed. Lyman Bryson, 37–52. New York: Institute for Religious and Social Studies, 1948.

Lazarsfeld, Paul F. *Radio and the Printed Page*. New York: Duell, Sloan, and Pearce, 1940.

Lazarsfeld, Paul F., Bernard Berelson, and Hazel Gaudet. *The People's Choice*. New York: Columbia University Press, 1944.

Leubsdorf, Carl P. "The Reporter and the Presidential Candidate." *The Annals of the American Academy of Political and Social Sciences: The Role of the Mass Media in American Politics* 427 (1976): 1–11.

Levy, Mark R. "The Audience Experience with Television News." *Journalism Monographs*, no. 55 (1978a): 1–29.

Levy, Mark R. "Opinion Leadership and Television News Use." *Public Opinion Quarterly* (1978b): 402–406.

Levy, Mark R. "Conceptualizing and Measuring Aspects of Audience 'Activity.' " *Journalism Quarterly* (1983): 109–115.

Levy, Mark R., and Sven Windahl. "Audience Activity and Gratifications: A Conceptual Clarification and Exploration." *Communication Research* (1984): 51–78.

Levy, Mark R., and Sven Windahl. "The Concept of Audience Activity." In *Media Gratifications Research: Current Perspectives*, eds. Karl Erik Rosergren, Lawrence A. Wenner, and Philip Palmgreen, 109–122. Beverly Hills, CA: Sage Publications, 1985.

Lichtenstein, Allen. "Differences in Impact between Local and National Televised Political Candidates' Debates." *Western Journal of Speech Communication* (1982): 291–298.

Lichty, Lawrence W. "Video versus Print." *Wilson Quarterly* (1982): 49–57.

Lometti, Guy E., Byron Reeves, and Carl R. Bybee. "Investigating the Assumptions of Uses and Gratifications Research." *Communication Research* (1977): 321–337.

Lowery, Sharon A., and Melvin L. DeFleur. *Milestones in Mass Communication Research: Media Effects*. New York: Longman, 1988.

Lucas, William, and William C. Adams, "Talking, Television, and Voter Indecision." *Journal of Communication* (1978): 120–131.

Macaluso, Theodore. "Political Information, Party Identification, and Voting Defection." *Public Opinion Quarterly* (1977): 255–260.

Mansfield, Michael W., and Katherine Hale. "Uses and Perceptions of Political Television: An Application of Q-Technique." In *New Perspectives on Political Advertising*, eds. Lynda Lee Kaid, Dan Nimmo, and Keith R. Sanders, 268–292. Carbondale, IL: Southern Illinois University Press, 1986.

Marsh, Catherine. "Back on the Bandwagon: The Effect of Opinion Polls on Public Opinion." *British Journal of Political Science* (1985): 51–74.

Marshall, Thomas R. "Evaluating Presidential Nominees: Opinion Polls, Issues, and Personalities." *Western Political Quarterly* (1983): 650–659.

Martel, Myles. *Political Campaign Debates*. New York: Longman, 1983.

McClure, Robert D., and Thomas E. Patterson. "Television News and Political Advertising: The Impact of Exposure on Voter Beliefs." *Communication Research* (1974): 3–32.

McClure, Robert D., and Thomas E. Patterson. "Print vs. Network News." *Journal of Communication* (1976): 23–38.

McCombs, Maxwell E., and Lee B. Becker. *Using Mass Communication Theory.* Englewood Cliffs, NJ: Prentice-Hall, 1979.

McCombs, Maxwell E., and Paula Poindexter. "The Duty to Keep Informed: News Exposure and Civic Obligation." *Journal of Communication* (1983): 88–96.

McCombs, Maxwell E., and Donald Shaw. "The Agenda Setting Function of the Mass Media." *Public Opinion Quarterly* (1972): 176–187.

McDonald, Daniel G. "Investigating the Assumptions of Media Dependency Research." *Communication Research* (1983): 509–528.

McDonald, Daniel G., and Stephen D. Reese. "Television News and Audience Selectivity." *Journalism Quarterly* (1987): 763–768.

McLeod, Jack M., and Lee B. Becker. "The Uses and Gratifications Approach." In *Handbook of Political Communication*, eds. Dan D. Nimmo and Keith R. Sanders, 67–100. Beverly Hills, CA: Sage Publications, 1981.

McLeod, Jack M., and Jay G. Blumler. "The Macro-social Level of Communication Science. In *Handbook of Communication Science*, eds. Charles R. Berger and Steven H. Chaffee, 271–324. Newbury Park, CA: Sage Publications, 1987.

McLeod, Jack M., and Daniel G. McDonald. "Beyond Simple Exposure: Media Orientations and Their Impact on Political Processes." *Communication Research* (1985): 3–33.

McLeod, Jack M., and Byron Reeves. "On the Nature of Mass Media Effects." In *Television and Social Behavior: Beyond Violence and Children*, eds. Stephen B. Withey and Ronald Abeles, 17–54. Hillsdale, NJ: Lawrence Erlbaum Associates, 1980.

McLeod, Jack M., Carl R. Bybee, and Jean A. Durall. "Equivalence of Informed Political Participation." *Communication Research* (1979): 463–487.

McLeod, Jack M., Carroll J. Glynn, and Daniel G. McDonald. "Issues and Images: The Influence of Media Reliance in Voting Decisions." *Communication Research* (1983): 37–58.

McQuail, Denis, and Sven Windahl. *Communication Models for the Study of Mass Communications.* New York: Longman, 1981.

McQuail, Denis, Jay G. Blumler, and J. R. Brown. "The Television Audience: A Revised Perspective." In *Sociology of Mass Communications*, ed. Denis McQuail, 135–165. Baltimore, MD: Penguin Press, 1972.

Meadow, Robert G. "Televised Campaign Debates as Whistle-Stop Speeches." In *Television Coverage of the 1980 Presidential Campaign*, ed. William C. Adams, 89–101. Norwood, NJ: Ablex Publishing, 1983.

Meadow, Robert G., and Lee Sigelman. "Some Effects and Noneffects of Campaign Commercials: An Experimental Study." *Political Behavior* (1982): 163–175.

Mendelson, Harold. "Election Day Broadcasts and Terminal Voting Decisions." *Public Opinion Quarterly* (1966): 212–225.

Mendelson, Harold, and Garrett J. O'Keefe. *The People Choose a President.* New York: Praeger, 1976.

Merrill, John C., and Ralph L. Lowenstein. *Media Messages and Men*. New York: David McKay, 1971.

Meyer, Timothy P., and Thomas R. Donahue. "Perceptions and Misperceptions of Political Advertising." *Journal of Business Communication* (1973): 29–40.

Mickelson, Sig. *The Electric Mirror*. New York: Dodd, Mead, 1972.

Milavsky, J. Ronald. "Early Calls of Election Results and Exit Polls: Pros, Cons, and Constitutional Consideration." *Public Opinion Quarterly* (1985): 1–2.

Miller, Arthur H., and Michael MacKuen. "Learning about the Candidates: The 1976 Presidential Debates." *Public Opinion Quarterly* (1979): 326–346.

Miller, Arthur H., and Michael MacKuen. "Informing the Electorate: A National Study." In *The Great Debates*, ed. Sidney Kraus, 269–297. Bloomington, IN: Indiana University Press, 1980.

Miller, M. Mark, Michael W. Singletary, and Shu-Ling Chen. "The Roper Question and Television vs. Newspapers as Sources of News." *Journalism Quarterly* (1988): 12–19.

Morganthau, Tom. "The Veepstakes: Bush Prepares to Debate Ferraro—Gently." *Newsweek*, 15 October 1984: 41–42.

Morrison, Donald, ed. *The Winning of the White House 1988*. New York: Time, Inc., 1988.

Morrow, Lance. "Of Myth and Memory: Dreaming of 1960 in the New World." *Time* 24 October 1988: 21–27.

Newton, James S., Roger D. Masters, Gregory J. McHugo, and Denis G. Sullivan. "Making up Our Minds: Effects of Network Coverage on Viewer Impressions of Leaders."*Polity* (1987): 226–246.

Nimmo, Dan D. *The Political Persuaders: The Techniques of Modern Election Campaigns*. Englewood Cliffs, NJ: Prentice-Hall, 1970.

Nimmo, Dan. "Episodes, Incidents, and Eruptions." *American Behavioral Scientist* (1989): 464–478.

Nimmo, Dan D., and Robert L. Savage. *Candidates and Their Images: Concepts, Methods and Findings*. Pacific Palisades, CA: Goodyear Publishing Company, 1976.

O'Keefe, Garrett J. "Political Campaigns and Mass Communications Research." In *Political Communication: Issues and Strategies for Research*, ed. Steven E. Chaffee, 129–158. Beverly Hills, CA: Sage Publications, 1975.

O'Keefe, Garrett J. "Political Malaise and Reliance on Media." *Journalism Quarterly* (1980): 122–128.

O'Keefe, Garrett J., and L. Erwin Atwood. "Communication and Election Campaigns." In *Handbook of Political Communication*, eds. Dan D. Nimmo and Keith R. Sanders, 329–358. Beverly Hills, CA: Sage Publications, 1981.

O'Keefe, Garrett J., and Kenneth G. Sheinkopf, "The Voter Decides: Candidate Image or Campaign Issue." *Journal of Broadcasting* (1974): 403–412.

Owen, Diana. "The Effect of Public Opinion Polls on Candidate Preference in Presidential Elections: An Experimental Study" (unpublished), Rutgers University, New Brunswick, NJ, 1983.

Palmgreen, Philip, Lawrence A. Wenner, and J. D. Rayburn II. "Gratification Discrepancies and News Program Choice." *Communication Research* (1981): 451–478.

Palmgreen, Philip, Lawrence A. Wenner, and Karl Erik Rosengren, "Uses and Gratifications Research: The Past Ten Years." In *Media Gratifications Research: Current Perspectives*, eds. Karl Erik Rosengren, Lawrence A. Wenner, and Philip Palmgreen, 11–37. Beverly Hills, CA: Sage Publications, 1985.

Papert, Frederic. "Good Candidates Make Advertising Experts." In *The Political Image Merchants*, ed. Ray E. Hiebert, 96–99. Washington: Acropolis Books, 1975.

Patterson, Thomas E. *The Mass Media Election*. New York: Praeger Publishers, 1980.

Patterson, Thomas E. "Television and Election Strategy." In *The Communications Revolution in Politics*, ed. Gerald Benjamin, 24–35. New York: Academy of Political Science, 1982.

Patterson, Thomas E., and Richard E. Davis. "The Media Campaign: Struggle for the Agenda." In *The Elections of 1984*, ed. Michael Nelson, 111–127. Washington: Congressional Quarterly Press, 1985.

Patterson, Thomas E., and Robert D. McClure. "Political Advertising on Television: Spot Commercials in the 1972 Presidential Election." *Maxwell Review* (1973): 57–69.

Patterson, Thomas E., and Robert D. McClure. *Political Advertising: Voter Reaction to Televised Political Commercials*. Princeton, NJ: Citizens Research Foundation, 1974.

Patterson, Thomas E., and Robert D. McClure. *The Unseeing Eye: The Myth of Television Power in National Elections*. New York: G. P. Putnam's Sons, 1976.

Payne, J. Gregory, John Marlier, and Robert A. Baukus. "Polispots in the 1988 Presidential Primaries." *American Behavioral Scientist* (1989): 365–381.

Payne, J. Gregory, James L. Golden, John Marlier, and Scott C. Ratzan. "Perceptions of the 1988 Presidential and Vice-Presidential Debates." *American Behavioral Scientist* (1989): 425–435.

Perloff, Richard M. "Personal Relevance and Campaign Information Seeking: A Cognitive Response-Based Approach." In *Mass Media and Political Thought: An Information-Processing Approach*, eds. Sidney Kraus and Richard M. Peroff, 177–200. Beverly Hills, CA: Sage Publications, 1985.

Polsby, Nelson W. *Consequences of Party Reform*. New York: Oxford University Press, 1983.

Pomper, Gerald M. *The Voters' Choice*. New York: Harper & Row, 1975.

Pool, Ithiel de Sola, and Barry Sussman. "Comments and Observations." In *Polling on the Issues*, ed. Albert H. Cantril, 46–51. Cabin John, MD: Seven Locks Press, 1980.

Ranney, Austin. *Channels of Power*. New York: Basic Books, 1983.

Ratzan, Scott C. "The Real Agenda Setters." *American Behavioral Scientist* (1989): 451–463.

Rayburn, J. D., II, and Philip Palmgreen. "Merging Uses and Gratifications and Expectancy-Value Theory." *Communication Research* (1984): 537–562.

Reese, Stephen D., and Mark M. Miller. "Political Attitude Holding and Structure: The Effects of Newspaper and Television News." *Communication Research* (1981): 167–187.

Rimmer, Tony, and David Weaver. "Different Questions, Different Answers? Media Use and Media Credibility." *Journalism Quarterly* (1987): 28–36, 44.

Rippey, John N. "The Use of Polls as a Reporting Tool." *Journalism Quarterly* (1980): 642–646.

Roberts, Donald R., and Christine M. Bachen. "Mass Communication Effects." *Annual Review of Psychology* (1981): 307–356.

Robinson, John P. "The Polls." In *The Great Debates*, ed. Sidney Kraus, 262–268. Bloomington, IN: Indiana University Press, 1980.

Robinson, John P., and Leo W. Jeffres. "The Changing Role of Newspapers in the Age of Television." *Journalism Monographs*, no. 63 (1979): 1–31.

Robinson, Michael J. "Public Affairs Television and the Growth of Political Malaise: The Case of 'The Selling of the Pentagon.' " *American Political Science Review* (1976): 409–432.

Robinson, Michael J. "A Statesman Is a Dead Politician: Candidate Images on Network News." In *What's News: The Media in American Society*, ed. Elie Abel, 159–186. San Francisco: Institute for Contemporary Studies, 1981.

Robinson, Michael J. "The Media in Campaign '84, Part II: Wingless, Toothless, and Hopeless." In *The Mass Media in Campaign '84*, eds. Michael J. Robinson and Austin Ranney, 34–39. Washington: American Enterprise Institute, 1985.

Robinson, Michael J. "News Media Myths and Realities: What Network News Did and Didn't Do in the 1984 General Campaign." In *Elections in America*, ed. Kay Lehman Schlozman, 143–170. Boston: Allen and Unwin, 1987.

Robinson, Michael J., and Margaret A. Sheehan. *Over the Wire and on TV*. New York: Russell Sage Foundation, 1983.

Roddy, Brian L., and Gina M. Garramone. "Appeals and Strategies of Negative Political Advertising." *Journal of Broadcasting and Electronic Media* (1988): 415–427.

Roll, Charles W., and Albert H. Cantril. *Polls: Their Use and Misuse in Politics*. Cabin John, MD: Seven Locks Press, 1980.

Roper, Burns W. "The Impact of Journalism on Polling." In *Polling on the Issues*, ed. Albert H. Cantrill, 15–19. Cabin John, MD: Seven Locks Press, 1980.

Roper, Burns W. "Early Election Calls: The Larger Dangers." *Public Opinion Quarterly* (1985): 5–9.

Roper, Burns W. "Evaluating Polls with Poll Data." *Public Opinion Quarterly* (1986): 10–16.

Rosenberg, Shawn W., Lisa Bohan, Patrick McCafferty, and Kevin Harris. "The Image and the Vote: The Effect of Candidate Presentation on Voter Preference." *American Journal of Political Science* (1986): 108–127.

Rosenberg, William L., and William R. Elliot. "Effect of Debate Exposure on Evaluation of 1984 Vice-Presidential Candidates." *Journalism Quarterly* (1987): 55–64, 262.

Rosengren, Karl Erik, and Sven Windahl. "Mass Media Consumption as a Functional Alternative." In *Sociology of Mass Communications*, ed. Denis McQuail, 166–194. Baltimore: Penguin Books, 1972.

Ross, Marc Howard, and Richard Joslyn. "Election Night News Coverage as Political Ritual." *Polity* (1988): 301–319.

Rothschild, Michael L., and Michael L. Ray. "Involvement and Political Advertising Effects: An Exploratory Experiment." *Communication Research* (1974): 264–283.

Rouner, Donna, and Richard M. Perloff. "Selective Perception of Outcome of First 1984 Presidential Debate." *Journalism Quarterly* (1988): 141–147, 240.

Rubin, Alan M. "Uses and Gratifications and Media Effects Research." In *Perspectives on Media Effects*, eds. Jennings Bryant and Dolf Zillman, 281–302. Hillsdale, NJ: Lawrence Erlbaum Associates, 1986.

Rubin, Richard L. *Press, Party, and Presidency.* New York: W. W. Norton, 1981.

Runkel, David R. *Campaign for President: The Managers Look at '88.* Dover, MA: Auburn House Publishing, 1989.

Ruotolo, A. Carlos. "A Typology of Newspaper Readers." *Journalism Quarterly* (1988): 126–130.

Sabato, Larry J. *The Rise of Political Consultants.* New York: Basic Books, 1981.

Sabato, Larry J. "TV Politics: The Influence of Television in Political Campaigns." *Vital Issues* 19 (1982): 1–6.

Salant, Richard. "Projections and Exit Polls." *Public Opinion Quarterly* (1985): 9–15.

Salwen, Michael B. "The Reporting of Public Opinion Polls during Presidential Years, 1968–1984." *Journalism Quarterly* (1985a): 272–277.

Salwen, Michael B. "Does Poll Coverage Improve as Presidential Vote Nears?" *Journalism Quarterly* (1985b): 887–891.

Salwen, Michael B. "Credibility of Newspaper Opinion Polls: Source Intent and Precision." *Journalism Quarterly* (1987): 818–819.

Sanoff, Alvin P. "Behind All Those Jumpy Political Polls." *U.S. News and World Report,* 17 September 1984: 33.

Schram, Martin. "Channeling the Message: Candidates' Words Compete with the Trappings." *The Washington Post,* 9 Sept. 1984: A8–A9.

Schram, Martin. "Group of Viewers Shifts Opinions but Not Its Votes." *The Washington Post,* 9 October 1984: A1.

Schram, Martin. *The Great American Video Game: Presidential Politics in the Television Age.* New York: William Morrow, 1987.

Schramm, Wilbur. "Channels and Audiences." In *Handbook of Communication,* eds. Ithiel de Sola Pool, Frederick W. Frey, Wilbur Schramm, Nathan Maccoby, and Edwin B. Parker, 116–140. Chicago: Rand McNally College Publishing, 1973.

Schramm, Wilbur. "The Nature of Mass Communication between Humans." In *The Process and Effects of Mass Communications,* eds. Wilbur Schramm and Donald R. Roberts, 3–53. Chicago: University of Illinois Press, 1974.

Sears, David O., and Steven H. Chaffee. "Uses and Effects of the 1976 Debates: An Overview of Empirical Studies." In *The Great Debates,* ed. Sidney Kraus, 223–261. Bloomington, IN: Indiana University Press, 1979.

Sears, David O., and Jonathan L. Freedman. "Selective Exposure to Information: A Critical Review." In *The Process and Effects of Mass Communication,* eds. Wilbur Schramm and Donald R. Roberts, 209–234. Urbana, IL: University of Illinois Press, 1974.

Seymour-Ure, Colin. *The Political Impact of Mass Media.* Beverly Hills, CA: Sage Publications, 1974.

Shapiro, Walter. "Reagan Wins a Draw." *Newsweek,* 29 October 1984: 26–28.

Shapiro, Walter. "Bush Scores a Warm Win." *Time,* 24 October 1988: 18–20.

Shyles, Leonard. "Defining the Issues of the Presidential Election from Televised Political Spot Advertisements." *Journal of Broadcasting* (1983): 333–343.

Shyles, Leonard. "The Televised Political Spot Advertisement: Its Structure, Content, and Role in the Political System." In *New Perspectives on Political Advertising,* eds. Lynda Lee Kaid, Dan Nimmo, and Keith R. Sanders, 107–138. Carbondale, IL: Southern Illinois University Press, 1986.

Shyles, Leonard. "Profiling Candidate Images in Televised Spot Advertisements for

1984: Roles and Realities of Presidential Jousters at the Height of the Reagan Era." *Political Communication and Persuasion* (1988): 15–31.

Sigelman, Lee, and Carol K. Sigelman. "Judgments of the Carter-Reagan Debate: The Eyes of the Beholders." *Public Opinion Quarterly* (1984): 624–628.

Spero, Robert. *The Duping of the American Voter.* New York: Lippincott and Crowell, 1980.

Squire, Peverill. "Why the 1936 Literary Digest Poll Failed." *Public Opinion Quarterly* (1988): 125–133.

Stengel, Richard. "The Likability Sweepstakes." *Time*, 24 October 1988: 20.

Stewart, Charles J. "Voter Perception of Mudslinging in Political Communication." *Central States Speech Journal* (1975): 279–286.

Stovall, James Glenn. "Foreign Policy Issue Coverage in the 1980 Presidential Campaign." *Journalism Quarterly* (1982): 531–540.

Stovall, James Glenn. "Coverage of the 1984 Presidential Campaign." *Journalism Quarterly* (1988): 443–449, 484.

Stovall, James Glenn, and Jacqueline H. Solomon. "The Poll as a News Event in the 1980 Presidential Campaign." *Public Opinion Quarterly* (1984): 615–623.

Sudman, Seymour. "The Network Polls: A Critical Review." *Public Opinion Quarterly* (1983): 490–496.

Sudman, Seymour. "Do Exit Polls Influence Voting Behavior?" *Public Opinion Quarterly* (1986): 331–339.

Surlin, Stuart H., and Thomas F. Gordon. "How Values Affect Attitudes toward Direct Reference Political Advertising." *Journalism Quarterly* (1977): 89–98.

Swanson, David L. "Gratification Seeking, Media Exposure, and Audience Interpretations: Some Directions for Research." *Journal of Broadcasting and Electronic Media* (1987): 237–254.

Swanson, David L., and Austin S. Babrow. "Uses and Gratifications: The Influence of Gratification-Seeking and Expectancy-Value Judgments on the Viewing of Television News." In *Rethinking Communication.* Volume 2 *Paradigm Exemplars*, eds. Brenda Dervin, Lawrence Grossberg, Barbara J. O'Keefe, and Ellen Wartella, 361–375. Newbury Park, CA: Sage Publications, 1989.

Swanson, Linda L., and David L. Swanson. "The Agenda-Setting Function of the First Ford-Carter Debate." *Communication Monographs*, no. 45 (1978): 347–353.

Swift, Al. "The Congressional Concern about Early Calls." *Public Opinion Quarterly* (1985): 2–5.

Tarrance, V. Lance. *Negative Campaigns and Negative Votes.* Washington: Free Congress Research and Education Foundation, 1982.

Taylor, Paul, and Milton Coleman. "Mondale's Polls Show Reagan's Lead Widening." *The Washington Post.* 2 October 1984: A3.

Todd, Rusty, and Richard A. Brody. "Mass Media and Stability of Party Identification: Are There Floating Partisans." *Communication Research* (1980): 361–376.

Trebbe, Ann L., and Charlotte Sutton. "Keeping Score, Party by Party." *The Washington Post*, 8 October 1984: D1, D4.

Trent, Judith S., and Robert V. Friedenberg. "Debates in Political Campaigns." In *Political Campaign Communication: Principles and Practices*, eds. Judith S. Trent and Robert V. Friedenberg, 233–279. New York: Praeger, 1983.

Vancil, David L., and Sue D. Pendell. "Winning Presidential Debates: An Analysis of

Criteria Influencing Audience Response." *Western Journal of Speech Communication* (1984): 62–74.

Walker, James R. "How Media Reliance Affects Political Efficacy in the South." *Journalism Quarterly* (1988): 746–750.

Wall, Victor, James L. Golden, and Herbert James. "Perceptions of the 1984 Presidential Debates and a Select 1988 Presidential Primary Debate." *Presidential Studies Quarterly* (1988): 541–563.

Wanat, John. "Political Broadcast Advertising and Primary Election Voting." *Journal of Broadcasting* (1974): 413–422.

Wattenberg, Ben J., and Everett Ladd. "Moving Right Along? Campaign '84's Lessons for 1988: An Interview with Peter Hart and Richard Wirthlin." *Public Opinion* (1985): 8–11, 59–63.

Weaver, David H. "Audience Need for Orientation and Media Effects." *Communication Research* (1980): 361–376.

Weaver, David H., and Maxwell E. McCombs. "Journalism and Social Science: A New Relationship." *Public Opinion Quarterly* (1980): 455.

Weaver, David H., Doris A. Graber, Maxwell E. McCombs, and Chaim E. Eyal. *Media Agenda-Setting in a Presidential Election: Issues, Images, and Interest.* New York: Praeger Publishers, 1981.

Weaver, Paul H. "Is Television News Biased?" *Public Interest* (1972): 57–67.

Weitzner, Jay. "Handling the Candidate on Television." In *The Political Image Merchants*, ed. Ray E. Hiebert, 100–107. Washington: Acropolis Books, 1975.

Wenner, Lawrence A. "Political News on Television: A Reconsideration of Audience Orientations." *Western Journal of Speech Communication* (1983): 380–395.

West, Darrell M. "Press Coverage in the 1980 Presidential Campaign." *Social Science Quarterly* (1983): 624–633.

Williams, Raymond. *Television: Technology and Cultural Form.* New York: Schocken Books, 1972.

Williams, Wenmouth, Jr., and William D. Semlak. "Structural Effects of TV Coverage on Political Agendas." *Journal of Communication* (1978): 114–119.

Williams, Wenmouth, Jr., Mitchell Shapiro, and Craig Cutbirth. "The Impact of Campaign Agendas on Perceptions of Issues in the 1980 Campaign." *Journalism Quarterly* (1981): 226–231.

Wolfinger, Raymond L., and Peter Linquitti. "Network Election Day Predictions and Western Voters." *Public Opinion* (1981): 56–60.

Yum, June O., and Kathleen E. Kendall. "Sources of Political Information in a Presidential Primary Campaign." *Journalism Quarterly* (1988): 148–151, 177.

Zapple, Nicholas. "Historical Evaluation of Section 315." In *The Past and Future of Presidential Debates*, ed. Austin Ranney, 56–69. Washington: American Enterprise Institute, 1979.

Zillmann, Dolf, and Jennings Bryant. "Selective-Exposure Phenomena." In *Selective Exposure to Communication*, eds. Dolf Zillmann and Jennings Bryant, 1–10. Hillsdale, NJ: Lawrence Erlbaum Associates, 1985.

Zukin, Cliff. "A Reconsideration of the Effects of Information on Partisan Stability." *Public Opinion Quarterly* (1971): 244–253.

Index

About the Author

DIANA OWEN is an Assistant Professor of Political Science at Rutgers University. Her articles have been published in *Political Psychology, Women and Politics,* and *Transaction/Society.* Another article by her is forthcoming in *Communication Research.*